THE DIARIES OF
FRANK HURLEY
1912–1941

THE DIARIES OF
FRANK HURLEY
1912–1941

Edited by Robert Dixon
and Christopher Lee

ANTHEM PRESS
LONDON · NEW YORK · DELHI

Anthem Press
An imprint of Wimbledon Publishing Company
www.anthempress.com

This edition first published in UK and USA 2011
by ANTHEM PRESS
75-76 Blackfriars Road, London SE1 8HA, UK
or PO Box 9779, London SW19 7ZG, UK
and
244 Madison Ave. #116, New York, NY 10016, USA

British Library Cataloguing in Publication Data
A catalogue record for this book is available from the British Library.

Library of Congress Cataloging in Publication Data
Hurley, Frank, 1885–1962.
The diaries of Frank Hurley, 1912–1941 / edited by Robert Dixon and
Christopher Lee.
p. cm.
Includes bibliographical references and index.
ISBN 978-0-85728-774-8 (hardcover : alk. paper) –
ISBN 978-0-85728-775-5 (papercover : alk. paper)
1. Hurley, Frank, 1885–1962–Diaries. 2. Explorers–Biography. 3.
Photographers–Biography. 4. Endurance (Ship) 5. Imperial
Trans-Antarctic Expedition (1914–1917) 6. World War,
1914–1918–Campaigns–Pictorial works. 7. World War,
1939–1945–Campaigns–Pictorial works. 8. Antarctic–Discovery and
exploration–British. 9. Papua New Guinea–Description and travel.
10. Middle East–Description and travel. I. Dixon, Robert. II. Lee,
Christopher. III. Title.
G585.H87A3 2011
910.92–dc22
[B]
2011007393

ISBN-13: 978 0 85728 774 8 (Hbk)
ISBN-10: 0 85728 774 5 (Hbk)

ISBN-13: 978 0 85728 775 5 (Pbk)
ISBN-10: 0 85728 775 3 (Pbk)

This title is also available as an eBook.

Contents

List of Illustrations

List of Illustrations

Introduction

Frank Hurley is best known today as a photographer and filmmaker, and it has become common to refer to his major works by the titles of his documentary films: *The Home of the Blizzard, In the Grip of the Polar Pack-Ice, Sir Ross Smith's Flight* and *Pearls and Savages*. But Hurley did not work in a single medium: he was an old-fashioned showman whose repertoire included both traditional and modern media, which he used in both old and new ways.[1] The shows he put on at the height of his fame in the 1910s and 1920s were not documentary films in the modern sense, but complex multimedia performances that he called 'synchronized lecture entertainments'.[2] They used a combination of photographic exhibition, saturation newspaper coverage, the presence of a celebrity lecturer or 'platform personality', silent cinema projection, coloured glass lantern slides, live musical accompaniment, themed theatre decorations, and mainstream book publication, all 'tied in' to achieve maximum advertising exposure. The performances were entertaining as well as educational, drawing as much attention to their own attractions as to the events they purported to represent. There was about them a sense of self-promotion and opportunistic contrivance that sometimes attracted criticism: they smacked of what contemporary pressmen called stunts. Hurley's shows toured Australia's capital cities and regional towns and they often took place simultaneously overseas by arrangement with various entertainment agencies in New Zealand, Great Britain, Europe, the United States and Canada. They made Captain Frank Hurley a household name and earned him an international reputation.[3]

We are familiar with the *images* of Hurley's professional life. His photographs of Douglas Mawson's Australasian Antarctic Expedition, Ernest Shackleton's Imperial Trans-Antarctic Expedition and the two World Wars have been so widely exhibited and reproduced that in many cases they are the principal means by which we have come to *see* those world-historical events. Hurley's photographs of the men of Mawson's expedition leaning on the wind; of Shackleton's ship, *Endurance*, crushed by pack ice during the fateful winter of 1916; of shell-shocked diggers of the first Australian Imperial Force (AIF), whose eyes meet ours as they walk on duckboards from the smoking ruins of Chateau Wood in the winter of 1917 – these have become, in that overly used but still suggestive phrase, iconic images.

Four biographies record Hurley's life and personality and his career as an adventurer-photographer.[4] The most recent of them begins with an account of biographer Alasdair McGregor's personal quest to 'meet' Hurley – his own voyage to Antarctica, his pilgrimage to Mawson's hut, and his entry into Hurley's old darkroom, where he encounters the ghostly traces of his subject:

> And so we cut, dug and shovelled [away] ... decades of accumulated drift. ... The hut's interior was gradually revealed, and the presence of its long-departed builders and occupants seemed to return to that chill space. As the expedition's photographer, I naturally sensed the rather daunting presence of a young Hurley looking over my shoulder. ... The darkroom in particular seemed almost to ring with Hurley's yelps of delight over his latest photographic triumph.[5]

Perhaps biography really does begin, as Stephen Greenblatt once said of history, with a desire to speak with the dead.[6] Yet despite their many strengths, in each of these books the voice of the biographer stands between us and Hurley. None of them grants us an intimate encounter with Hurley himself; the inner life of this complex man remains elusive.

Yet there is another source, so far little known to the public, that also gives us a startling sense of the presence of the past: it is Hurley's voluminous manuscript diaries, only brief extracts from which have so far been published.[7] Originally written in the field in Antarctica, South Georgia, England, France, the Middle East, Papua and Australia, and later raided and revised for his many publications and stage performances, they have survived years of world travel and are now carefully preserved in the archives of the National Library of Australia in Canberra and the Mitchell Library in Sydney. Alongside thousands of Hurley's articles and advertisements, press notices, photographic illustrations, interviews and reviews clipped from hundreds of newspapers and magazines throughout the English-speaking world and pasted into his scrapbooks, they are now quietly crumbling to pieces, wrapped in acid-free paper and protective plastic. By republishing this illustrated edition of his diaries we hope to re-present Frank Hurley in his own words, explore his testimony to these significant events, and review the part he played in imagining them for an international as well as an Australian public.

A Life of Adventure and Controversy

James Francis (Frank) Hurley was born on 15 October 1885 in a single-story terrace house at 63 Derwent Street in Sydney's Glebe. He ran away from the nearby public school at the age of 13 and found work in the Lithgow steel mills, where he began to acquire the mechanical skills that helped make him such a resourceful traveller. By the age of 20, he was a leading figure in local camera clubs and soon developed a reputation for sensational photography in Sydney's competitive postcard industry. His first one-man exhibition was held in Kodak's George Street salon in 1910. The following year, Douglas Mawson called him on to the stage of history when he invited him to serve as the official 'camera artist' on the Australasian Antarctic Expedition. Hurley's film of the expedition, *The Home of the Blizzard*, whose earliest form dates from 1912, brought him international fame as an adventurer-photographer and cinematographer. After making a documentary of Francis Birtles' expedition by car across Northern Australia, he was invited to join Sir Ernest Shackleton's ill-fated Imperial Trans-Antarctic Expedition. The loss of the expedition's ship, *Endurance*, and the epic story of the party's survival and rescue, provided Hurley with photographic opportunities that made him a legend. In wartime London in 1916, he developed his film and photographs of the expedition, and learned something of the showman's craft by attending performances of Hubert Ponting's *With Captain Scott in the Antarctic*. Ponting's synchronized lecture entertainment was based on Robert Falcon Scott's fatal race for the Pole, and it gave Hurley a commercial format in which he could exploit his own expedition work.

Once again in the right place at the right time, Hurley was appointed an official photographer to the Australian Imperial Forces in France in June 1917. At the Third Battle of Ypres he won the respect of Australian soldiers for displays of great courage under fire as he attempted to capture an authentic experience of modern warfare. Hurley's use of composite printing to convey this grand spectacle, which was otherwise impossible to capture under the combat conditions of the Western Front, drew him into conflict with the head of the Australian War Records section, Charles Bean, who openly favoured the work of his second photographer, Hubert Wilkins. One result of their conflict was that Hurley was sent to Palestine and the Middle East to capture the achievements of the Light Horse; another was that when he returned to London to exhibit this work in 1918, he was censured for 'fakery' and self-promotion and lost control of his images to the Australian War Museum, the organization that would later become the Australian War Memorial.

Hurley resigned from the AIF in indignation and returned to Sydney, determined to exploit commercially the photographs and films of his polar adventures. In 1919 he joined Ross and Keith Smith in their Vickers Vimy on the final Australian leg of their record-breaking flight from England to Australia. He then made two separate trips to the Torres Strait and Papua in the early 1920s to gather material for newspaper articles, radio talks, lecture entertainments and documentary films. His handling of the indigenous population led him once again into conflict with officialdom, and he was accused by the Territorial Administration of stealing artefacts and intimidating the natives. As when he fell foul of the AIF, he used his celebrity and his contacts in the press to vent his spleen.

Following the success of his Melanesian travelogue, *Pearls and Savages*, in Australia, Great Britain and North America, Hurley ventured into feature filmmaking with *The Jungle Woman* and *The Hound of the Deep* (1926). When territory officials refused to let him return to Papua, he moved production to Dutch New Guinea and the Torres Strait. In 1927 he was briefly named pictorial editor for Sydney's *Sun* newspaper. It was an era when the spectacle of flight was exciting the popular imagination and inspiring nationalist sentiment across the world, and Hurley tried – and failed – to fly from Australia to England.[8] He was back in the saddle with Mawson at the end of the twenties when he joined the British, Australian and New Zealand Antarctic Research Expedition (BANZARE), during which he shot the photograph of Mawson that was later used in the design for the first Australian $100 note. BANZARE was a scientific success but did not provide the stirring narrative of earlier polar expeditions. Nevertheless, Hurley produced *Southward Ho with Mawson* and *Siege of the South*, with which he toured in 1930 and 1931 until the Great Depression forced him to turn to short feature films for Greater Union cinemas. A stint as cameraman for Cinesound followed, and he worked on Ken G. Hall's feature films, *The Squatter's Daughter* (1933), *The Silence of Dean Maitland* (1934), *Strike Me Lucky* (1934), *Grandad Rudd* (1935) and *Lovers and Luggers* (1937). New techniques from Hollywood increasingly moved production indoors and called for a softer focus, and Hurley was gradually supplanted by younger cameramen.[9] He moved to short documentary film making for business and government, making *Silver City, Vulcan's Crucible, Treasures of Katoomba* (1936) and *A Nation is Built* (1938).

The Second World War provided Hurley with another international event that he could conjure in images. He returned to his beloved Middle East, leaving from Sydney's Rose Bay on 3 September 1940 aboard a Qantas Empire Airways flying boat, and landed nine days later on the Sea of Galilee in Palestine. As head of the Department of Information's Photographic Unit, he covered the Australians' fighting at Bardia, Tobruk and El Alamein, but his preference for bulky, old-fashioned camera equipment and high production values meant that it was the younger photographers Damien Parer and George Silk who made their reputations by getting in close to the action with their new 35mm single-lens reflex still cameras and light Eyemo movie cameras. Hurley found himself behind the times in North Africa, just as he had when working at Cinesound in the 1930s. He covered Australian Prime Minister Robert Menzies's tour of the North African theatre en route to London in 1941 and then embarked on a number of nostalgic tours of Palestine, Syria and Lebanon. But Hurley's penchant for travelogues failed to satisfy the demand of Australian cinema audiences for up-to-date news footage about the progress of the war. He left his Australian post to become Middle East Director of Army Features and Propaganda Films for the British Ministry of Information, and did not return to Australia until 1946.

Sledging Diary, the Australasian Antarctic Expedition (November 1912–January 1913)

The earliest of Hurley's diaries known to have survived was written during Mawson's Australasian Antarctic Expedition (AAE) between 10 November 1912 and 10 January 1913.[10] The AAE set out to map the depth of the ocean floor between Australia and Antarctica, conduct a scientific examination of the sub-Antarctic territory of Macquarie Island, and explore a two thousand mile stretch of uncharted Antarctic coast to the south of Australia. The expedition left Hobart on board the *Aurora* on 2 December 1911 and after a brief stop at Macquarie Island, landed the scientific party at Cape Denison, Commonwealth Bay, in January 1912. They spent the summer and autumn months establishing a winter camp and conducting scientific experiments while preparing for the following summer, when they would split up into sledging parties, exploring to the west, east and south.[11]

Hurley was a member of the southern party, which gathered information on magnetic variation in proximity to the south magnetic pole. Mawson thought they could expect 'the most adverse weather conditions', for 'they were to set their backs to the coast and traverse an icy desolation, an unbroken wilderness', but it was the expedition leader's own far-eastern party that met with disaster.[12] Mawson's sledging partner, Lieutenant Belgrave Ninnis, was lost in a crevasse with the best of the dogs and most of their provisions, while Dr Xavier Mertz died of starvation and exhaustion on the return trip. Mawson struggled back alone to Cape Denison, arriving a few hours after the relief ship had departed, and was forced to spend a second winter there. Hurley returned to Australia with *Aurora* in March and *Dr Mawson's Antarctic Film Series* was shown in Melbourne, Sydney, Adelaide and Perth over the next few months. During the winter he took on an assignment in Java to promote tourism for the Royal Dutch Steam Packet Company, but rejoined *Aurora* when it departed Hobart for the relief of Mawson's party on 13 December 1913.

Hurley's diary concentrates on the search for the south magnetic pole with his sledging companions Robert Bage and Eric 'Azzi' Webb. Simply titled, 'My Diary with Bage and Webb to the South Magnetic Pole', it is a surprisingly well-crafted narrative of heroic aspirations modified by the realities of Antarctic travel. The party falls fifty miles short of its objective and narrowly cheats death when, low on food and lost in a blizzard, they make a dash for the safety of Mawson's hut. Like other exploration diaries, it is influenced by period expectations of the style and content appropriate to British Antarctic explorers of the classic age. Some of these conventions, exaggerated in the interests of sensation, anticipate Bean's later pejorative description of Hurley as a 'commercial' man.[13] The AAE diary records hardships that affirm the explorers' qualities of character, and includes several descriptive set pieces that reflect Hurley's trained eye as a photographer and cinematographer. There are also signs of anxiety that the self-taught, working-class boy from Glebe had to prove himself worthy of his better-educated companions. Part imperial adventurers and part objective men of science, they are both tested and united by the sublime beauties of a wilderness supremely indifferent to human weakness.

In the nineteenth century, the Royal Society and the Admiralty had established protocols to ensure the authority of exploration journals as a source of new knowledge. Late in the century, however, tensions developed between the values of naval and scientific personnel and the mass media's increasingly active role in exploration. The reality was that Antarctic exploration of the so-called classic age was commercially dependent upon the new century's mass media. The books, photographs, films, newspaper articles and illustrated lecture tours that followed the expeditions of Scott, Mawson, and Shackleton were not merely incidental to the events they recorded; without the funds they raised, the expeditions could not have taken place. In some instances, the possibility of producing profit-making entertainments was part of the raison d'etre for exploration and not merely incidental to it. As Beau Riffenburgh has shown, by the late nineteenth century, explorers and their adventures were 'widely desired and highly paid as public speakers. They ... were the subjects of painters, sculptors, and early photographers, ... [they] were featured in both theatres and music halls [and] most importantly ... explorers were assiduously promoted in print ... [in] popular biographies, juvenile literature, and the popular press'.[14] Although Mawson's AAE was among the most scientifically rigorous of the classic age, it was as much a media event as any other.

Exploration journals often focused on the expedition leader, and diaries kept by other members of the party were sometimes suppressed or editorially incorporated in the interests of a singular official perspective. *The Home of the Blizzard* was published in 1915 in Mawson's name, but was written by Dr Archie McLean from expedition records by various hands, and the southern sledging trip was represented by Bage's journal, not Hurley's.[15] At the insistence of the publisher, William Heinemann, it addressed a popular, not a scientific readership. The explorer was cast as a romantic imperial adventurer whose heroic individuality and sensational testimony excited the public imagination. At the same time, he needed to be a reliable empiricist capable of describing without emotion the objective facts as any man of science might recognize them.[16] The difference between these two modes suggests some tension between science and high culture's concern to educate, and popular culture's need to entertain. As a showman, Hurley marketed his accounts of travel, exploration and adventure through commercial mass media, though he often met with the disapproval of professionals and public servants such as Mawson, Bean, and Sir Hubert Murray, the Lieutenant Governor of Papua. Hurley worked in the media at a time when their commercial imperatives and professional codes of practice were undergoing profound and often incompatible transformations. Even different kinds of photographers – the postcard photographer, the portraitist, the scientific illustrator, the newsman and the adventurer-cameraman – did not share the same social status and codes of practice, or sell to the same markets. Yet Frank Hurley, at one time or another, was all of these things. How he charted his career across these different fields and negotiated their varying demands can be traced in the pages of his diaries of the 1910s and 1920s.

The Imperial Trans-Antarctic Expedition Diary (November 1914–April 1917)

Hurley returned from Commonwealth Bay with Mawson in February 1914. While Mawson went on to London to arrange for media exploitation of the expedition, which would help to defray its substantial debts, Hurley accompanied the adventurer Francis Birtles on a photographic tour to Queensland's Gulf Country and his unavailability meant that some of his images were left out of *The Home of the Blizzard*. By September, and against Mawson's advice, he was en route to South America to join Shackleton's Imperial Trans-Antarctic Expedition (ITAE).

The ITAE had been organized in the aftermath of the tragic death of Robert Falcon Scott, who arrived at the South Pole just thirty-five days after Norwegian explorer Roald Amundsen. Since attaining his 'furthest south' on the British Antarctic Expedition of 1907, Shackleton had been locked in intense competition with Scott for the honour of being the premier British explorer. With Scott dead and the prize of the pole lost to Amundsen, the ITAE now sought to make the first coast-to-coast crossing of the Antarctic continent, starting at the Weddell Sea and finishing at the Ross Sea in the Southern Ocean.[17] The expedition's ship, *Endurance*, failed to make it through the frozen Weddell Sea, and by February 1915 Shackleton and his men were trapped in the ice for the winter. The pack ice drifted a thousand miles to the north, carrying *Endurance* with it, and the following spring the thaw caused huge floes to move against each other, crushing and sinking the ship, and marooning the expedition's personnel on the diminishing sea ice. By April 1916 the men were forced into three small lifeboats – the *James Caird*, the *Dudley Docker* and the *Stancomb Wills*. A hazardous open-boat voyage to the barren and uninhabited Elephant Island saved them from the sea, but they were still far from rescue. Shackleton, Frank Wild and Captain Frank Worsley's subsequent voyage in the *Caird* across 1,500 kilometres of tempestuous Southern Ocean to the Norwegian whaling station at Grytviken on the remote island of South Georgia saved them all. This astonishing feat of endurance and navigational skill was all the more incredible because the exhausted party – accompanied by a mysterious and ghostly fourth man – had also to make the first crossing of the island's rugged spine of glaciated mountains. Shackleton's achievement is best known to the reading public from his book, *South: A Memoir of the Endurance Voyage* (1919) and it does not form part of Hurley's own ITAE diary. Four months and three failed attempts after leaving Hurley and his fellow survivors on Elephant Island, Shackleton returned aboard the Chilean naval vessel *Yelcho*, and although three members of the Ross Sea party were lost, the entire Weddell Sea party was miraculously saved.

Unlike the AAE sledging diary, which survives in a relatively clean manuscript in Hurley's own hand, the ITAE diary was revised and extensively rewritten after the fact. Large sections survive only in edited typescript. Some of these revisions were probably Hurley's preparation for later publications, including his many newspaper articles and his books, *Argonauts of the South* (1925) and *Shackleton's Argonauts* (1948). The version we have chosen to reproduce here is one of the earliest of these edited typescripts, now held in the Mitchell Library, Sydney.

In the diaries we can see the beginnings of Hurley's attempt to craft his professional persona as an adventurer-cameraman distinct from other Antarctic celebrities, including Ponting and Shackleton. This persona was always a work in progress, and Hurley's anxieties about social class, already evident in the AAE diary, are undisguised in his account of tensions between the ship's crew and the expedition's scientists. On 1 February 1915 he writes, 'The idea of spending the winter in an ice-bound ship is not altogether pleasant, not only owing to the necessary curtailment of our work, but also the forced association with the sailors, who, although being an amiable crowd, are not altogether partial to the scientific staff.' By 8 June the following year Hurley is convinced that the sailors 'are a very meagre set, ignorant and illiterate, and of far more complaining disposition than the shore party'. These tensions are counterpointed by the constant grinding of the sea ice, the pressure buckling the ship's timbers, and the menacing presence of the killer whales.

The revised ITAE diaries also show Hurley's first great success as a writer, consciously creating a range of reading pleasures. There are sweeping narrative accounts of the crushing of *Endurance*, the months adrift on the pack ice, the move to the open boats, and the final rescue from Elephant Island. The photographer in Hurley responds to the sublime qualities of the Antarctic landscape in effusive, impressionistic descriptions of snow and ice and light. Closely observed pseudo-scientific accounts of the teeming wildlife and intimate reportage of the class tensions developing between the ship's crew and expedition personnel are interspersed by diverting episodes such as the grim whaling operations at Grytviken, the handling of the dog teams, football matches on the ice, mid-winter concerts and the constant struggle for food and warmth. Fine character portraits of Shackleton, Worsley, and Wild illustrate the Edwardian cult of the hero.

The final pages of the ITAE diary describe Hurley's response to wartime London and serve as a prelude to his Great War Diary. After the rescue from Elephant Island, Shackleton and his men were wined and dined through South America before a disapproving Hurley could return to England to arrange for the promotion of his photographs and cine film. The contrast between Antarctica, with its white silence, and the hectic confusion of the capital transported him abruptly, as it were, from the nineteenth into the twentieth century. London's streets were full of wounded soldiers, officers on leave, prostitutes and women freed from domestic confinement. This moment in the diaries reveals recurring aspects of Hurley's character: the dedicated, self-made professional is a loner, scornful of self-gratification in himself and in others; a self-educated colonial in London, he did not enjoy Mawson's access to high society, yet he is equally scornful of working-class pleasures and defensive about his prudish attitudes to alcohol and sex.

Hurley enjoyed himself in London but he was not there to play. The British capital was at the centre of new developments in photographic and cinematic technology, and he was eager to learn about the latest equipment and techniques and to capitalize on his growing reputation in the media. The Australian photographer was inspired by Ponting's travelogue, *With Captain Scott in the Antarctic*, then showing at the Philharmonic Hall in New Bond Street. The term 'travelogue' had been coined in 1904 by the leading American platform personality, E. Burton Holmes, to describe his new multimedia travel entertainments, which incorporated lecturing, cinema projection and lantern slides. Ponting's was the most complete entertainment of the kind yet performed in London, and Hurley thought it 'the acme of photographic perfection'.

He noted in his diary that Ponting's 'patter is splendid and gives one the impression the penguins were actually performing to his words. Ponting's manner and delivery is excellent' (18 November 1916). The show became the model for Hurley's own 'synchronized lecture entertainments' after his return to Australia in 1918.

The Great War Diary (August 1917–August 1918)

In August 1917 Hurley crossed over to France and Belgium, where the Australian Imperial Forces were soon engaged in the Third Battle of Ypres. It was during this intense period of work in the winter of 1917 that he produced many of his most famous images of the Great War, including 'Death's Highway', 'Death the Reaper', 'Ruins of the Cloth Hall, Ypres', 'The Morning of Passchendaele', 'Chateau Wood', and 'Over the Top' (or 'The Raid'). It is quite clear from the diary that his preoccupation during these months in the field was not with dutifully recording events exactly as they happened, as Bean expected of him, but with assembling a powerful collection of photographs, lantern slides and cine films suitable for mounting a show that might compete with those the Canadian War Records Section had already staged in London.[18]

Like so many of the young combatants from both sides, Hurley was stunned by the violent contrast between the pastoral character of the French countryside and the deadly energies and blasted landscapes of the Western Front.[19] The 'tents surrounded by wheat fields and great hayricks', 'the gay tiled cottages' and the 'beauty and glorious colour contained in this country' tenderised his senses for the pandemonium of Hill 60: 'What an awful scene of desolation! … Everywhere the ground is littered with bits of guns, bayonets, shells and men. … It might be the end of the world where two irresistible forces are slowly wearing each other away' (23 August 1917).

In the ruined town of Ypres, the flotsam and jetsam of domestic life prompt further reflections on the horrors of war, and Hurley reverts to the conventions of the sublime to make sense of the chaotic scenes of urban destruction. He saw a 'somehow wildly beautiful' character in that 'weird, awful and terrible sight' which was 'aesthetically … far more interesting than the Ypres that was.' This sentiment is expressed in his many romantic camera studies of the ruins of the famous Cloth Hall. The presence of beauty in Hurley's images of the Great War is one of their most striking and controversial features, and he remained both sentimental and melodramatic about the human cost of industrial warfare: 'There is a touch of pathos and sadness in these new ruins, little patches of clothing and domestic things; each speaks its own tale of suffering, of homes wrecked, of death and ruination' (4 September 1917).

Hurley's view of the Australian soldiers is consistent with the emerging Anzac legend, which his photography helped to build. The Australians are the ones sent to take 'any objective which other troops cannot take', and although they 'have the reputation of being unkempt and undisciplined, they always achieve their object' because they 'have the dash and resource and are unsurpassed' (5 September 1917). The horrors of the Western Front are described firsthand, calling forth a national expression of male heroism: 'The way was gruesome and awful beyond words. The ... dead and wounded lay about everywhere. ... Those murderous weapons the machine guns, maintained their endless clatter, as if a million hands were encoring and applauding the brilliant victory of our countrymen. It was ineffably grand and terrible' (20 September 1917).

Despite his admiration for the Australian diggers, the real hero of Hurley's diaries is Hurley himself. As even Bean conceded, Hurley and Wilkins narrowly escaped death many times in their attempts to obtain the authentic photographs that Bean demanded. Hurley decided that the epic scale and complexity of modern warfare could only be represented through composite printing, in which two or more negatives were used to print a single photograph. Bean believed that these 'fakes' would undermine the status of his historical records by association with the staged photographs widely used in the popular press. Hurley defended composites as the only way to pay adequate tribute to the sacrifice of the troops and if he could not produce them he would resign. In the end, General Sir William Douglas Birdwood, the commander of the AIF, granted permission for six combination prints to be made for an exhibition at the Grafton Galleries in May 1918. Bean was incensed, noting in his diary that although the exhibition was a success, it contained 'too much Hurley'.[20]

The dispute was probably responsible for Hurley's reassignment to the Middle East in November 1917, where the Australian Light Horse were sensitive to the lack of publicity they were receiving compared with those on the Western Front. In France, Hurley had experienced the fighting firsthand, but in Palestine many of the key engagements, including the charge of the Light Horse at Beersheba, were already history. Hurley was effectively beyond Bean's reach, however, and this left him free to organize re-enactments and craft his composite prints. The officers in charge of the Light Horse were so enthusiastic about reenacting old battles for his camera that eventually even he expressed reservations: 'It is amusing the keenness of the staff and brigades to have their photos taken. I have had three brigades turned out! Generals coming from distant parts of the country! and all the impossible stunts enacted for the cinema' (30 January 1918).

The Middle East allowed Hurley the freedom to create highly romanticized images of Australian airmen and the Light Horse in the richly associated geography of the Holy Land. His fascination with the Middle East reflects a deeply felt belief that the Bible lands were part of the cultural heritage of the British people. Photographic historian Kathleen Stewart Howe calls this sentiment 'geopiety', and it was widely expressed in photographs showing British and Australian troops standing proprietarily in the foreground of biblical scenes.[21] In the official history of Australia's role in Sinai and Palestine (1923), H. S. Gullett imagines the campaigns as a modern crusade in which the British reclaim the Bible Lands from the Turks and make good Richard the Lionheart's failure in the twelfth century.[22]

The exotic location and multicultural character of the Middle East also provided Hurley with unlimited opportunities to indulge his interest in the travelogue. Cairo's native quarter presented the familiar pleasures of the orient: 'Every turn a new picture is presented; every shop is a picture, every face a study. ... How quaint and beautifully oriental it all is' (18 December 1917). Gullett's volume of the Official History places the native types within a hierarchy of races and civilizations based on ideas of hygiene and industry, and Hurley adopts a similar practice. The Jews of Yebna, for example, receive a nod of approval because their clean houses, neat village and Australian gum trees transport him back to the eastern suburbs of Sydney. The likeness of the Middle East landscapes to Australia also preserves a more authentic Australian fighting man than those the photographer encountered in Europe: 'Here a life more nearer to home is lived' and the Australian horsemen remain 'hospitable, warm-hearted and ingenuous' (31 December 1917). The 'rigid militarism which is so obvious in France' is relaxed in the Middle East 'and so one finds more harmony, sympathy and kinship'. The 'open', 'expansive', 'more Australian' atmosphere is also related both to the relative absence of risk and the freedom from contact with cosmopolitan peoples: 'It would be a man's bad luck to be killed here in action, whilst in France, he might consider himself fortunate to escape with life. France is hell, Palestine more or less a holiday' (31 December 1917).

Hurley had ascended in observation balloons at Ypres, but it was in Palestine that he began his life-long passion for aviation. He experimented with aerial photography and cinematography when he made several flights with No. 1 Australian Flying Squadron's air ace, Captain Ross Smith, in the new Bristol F2B Fighter. After his first flight, Hurley wrote, 'This day ranks as one of the most salient in my life' (16 February 1918). He planned to make a film of a bombing raid and conducted 'experiments to ascertain the points of minimum vibration' on the airframe, clamping his camera across the gun cockpit and 'insulating it by means of flat rubber sponges' (14 February 1918). In the early part of the century, flight was celebrated as a transformative experience for the modern artist, yet Hurley's descriptions and aerial photographs continued to mask the reality – and modernity – of warfare with romantic pictorial effects:[23] 'One is too absorbed in contemplation, in fact intoxicated by the mighty works of nature, to heed the vile endeavours of Turkish rabble to shoot us down. From the ground, we appear as a tiny humming bird flitting through the infinity of cloudless blue; from my seat, we are hurtling along on the wings of a tornado, poised over the deep blue waters of the Mystic Sea!' (16 February 1918).

Hurley returned to London in May 1918 to prepare the exhibition of Australian war photographs and paintings at the Grafton Galleries. His images were displayed to public acclaim, but Bean objected to the photographer's self-promotion. Hurley was denied permission to take the exhibition to Australia, the exhibition prints were taken out of his control, and he resigned from the AIF in disgust. When *The Photographic Record of the War* was published in 1923, Bean made it clear in the preface that Hurley departed before the job was done and the war had finished.[24] He wrote that 'The Australian official photographers, in as much as they maintained such accuracy as the ideal of their service to their country, played their part as Australian soldiers'.[25] On his return to Australia, Hurley used his press connections to embarrass Bean and to pursue the commercial exploitation of the Scott, Mawson and Shackleton expedition films. His disagreement with Bean and his eagerness after 1920 to pursue new travelogue projects repeated the pattern of his relationship with Mawson before the War.

Tour Diary – *In the Grip of the Polar Pack-Ice* (December 1919–January 1920)

Back home in Sydney, Hurley set about launching his new career as a platform personality. The worldwide, postwar influenza pandemic closed cinemas and theatres in Australia until March 1919, when Hurley's *With the Australians in Palestine* screened briefly in Sydney. That same month, at the Kodak Salon in George Street, he staged an exhibition of war pictures from his own private collection in aid of the Red Cross. The philanthropic cause helped him to avoid the appearance of commercial exploitation, but he did not miss his opportunity to further embarrass Australia House for preventing an Australian exhibition of the spectacular enlargements shown in London.

The Mawson film had been screened in Australia during the war and so Hurley contracted with West's and Union Theatres to perform his Shackleton film on a tour of eastern Australia from November 1919 to January 1920. It was a mixed form of lecture, film and lantern-slide show, which Hurley modelled on Ponting's *With Captain Scott in the Antarctic*. Another influence was the American journalist Lowell

Thomas, who toured England and Australia from 1919 to 1920 with his show, *With Allenby in Palestine and Lawrence in Arabia*.

In the Grip of the Polar Pack-Ice opened at the New Lyceum Theatre in Sydney on 22 November 1919, and from there it played to a range of audiences in different venues in Brisbane, Wagga Wagga, Adelaide, Geelong and Melbourne. Travelling interstate by train, Hurley took with him an assistant lecturer, William Mazengarb, and an operator, Terry O'Shea. His show was integrated into West's and Union Theatres' variety programs, and sometimes preceded by gazettes, or newsreels, and one or two feature films. Using other people's projection equipment and performing in unfamiliar venues was a physically challenging experience. Hurley wrote scathingly in his diary about the poor equipment and maintenance standards of West's theatres. At the Brisbane *Olympia*, for example, O'Shea found an operating box made of galvanized iron and 'installed with two primeval machines, which had to be rewired and adjusted and got as hot as an oven' (6 December 1919). Hurley described the venue as 'a characteristic big barn, typical of West's theatres. ... It is a filthy, ill kept, dirty and dusty house and the last place in the world to go in a decent suit of clothes' (6 December 1919). Although he shared lecturing duties with Mazengarb, his voice was often strained from the demands of constant lecturing in large houses with poor acoustics. The worst was the Palais de Danse at St Kilda, where he had to compete with the noisy attractions of the next-door Luna Park.

As the tour went on, Hurley became fascinated by 'the sociology of crowds' and noted his intention to 'scientifically investigat[e] the problem'. He understands the travelogue as a middlebrow form of entertainment that is culturally superior to popular romance and melodramas, which merely stimulate the emotions with drama and spectacle. The distinction is crucial to his sense of himself as a professional and an artist. His carefully recorded observations of audiences in different towns, theatres, and even sessions provided the basis for an article on 'Adventure Films and the Psychology of the Audience' (23 December 1919). For no apparent reason, his audiences responded differently to apparently identical performances: 'This evening I repeated precisely the same words, projected the same pictures ... and yet last night the audience were on the crest of enthusiasm and tonight they fell into the trough of apathy' (23 December 1919). Hurley knew that his films had the power to move audiences, but inconsistent responses meant that their effects were difficult to predict. 'The psychology of audiences', he came to see, 'is extremely capricious.'

The Tour Diary is one of the few to survive in which Hurley writes directly about Australia and the Australians. It contains unguarded and acerbic comments about his fellow countrymen reminiscent of his remarks about the ship's crew on the *Endurance*, Londoners during the

War and local people in the Middle East. These comments confirm our sense of him as a detached and often disapproving observer increasingly isolated from the routines of everyday life. On a visit to Brisbane's gardens, he approves of their condition and arrangement but the band reminds him of 'the gyppo band in the gardens at Cairo, each instrument vying with each other to make itself predominant'. The occasion is an opportunity to study 'the types of Brisbane beauty' and according to Hurley 'the Brisbanians are a weary-looking lot minus dash and energy, and the women do not suffer from good looks to any noticeable extent' (7 December 1919). In these misanthropic descriptions of his countrymen, Hurley is critical of everyday life in Australia for its mediocrity, reading the physical appearance of the people and their theatres, gardens and public buildings as an indication of their lack of a vital and authentic culture. Returning from Europe after the Second World War in 1948, the novelist Patrick White would famously call this 'The Great Australian Emptiness'.[26]

The Torres Strait and Papua Expedition Diaries (December 1920–August 1921)

With the Australian tour of *In the Grip of the Polar Pack-Ice*, Hurley established himself as a successful platform personality. To date, all of his exhibitions and shows had been based on projects initiated by others: the polar expeditions led by Mawson and Shackleton, for whom he had worked as a camera artist, and his coverage of the Great War for the AIF. In these previous adventures he had often to subordinate his artistic and commercial ambitions to scientific or historical imperatives. He now aspired to become an independent producer of adventure travelogues.

One challenge for Hurley was to raise the funds necessary to mount his own photographic expeditions. In September 1919, he issued a prospectus for 'The Hurley Australian Film Production Company Limited', but Mawson declined to lend his name to the project and the float failed to attract sufficient capital. At some time in the preceding two years, Hurley had also developed a connection with Lowell Thomas, who succeeded Burton Holmes as America's leading travelogue presenter. It is not clear when they met: whether in Palestine, where they were both filming in the final year of the war; during the London season of Thomas's *With Allenby in Palestine and Lawrence in Arabia*, or during Thomas's subsequent tour of Australia at the invitation of Prime Minister Billy Hughes. But in 1920, the Lowell Thomas Travelogues managed the London season of Hurley's *Sir Ross Smith's Flight*, while the later travelogue, *Pearls and Savages*, began as a collaborative venture between Thomas's and Hurley's companies.

Hurley's first independent travelogue was based on his tour of Torres Strait and Papua between December 1920 and August 1921. Papua, the southern half of present-day Papua New Guinea, had been annexed by Queensland in 1883 and the following year became a British protectorate called British New Guinea. It passed to Australia in 1905 as the Territory of Papua. The northern section of the country formed part of German New Guinea from 1884 to 1914 and was called Kaiser-Wilhelmsland. Occupied by Australian forces during the Great War, it was mandated to Australia by the League of Nations in 1920 as the Territory of New Guinea. Australian rule was reconfirmed by the United Nations in 1947, and the territories of Papua and New Guinea were merged administratively in 1949.

Hurley's first trip to Papua was supported by the Anglican Board of Missions (ABM) who engaged him to make a promotional film about their work in the territory. Hurley travelled aboard the ABM's lugger, the *Herald*, and stayed with the missionaries and their families, eventually complaining that he had become 'a shuttlecock of the missionaries' (2 February 1921). He also cultivated relationships with the Territorial Administration in Port Moresby and the Catholic Sacred Heart Mission at Yule Island, both providing additional transport and accommodation. At the same time, he was taking cinematograph films and photographs for his own travelogue, which he planned to present personally in Australia while ceding to Thomas the rights for wider distribution in North America and Europe. We will never know how firm Hurley's arrangements were with Thomas – 'Lowell Thomas', after all, was a name for the aspiring showman to conjure with in his publicity – but in the course of this and his subsequent photographic tour to Papua, he found the confidence to strike out on his own. On 4 April 1921 he writes, 'Cabled Thomas not to come to Papua'.

Hurley departed Sydney on 3 December 1920 on the *Taiynan*, arriving on Thursday Island on the 13th. From there he arranged passage to the islands of Darnley, Murray, Moa, Mabuiag, Coconut and Saibai, only kilometres from the Papuan coastline. Hurley's work in the islands covered the marine life of the reefs and the bêche-de-mer and pearling industries as well as the activities of the ABM. On 24 March, he left Torres Strait for Papua, arriving in Port Moresby on the 31st. He was immediately fascinated by the nearby villages of Hanuabada and Elavara, which were suspended upon platforms above the tidal shallows. At the beginning of April he travelled to the island of Samarai off the southeastern tip of the mainland, and from there began an eight-week cruise north along the eastern coast aboard the mission launch *Whitkirk*. After recording images and film of native life and customs in the villages of Dogura, Mukawa, Emo, Ambasi, Koira, Buna and Mailu, he returned to Port Moresby. In early July he left the coast for a journey into the Highlands and a visit to the village of Ononge in the rugged Owen Stanley Range.

Hurley was now developing a style of writing that complemented his new professional persona. He modelled his style on the personal reportage and quasi-ethnographic description common in travelogues, popular magazines and tabloid newspapers like London's *Daily Chronicle* and Sydney's *Sun*. During both tours of Papua he wrote and dispatched travel articles in the field that were serialized in the *Sun*, often lifting passages directly from the diaries. Other illustrated articles and photographic essays were later to appear in important travel magazines such as *Walkabout* and *National Geographic*. Hurley developed a range of themes and motifs including quasi-ethnographic descriptions of 'native' manners and customs, quasi-scientific accounts of tropical flora and fauna, and accounts of tropical industries such a pearling and bêche-de-mer gathering. His photographs and films of these activities were typically achieved by the practice of enacting stunts that had begun in Palestine with the Light Horse. Natives were now enlisted, paid and even coerced into performing for Hurley's camera.

Hurley's Papua diary and the travelogue later derived from it are coloured by his typically acerbic comments on a range of issues canvassed in the popular press of the day. These include the failure of the White Australia policy, the threat of Asian invasion, the degeneration of the white man and white civilization in the tropics, criticism of Papua's plantation and mining economy, and the effects of the Christian missions in Melanesia. Hurley was pro-development and pro-White Australia, and although he was working for the missionaries he was privately sceptical about their enterprise. He felt that the natives needed someone to protect them from marauding whites, especially the miners and planters, but at this point in time he thought that the Government was better suited to the task because of the Anglican clergy's 'indolent life of uselessness' (12 April 1921). Hurley worried that the natives were susceptible to 'the superstition' of the missionaries, but he also noted that they continued to practise many of their traditional beliefs and customs. He believed that industry and not salvation must be the priority if Northern Australia were to develop as a bulwark against Asian invasion, and it was the Catholics rather than the Anglicans who found favour because their work was 'of a practical, as well as spiritual nature' (30 March 1921).

The popular entertainer in Hurley wanted to romanticize an atavistic primitivism which he saw lingering in the post-contact population. During the dancing ceremonies contrived for his cameras he observed that 'a reminiscent expression comes over the faces of the old men and they live not in the present. The young men have the blood of their forefathers still hot in their veins, the wild look comes into their eyes, and their song and yells betoken the primitive man again' (2 January 1921). Later, when purchasing spears from old men in the village of Opi, Hurley found them useful in staging a mock attack: 'They are just out of the cannibal stage and all the old fire is still there and only wants kindling into war flames' (20 April 1921). While Hurley's travelogues are quasi-ethnographic, they abound in the stereotypes of popular racism expressed in tabloid journalism. His description of natives dancing in the village of Emo, for example, reflects the cross currents of indigenous traditions and religious evangelism observed through the filter of popular racial understanding (17 April 1921). Although they now seem dated and unacceptable, Hurley's racial attitudes appealed to contemporary metropolitan audiences. A review of *Pearls and Savages* in the Sydney magazine, the *Triad*, would later announce, 'Captain Hurley lectured in a delightful way on his adventures and experiences in those beautiful islands. It made me personally long to let down my hair, grab a few beads, and stain myself chocolate'.[27]

By the end of his first expedition to the Torres Strait and Papua, Hurley had taken 22,000 feet of film and produced over 1,200 negatives. He returned to Sydney in August 1921 and quickly organized an exhibition of the photographs at the Kodak Salon. *Pearls and Savages* premiered at the Globe Theatre in George Street in December, then toured nationally by arrangement with Union Theatres. Hurley supplied the ABM with films of the Torres Strait and Papua, and these were edited to form *The Heart of New Guinea*, which Hurley's biographer, Alasdair McGregor, wryly describes as 'more travelogue entertainment than evangelistic propaganda'.[28]

The Papua Expedition Diary (August 1922–January 1923)

At the conclusion of his first expedition, Hurley dined at Government House in Port Moresby as a guest of the Lieutenant Governor, Sir Hubert Murray. His imagination was stimulated by Murray's tales of the early history of the Territory and accounts of the great Fly River in Western Papua. The Fly and its dense rainforests were first explored by the Italian, Luigi D'Albertis, fifty years earlier. By the 1920s the river system was relatively well travelled but Hurley would represent himself as a pioneering explorer and was confident that he could secure on film an authentic moment of 'first contact'. To sharpen the contrast between the 'Stone Age' and the 'Air Age' and provide added sensation, he secured sponsorship from Amalgamated Wireless (Australasia), who provided a radio receiver and transmitter, and the loan of two seaplanes – a Fleetwings and a Seagull – from the wealthy Sydney aviation enthusiast, Lebbeus Hordern. Hurley boasted in his publicity that it was the best equipped expedition ever to set off for Papua. The addition of naturalist Allan McCulloch of the Sydney Museum lent a much-needed air of scientific credibility.

The expedition embarked for Papua on the Burns Philp vessel *Morinda* at the end of August 1922 and by 6 September it was dropping anchor in familiar waters off Port Moresby. Hurley enthusiastically described the natives' first encounter with an aeroplane:

> The amazing spectacle of the native canoes and man's supreme achievement – the aeroplane – moving off in procession across the bay, contrasting the most primitive and modern methods of progression, was indeed a unique and epoch-making event. ... The roar of the engine called everyone out of doors; natives decamped from their work and rushed out in wild excitement to watch the Seagull racing across the water before taking off. ... Opening the throttle, the machine raced over the water gaining speed each moment; everyone looked on bewildered and spoke not, then as she began to lift and clear the water, the wildest enthusiasm prevailed. (6 September 1922)

Hurley was once again a guest of Government House, making him unpopular with the plantation owners who resented government restrictions on their use of native labour. The adventurous cinematographer was happy in the bosom of officialdom and expresses his own high-minded contempt for their exploitative attitude to the natives. But on this trip his own commercial imperatives would once again place him on the wrong side of officialdom.

A small rented steamer, the *Kerema*, was refitted and renamed the *Eureka*, while Hurley and McCulloch made studies of the coral reefs outside the harbour. Preserving the fragile timber and canvass flying machines from physical damage and deterioration in the harsh tropical climate caused Hurley much anxiety, and his worries were exacerbated as the relationship between his pilot, Andrew Lang and his mechanic, A. J. Hill, also deteriorated. In early October the *Eureka* proceeded west along the southern coastline while Hurley and Lang followed in the Seagull. Tropical conditions forced them to fly early in the day to avoid violent thermals, strong winds and poor weather. Nearing the Purari River delta Hurley anxiously describes dense clouds and heavy rain as his 'machine was tossed about wildly'. Once safely on the ground at the village of Kaimare and reunited with his surface vessel, he could reflect with satisfaction on the contrast between his modern marvels and his primitive native subjects:

> The *Eureka* floats with her electric lights ablaze, a few hundred yards away; McCulloch has just finished speaking via wireless to

Thursday Island. The Seagull swings at her moorings nearby and around us rests the strangest of villages with its great dubus or ravis silhouetted against the moon. It is the realisation of a Jules Verne. The most ancient and modern resting by the shores of a time-old lake. White men and black men – the modern and the ancient strangely commingling. Truly, we seem to have entered another planet. (6 October 1922)

This was the contrast and these were the images that Hurley had come to Papua to collect, and a few days later he was delighted when the natives were moved to sacrifice a pig as a propitious offering to the aircraft.

The giant ravi of the village housed ceremonial masks and cane effigies which were screened from sight in a room that Hurley described as the 'holy of holies'. He was determined to capture them in his photographs and to acquire them as artefacts – supposedly for the Australian Museum, but also to be used as decorations in the theatre foyers where his travelogue was performed. When native reluctance and then outright resistance thwarted his intentions, he showed that he was prepared to use deception to get the job done. While the natives were occupied at a funeral, he stole into the ravi to photograph the cane effigies while McCulloch lit firecrackers to warn off a group that returned unexpectedly.

In October 1922 the fragile Seagull made a further flight from Kaimare to Daru, 150 miles along the coast. The turbulent air, low mist and cloud, and unsettled weather typical of the great delta formed by the Purari, Kikori, Aird, Auro, Omati, Urama, Bamu, Aramia and Fly Rivers, made it a precarious exercise. Hurley was more at ease over Palestine being shot at by the Turks than in the turbulent atmosphere of Papua's coastal wilderness. Following a brief trip to Thursday Island on the *Eureka*, he gladly dismissed back to Australia the troublesome pair of Lang and Hill, and their rapidly deteriorating aircraft. Hurley judged his ten flights without incident a worthy contribution to aviation in the Territory. More might have been achieved had his morose pilot and temperamental mechanic been better suited to the conditions, but he concluded that the rigors of tropical aviation required an aircraft with a metal airframe and more powerful engines.

Early in November the expedition turned north for a month's voyage up the Fly and its tributaries, the Strickland and Herbert Rivers, to the great inland lake, Lake Murray. There they spent a week removing native artefacts from temporarily deserted villages. In his diary and travel articles, Hurley was hammering out well-worn themes: 'We seem to be back in the remote Dark Ages amongst the prehistoric people dwelling on the shore of a primeval sea' (16 November 1922). When contact with the natives was finally made, a few were allowed aboard the *Eureka* to trade crafts and tools, and nervously pose for portraits.

On the return trip to Port Moresby, the *Eureka* paused at a number of coastal villages to shoot scenes of native dancing to be used in the Lake Murray episode. Hurley took the opportunity to acquire shields, masks, stone adzes and two ornately carved canoes. His greatest prize, however, was a complete skull rack from the Urama people that still resides in the Australian Museum in Sydney. Headhunting had been banned by the territory administration and the elders were reluctant to part with the skull rack. Hurley got what he wanted, but recorded feeling 'rather sad about the whole affair; to secure a head from a headhunter might sound a permissible action to most people; but when it is understood that many of these skulls were relics passed down by ancestors – fine old warriors – heads won in fair combat by strength of arms and valour and objects of religious reverence, it is natural that many must have felt a deep pang when parting with them' (8 January 1923). Not for the first time Hurley found himself caught up in the contradictions of the colonial situation. When the natives retained their original customs and cooperated with his expedition, they found favour; when they adopted modern tools and practices and resisted his depredations, they drew his ire. He could not see that he was part of the problem. At the villages of Urama and Kaimare he alternately cajoled and threatened the natives into organizing dances and displaying their sacred Kaiva-Kuku masks for the cinecamera. The *Eureka* was now 'a floating museum and menagerie of native objects' (9 January 1923). But there was another shock waiting for them when they arrived back in Port Moresby on 13 January. Their collection for the Australian Museum had been seized, and they stood accused of 'chasing and terrifying the people and robbing their villages'. Hurley's wheel had once again come full circle and his now well-practised response was to use his connections with the press to embarrass an unnecessarily officious administration for standing between him and an audience that had a right to know.

Hurley's problems with the Territory Administration did not prevent him from making a commercial success of his second trip. During the writing of the Torres Strait and Papua diaries he mastered a new genre of travel writing that led to the illustrated serialization of his travel articles and diaries in newspapers and magazines, and would later provide copy for radio broadcasts. As well as providing a profitable new outlet for his writing and still photography, these articles created a climate of anticipation for his travelogues in the major cities in Australia, Britain and North America, and enhanced the intelligibility of his silent films for their first audiences. He revised *Pearls and Savages* using the new material, and with the new title, *With the Headhunters of Unknown Papua*, it enjoyed successful tours of Australia (1923–24), the United States and Canada (1924), and England (1924–25). Attracting widespread publicity, he was approached by the New York publisher

George Putnam to prepare the illustrated travel book, *Pearls and Savages: Adventures in the Air, on Land and Sea – in New Guinea*. Addressed to an international readership, it appeared simultaneously in New York and London in 1924, where it received positive reviews both for the technical excellence of its illustrations and the quality of its letterpress. The text was taken more or less directly from Hurley's diaries, which he must have carried with him to New York in anticipation. In 1925 it was followed by *Argonauts of the South*, also with Putnam. An American reviewer observed, 'If proof had been wanting that Captain Frank Hurley is an artist with the pen as well as with the camera, that proof is supplied by his latest book.'[29]

Despite the international success of *Pearls and Savages*, by the late 1920s the growing world dominance of Hollywood cinema had begun to make Hurley's travelogues seem at once highbrow and old-fashioned, and the advent of the talkies in 1927 spelled an end to the kind of live synchronized lecture entertainments pioneered in the 1890s by E. Burton Holmes and carried on into the 1910s and 1920s by Hubert Ponting, Lowell Thomas and Frank Hurley. Hurley responded to the challenge by making two narrative feature films, *The Hound of the Deep* (1926) and *The Jungle Woman* (1926). Predictably, his directorial debut resulted in some quality scenes shot on location in the Torres Strait and Dutch New Guinea, but the two features were marred by clichéd characterization, semaphoric acting and melodramatic plots. They enjoyed only modest success at the Australian box office.

The World War II and Middle East Diaries (September 1940–April 1941)

In the late 1920s Hurley briefly settled down to a desk job as pictures editor for the *Sun* newspaper, but by the end of the decade he was back adventuring with an unsuccessful attempt to break Bert Hinkler's Australia-to-England record in the *Spirit of Australia*. He then accompanied the two BANZARE Expeditions in 1929 and 1930. During the 1930s, the ageing showman made documentaries for Greater Union theatres and Cinesound, and worked as a cameraman on the canonical Australian films *The Squatter's Daughter* (1933), *Strike Me Lucky* (1934) and *Grandad Rudd* (1935). His inflexible production values, however, meant that he was out of touch with the period's new visual styles and techniques. The outbreak of war in 1939 must have come as something of a relief for Hurley, for he quickly offered his services to the Department of Information (DOI). The Minister for External Affairs, H. S. Gullett, had been the official correspondent to the Middle East during the Great War and the first director of the Australian War Memorial. Unfortunately for Hurley, he was also a close friend of Hurley's old foe, Bean, and he conspicuously overlooked his application, appointing instead younger men in Damien Parer and George Silk.[30] Hurley had to make do with a position with the ABC in Western Australia. But when Sir Keith Murdoch replaced Gullett as Director-General of Information, Hurley was brought back into the fold, and on 3 September 1940 he left Sydney's Rose Bay on a Qantas Empire Airways flying boat bound for the Middle East.

The DOI's Photographic Unit, which Hurley had come to lead, included Parer, Silk, and Ron Maslyn Williams, the sound recordist Alan Anderson, and Hurley's batman and driver Ron 'Pambo' Morrison. Looking back on this period, Hurley would later title an essay of his war memoirs, '200,000 Miles Through the Middle East', an echo of his friend Ross Smith's book, *14,000 Miles Through the Air*. The Unit was headquartered in Cairo, but covered thousands of miles each year chasing the action of battle and indulging Hurley's personal interest in making travelogues as far afield as Lybia, Lebanon and Iran. Despite the appearance of action, in reality Hurley was again behind the times, and the rapid pace of mechanized warfare and the large distances of the desert theatre of operations did not suit him. While Parer and Silk used the new single-lens reflex cameras and small, hand-held Eyemo cinema cameras to keep pace with the ever moving front line, their older colleague lagged behind with his ponderous Debrie equipment.

The diaries that survive from World War II reflect Hurley's increasingly discontinuous engagement with the Australian Forces in North Africa and the Middle East. Unlike the earlier diaries, which were well crafted and often revised for various forms of publication, the World War II diaries are in a rough and chaotic state consistent with being written in the field, and there are many long gaps in the record. It is not known whether Hurley wrote these 'missing' diaries and they have not survived, or whether he failed to record significant passages of time. What does survive can be separated into a number of relatively discrete episodes, and we have chosen to reproduce a selection of the more significant and coherent sections. They are Hurley's arrival in the Middle East in September 1940, the assault on Tobruk in January 1941, the visit of Australian Prime Minister Robert Menzies the following month, the defense of Tobruk in April, and Hurley's account of his trip to Tel Aviv in August 1941.

In February 1941 the DOI Photographic Unit spent some weeks covering the visit of Prime Minister Menzies, who toured the Middle East en route to London, and Hurley then stayed behind in North Africa, while Parer and Silk accompanied the Australian forces on the disastrous Greek campaign. The landing of Erwin Rommel's *Afrika Korps* in Tripoli reversed the fortunes of the Allies in North Africa. Benghazi was lost and the fortress of Tobruk surrounded. In April 1941 Hurley covered the stubborn resistance of the garrison, and the destruction of the town and shipping in its harbour. He filmed the Battle of El Alamein in October of 1942, but the diaries suggest that he was more interested in making a number of nostalgic tours through Palestine, Syria and Lebanon. His personal interest in the old travelogue format failed to satisfy demands at home for up-to-date news footage at a time when the threat of Japanese invasion was shifting Australian attention to the Pacific. Once again, Hurley left his position covering the Australian forces, this time to take up the post of Middle East Director of Army Features and Propaganda Films for the British Ministry of Information, which post he held until his return to Australia in 1946.

Nearly twenty years separate the second Papua diary from the first of the World War II manuscripts. Hurley's style is less assertive now, in keeping with his sense of himself as an old hand at his profession and a seasoned campaigner at war. But Hurley has not adapted his now well-worn conventions. The luxurious Imperial Airways flying boat deposits him in yet another fine hotel in yet another exotic location. Rich historical associations and a picturesque native population provide familiar materials for Orientalist set pieces that remind the reader of his earliest experiences in the Middle East. Second impressions of Palestine, Jerusalem, and Gaza approvingly contrast their contemporary state of hygiene, order and civic development with their ravaged condition at the end of the last war, and this is an implicit endorsement of British occupation.

As Hurley first takes to the field, the battle for Bardia is over and the troops have moved on to lay siege to the Italian garrison at Tobruk. His intention is to go in with the first wave of the attack so that he can occupy an advanced position and film the oncoming waves of tanks and infantry, but he fails to gain adequate intelligence of the plan of battle and is left behind by the first wave. In a passage notable for its failure to reflect upon the lessons of the Great War, he speculates on his role in representing the events that are about to take place:

> The work of the official photographer ... constantly calls for a life stake and one must be prepared to play with chance, perhaps even more than in most branches of the service. One cannot crouch to shelter all the time. The infantryman and the gunner have at least the satisfaction of being able to shoot back, but we carry cameras to photograph them doing this, and unless one sets up where the barrage is sending up death shapes then the camera misses the most spectacular symbols of war. It is through the lens that the world sees the contest and so then it falls to one's duty to present as vivid and comprehensive a picture as possible. (21 January 1941)

In entries like this, Hurley reasserts himself as the daring and adventurous eyewitness for a new international audience. But he was now fifty-five years old, and his age and artistic temperament together with the highly mobile nature of the desert campaign and its harsh physical conditions were conspiring against him. He falls in with a unit of mechanized cavalry made up of Bren gun carriers and captured Italian tanks sporting hastily applied Kangaroo markings prior to moving on alone to a captured strongpoint. Ascending to the lookout post, Hurley reflects upon the differences between the two wars to which he has been witness: 'There was nothing frightful in the grand battle panorama over which I looked. ... There was no horror like we had in the last war – rather did this particular attack impress me as a spectacle made sublime by the great spirit of heroic men' (21 January 1941).

After the fall of Tobruk to the Allies, Hurley returns 1,000 miles behind the lines to cover Menzies' trip to the Middle East. His intention to shoot some additional travelogue footage in Jerusalem, however, is interrupted by Rommel's invasion of Libya and he reluctantly returns to the Libyan desert. Mid-April finds him aboard a small vessel, which slips into Tobruk Harbour as Rommel's *Afrika Korps* lays siege to the town. There are some anxious times as the small craft slowly slips past the enemy occupied town of Bardia on the coast, and on reaching their destination Hurley is moved by new scenes of desolation: 'Tobruk harbour presented a very sad sight. It is a graveyard of ships sunk in all attitudes of dereliction, nose pointing sky up, masts only above the surface others stranded and lying at abandoned angles' (22 April 1941).

Tobruk is under siege from the air as well as the land and Hurley describes hiding in bomb shelters, diving out of vehicles and running the gauntlet as screaming *Stuka* dive-bombers unload their bombs and machine-gun the roads. A prim condemnation of the prioritization of beer in his vessel's cargo reminds us of his attitude to the heedless recreations of London in the last war. For Hurley, the inefficiency of the exercise is exacerbated by the soldiers' practice of pillaging the cargo at every opportunity, for even 'during the air raids ... scores of cases disappear each time' (25 April 1941). A week later he is on his soapbox once more as a small ship valiantly makes its way into the harbour to offload a cargo of latrines. It was enough to convince Hurley that headquarters was 'heavily overstaffed, overfed, over-entertained, over-officered and under-efficient, under-worked, and under-brilliant' (1 May 1941).

Hurley does the rounds of Tobruk's defences, visiting the crack 25-pounders that destroy the formidable armour of the Germans, and the anti-aircraft gunners who blaze away at the waves of bombers decimating the harbour and the town. The wreckage of a *Stuka* is found and Hurley decides to re-enact its demise by setting fire to the wreck and filming it.

The exercise is interrupted three times by bombing raids and the diary provides an effective testimony to the incessant bombardment to which the troops were subjected. A visit to the Australians in the front line eight miles from town brings some relief from the incessant air attacks and in a revealing passage, Hurley notes the different character of the fighting against their new opponents. The Germans ruthlessly bomb hospitals and hospital ships; the Australian response is to take fewer prisoners: 'One hears of a natural desire for reprisals and we wage war with a ferocity unknown against the Italians' (5 May 1941).

*

When he returned to Australia after the war in 1946, Hurley found himself in the unenviable position of having to rebuild his family's finances. He did so as he had done in the past, by seeking new commercial opportunities in which to employ his skills as a photographer, travel writer and publicist in various media and formats, both old and new. Drawing on past adventures, he quickly published *Shakleton's Argonauts: A Saga of the Antarctic Ice-Packs* (1948), a rambling narrative drawing on his own diaries and other published sources. It was followed in 1949 by *The Holy City: A Camera Study*, utilizing the best of his still photographs taken in Palestine. But the postwar period was also a forward-looking era that brought a number of sweeping changes to Australian society: the influx of European migrants, the development of manufacturing and heavy industries, the expansion of pastoralism, agriculture and mining, the growth of cities and suburbs, the advent of modern beach culture, and the growth of domestic tourism promoted by increased car ownership and a bourgeoning pride in the national landscape. Sensing new opportunities, Hurley liaised with the tourist bureaus that were being established in each state and approached an old sponsor, the publisher John Sands, who had specialized in postcards and greeting cards. There followed a series of illustrated books, or 'Hurley Camera Studies', initially of individual states and regions, including *Queensland Calling!* (1940s), *Beautiful Hobart* (1950s), *The Blue Mountains and Jenolan Caves: A Camera Study* (1952), *Perth and South-Western Australia in Natural Colour* (1957), *Brisbane and the Gold Coast in Natural Colour* (1958), and *The Snowy Mountains: A Camera Study* (1961). These were eventually consolidated into his magnum opus, *Australia: A Camera Study*, first published by Angus & Robertson in 1955, and revised and reprinted many times throughout the 1950s and 1960s. Although Hurley's camera studies were familiar books in many Australian homes of the 1960s, they have more recently been forgotten in favour of his earlier Antarctic and war photography. In an important book published by the National Library of Australia in 1999, John

Thomson argues for a reconsideration of Hurley's 'late period Australian photography' as an iconic 'distillation of Australia in the 1950s'. 'In his mission to capture Australia for Australians, he travelled throughout the country photographing its vast landscape, its modern cities, its industrial strength and its agricultural riches. The vision he created captures the essence of a younger, more innocent nation'.[31] The National Library holds a diary from 1961 ambitiously titled 'Round Australia Tour', but the entries are brief, fragmentary and incomplete. Hurley's best years as a writer had been in the 1910s and 1920s, when he responded as a younger man to a series of world-historical events and the limitless commercial opportunities they offered him.

Frank Hurley passed away after a heart attack at his home in Collaroy on 16 January 1962. He was 77.

Notes

1 See Julian Thomas, *Showman: The Photography of Frank Hurley* (Canberra: National Library of Australia, 1990); and Jeffrey Ruoff, ed., *Virtual Voyages: Cinema and Travel* (Durham and London: Duke University Press, 2006).

2 Hurley to Mawson, 22 July 1922. MAC, 6DM.

3 Robert Dixon, 'Travelling Mass-Media Circus: Frank Hurley's Synchronized Lecture Entertainments', *Nineteenth-Century Theatre and Film* 33.1 (Summer 2006): 60–87; and 'What Was Travel Writing? Frank Hurley and the Media Contexts of Early Twentieth-Century Australian Travel Writing', *Studies in Travel Writing* 11.1 (2007): 59–81.

4 Frank Legg and Toni Hurley, *Once More on My Adventure* (Sydney: Ure Smith, 1966); Lennard Bickel, *In Search of Frank Hurley* (Melbourne: Macmillan, 1980); David P. Millar, *From Snowdrift to Shellfire* (Sydney: David Ell Press, 1984); and Alasdair McGregor, *Frank Hurley: A Photographer's Life* (Camberwell, Vic.: Viking Penguin, 2004).

5 Alasdair McGregor, *Frank Hurley*, p. 3.

6 Stephen Greenblatt, *Shakespearean Negotiations: The Circulation of Social Energy in Renaissance England* (Berkeley and Los Angeles: University of California Press, 1988), p. 1.

7 Daniel O'Keefe, *Hurley at War: The Photographs and Diaries of Frank Hurley in Two World Wars* (Sydney: Fairfax Library, 1986). A transcript of Hurley's ITAE diary is available on cd-rom, edited by Shane Murphy as *Shackleton's Photographer: The Standard Edition*, though the text is an unscholarly conflation of material from many sources.

8 Robert Wohl, *The Spectacle of Flight: Aviation and the Western Imagination, 1920–1950.* (New Haven and London: Yale University Press, 2005).

9 McGregor, *Frank Hurley*, p. 346.

10 NLA, Ms 883, Series 1, Item 1.

11 See Douglas Mawson, *The Home of the Blizzard* (1930; Kent Town, SA: Wakefield Press, 1996).

12 Mawson, p. 204.

13 C. E. W. Bean, *Gallipoli Mission* (Canberra: Australian War Memorial, 1948), p. 20.

14 Beau Riffenburgh, *The Press, Sensationalism, and Geographical Discovery* (1993; Oxford and New York: Oxford University Press, 1994), pp. 1–2.

15 Philip Ayers, *Mawson: A Life* (Carlton, Vic.: Melbourne University Press, 1999), pp. 101–2.

16 Simon Ryan, *The Cartographic Eye: How Explorers saw the Country* (Cambridge: Cambridge University Press, 1996), pp. 38–53.

17 Roland Huntford, *Shackleton* (1985; London: Abacus, 2000).

18 Martyn Jolly, 'Composite Propaganda Photographs during the First World War', *History of Photography* 27.2 (Summer 2003): 154–203.

19 Robert Dixon, 'Where are the Dead? Spiritualism, Photography and the Great War', *History of Photography* 28.3 (Autumn 2004): 247–260.

20 Martin Jolly, 'Australian First-World-War Photography Frank Hurley and Charles Bean', *History of Photography* 23.2 (1999): 141–48; and Robert Dixon, 'Spotting the Fake: CEW Bean, Frank Hurley and the Making of the 1923 Photographic Record of the War', *History of Photography* 31.2 (Summer 2007): 165–179.

21 Kathleen Stewart Howe, *Revealing the Holy Land: The Photographic Exploration of Palestine* (Santa Barbara: Santa Barbara Museum of Art, 1997), p.28.

22 H. S. Gullett, *The Australian Imperial Force in Sinai and Palestine 1914–1918* (Sydney: Angus & Robertson, 1923); and Christopher Lee, '"War is not a Christian Mission": Racial Invasion and Religious Crusade in H. S. Gullett's *Official History of the Australian Imperial Force in Sinai and Palestine*', *Journal of the Association for the Study of Australian Literature* 7 (2007): 85–96.

23 Robert Wohl, *A Passion for Wings: Aviation and the Western Imagination 1908–1918* (New Haven and London: Yale University Press, 1994), pp. 157–202.

24 Dixon, 'Spotting the Fake', p. 178.

25 *Photographic Record of the War*, edited by C. E. W. Bean and H. S. Gullett (Sydney: Angus & Robertson, 1923), p. viii.

26 Patrick White, 'The Prodigal Son' (1958), in *Patrick White Speaks*, ed. Paul Brennan and Christine Flynn (Sydney: Primavera Press, 1989).

27 Lalie Setton Cray, 'The Shadow Show', *Triad* 10 January 1922.

28 McGregor, *Frank Hurley*, p. 239.

29 Unsigned review of *Argonauts of the South*, *Buffalo Express*, 18 October 1925, NLA, Ms 883, Series 2, Item 71a.

30 See Neil McDonald, *Damien Parer's War* (South Melbourne: Lothian, 1994).

31 John Thomson, *Frank Hurley: Myth, Dream, Reality* (Canberra: National Library of Australia, 1999), viii, p. 7.

Acknowledgements and Notes on the Text

Frank Hurley's diaries are at once too extensive and too detailed for their complete publication to be commercially feasible, and so our selection aims to be representative rather than comprehensive. Nor is this a scholarly edition in the sense in which that term is now understood. In Australia, for example, the standards of computer-assisted scholarly editing have been set by the authoritative Academy Editions of Australian Literature series. Our aim, by contrast, has been to bring as much of Hurley's diaries before the public as practicable, and in an accessible, readable and illustrated format. We have carefully made cuts both to reduce the length of the diaries and to eliminate repetition and circumstantial detail. There is a precedent for this in Hurley's own practice, which was to raid the diaries as a resource for his subsequent books, magazine articles, advertisements and lectures. As a consequence, we believe that the forward thrust of Hurley's narrative has been enhanced and that his many set pieces of description have been foregrounded.

Hurley's diaries were usually written at night in the field. On some occasions, when events prevented this, he either omitted whole days or else wrote up several days together in retrospect. Essentially a self-educated man, his punctuation and spelling vary considerably. While we have tended to preserve the rhythm of his punctuation, his spelling of the names of places and people has been silently regularized, modernized and corrected. The form of entry for dates has also been regularized. Elision marks indicate where editorial cuts have been made either within a day's entry or to whole days.

Permission to reproduce Hurley's diaries and images was kindly granted by his daughter, Toni Hurley. The text of the diaries was transcribed by Joan Garvan and Alison Baxter from the manuscripts and typescript sources held in the National Library of Australia and the Mitchell Library, State Library of New South Wales. The transcript was edited by Stephanie Owen Reeder. The images and related Hurley materials have been sourced from those institutions, and from the Australian War Memorial, the National Gallery of Australia, and the Mawson Antarctic

Collection, South Australian Museum. The editors wish to acknowledge the assistance of the staff of those institutions, and the editorial and research assistance provided by Lachlan Brown, Nathan Garvey, Meegan Hasted and Jacinta van den Berg at the University of Sydney, and Ian Herbertson at the University of Southern Queensland. They also acknowledge the collegial support provided by Natalie Adamson, Bryce Barker, David Carter, Barbara Creed, Richard Fotheringham, Ian Henderson, Jeanette Hoorn, Veronica Kelly, Lara Lamb, Steve Martin, Tom O'Regan, Mark Pharoe, Simon Ryan, Graeme Turner, Elizabeth Webby and Gillian Whitlock.

Research on the Hurley project was supported by Robert Dixon's Australian Research Council Professorial Fellowship at the University of Queensland (2003—2006) and the University of Sydney (2007). This illustrated edition of the diaries was conceived as a companion to Robert Dixon's book on Hurley's stage and screen practice, *Photography, Early Cinema and Colonial Modernity: Frank Hurley's Synchronized Lecture Entertainments*, also published by Anthem Press.

The diary extracts in this edition are taken from the following sources:

Chapter One: NLA MS883.1.1

Chapter Two: NLA MS883.1.2–4

Chapter Three: NLA MS883.1.5

Chapter Four: NLA MS883.1.6

Chapter Five: NLA MS883.1.7–9

Chapter Six: NLA MS883.1.10–13

Chapter Seven: NLA MS883.1.18–23

Acronyms

AAE	Australasian Antarctic Expedition
AM	Australian Museum
AIF	Australian Imperial Force
ABM	Anglican Board of Mission
AWM	Australian War Memorial
ITAE	Imperial Trans-Antarctic Expedition
MAC	Mawson Antarctic Collection, Museum of South Australia
ML	Mitchell Library, State Library of New South Wales
NGA	National Gallery of Australia
NLA	National Library of Australia

Glossary

aannock	flat Scottish cake made of oatmeal and cooked on a griddle
alpengluhen	radiance of snow-capped mountains at sunset
archies	military slang for anti-aircraft guns
baksheesh	Oriental term for a gratuity, present of money or tip
beche-de-mer	sea cucumber
bidi-bidi	breast ornaments
billy	a metal canister used for brewing tea on a campfire
bogie	stove
brash ice	loose floating ice
Burberrys	waterproof, gaberdine raincoat
coo-ee	a call used to attract attention, imitative of a signal used by Australian aboriginals
crampons	metal spikes worn on the soles of shoes for traction in ice
digger	Australian soldier
dim-dim	white man
dubu	Papuan long house
enfilade	fire from guns which is directed along the length of enemy positions or troop formations
feu de joys	bonfire or gun salute
finneskos	fur boots
fumarole	hole in or near a volcano from which steam arises
gammon	humbug
gopi board	a wooden tribal shield with decorative carving
gyppo	an Egyptian
hoosh	a stew
humpy	a native Australian hut, hence, applied to a small and primitive house
lava-lava	rectangular cloth worn like a kilt or skirt
lead	an open channel through a field of ice
limber	detached forepart of a gun carriage, consisting of two wheels, an axle, a pole etc
lugger	a small sailing ship used for pearling
lumper	wharfie or wharf labourer
mamoose	headman of the village
nunatak	isolated rocky peak completely enclosed by a glacier or icesheet
Paget plate	an earlier form of colour photography
pampero	cool polar air from the south bringing thunderstorms
puri-puri	sorcery
raddle	a red variety of ochre

rami	woman's mourning tapa cloth
ravi	Papuan house or dwelling
sastrugi	ridges carved in compact snow or ice surfaces, and caused by constant abrasions
serace	large block or pinnacle-like mass of ice on a glacier
skrott	stripped whale carcass
spruiker	a speaker employed to attract customers to a sideshow
trochus	a genus of gastropod mollusk with a conical shell
trumilk	a brand of powdered milk used on expeditions
volplane	a dive, descent, or downward flight of an aeroplane, under control but with the engine shut off
wowser	Australian term for a puritanical person, especially one opposed to intoxicating drink

1

Sledging Diary, the Australasian Antarctic Expedition (November 1912–January 1913)

10 November 1912

Temperature at midnight: −12°

After numerous attempts to push forward the sledging section of the expedition, we have at last been able to make a start. The continuous blizzard conditions have every evidence of breaking up or at least abating. ... Our party left the hut at 12.30 p.m. Robert Bage in command, Eric N. Webb, magnetician, and myself, general handyman and photographic. It is our intention to steer magnetic south, reaching a point, as near as possible, to the south magnetic pole. ... Our supporting party ... are to proceed inland 100 miles, if possible. .... The provisions of our supports and our own are ample for nine weeks sledging, enabling us to return to the hut about the 15th January. Arriving at the Five Mile Depot ... we met Dr Mawson, Mertz and Ninnis with the dogs. I took some cinefilm of the party, also a few snaps and after a hearty handshake and good wishes on both sides we bid farewell. ... After 'The Five Mile', our way lay up a steep slope. Going was very hard, and ... we fell through many crevasses to our waists, but without any serious mishap. ...

11 November 1912

... We slept poorly owing to the novelty of our surroundings and also the excitement in pushing out into new fields. The wind was freshening and shortly after starting, snow began to fall. The conditions gradually accelerated into our usual blizzard conditions. ... [T]he wind attained a velocity of 70 miles per hour, with drifting snow. We only made three miles and were then right glad to pitch camp. ...

12 November 1912

The blizzard raged throughout the night. ... In our tiny tent we can barely move about, while to converse with one another we have to raise our voices to a shout so terrific is the swish of drift and the blizzard din. Yet it is not without its humour. ... To see Bob endeavouring to light the Primus and make hoosh, is even more amusing than watching 'Azzi' (Webb) donning his frozen Burberrys. These indispensable garments are frozen as stiff as boards, and it feels like putting one's legs into stovepipes to don the trousers. ... All day we have been confined to the tent and as it is now 8.45 p.m. we are toggling up into our bags to await favourable conditions.

13 November 1912

Although only confined to the tent for a day and a half, we were pleased when the weather moderated to enable us to resume the trail. ...

14 November 1912

... [A]lthough our light tent is pitched in the lee of our supporting party's, we have grave apprehensions of whirling away in these 'Gentle Zephyrs'. It is now 9 p.m. and the wind is bellowing at 80 miles per hour! The thin tent threatens to rip at any moment, while the seething drift pelts like a sandblast. It would be fatal to have our thin calico walls ripped by these terrific conditions, yet it seems impossible they can hold out much longer. Got out of our bags at 3.30 p.m. and it took us nearly two hours to put on our frozen garments and get the few necessaries off the sledge to make hoosh. We all got frostbitten, though not very severely, and were glad to return to our sleeping bags again. If one once gets cold it is a hard job to warm up again and much of the calorific value of the food is wasted; so we find the bags the best and only place. We long for a fine day. ... Our supports, although in a tent a few yards away, have not been seen or heard the whole of the day. ...

16 November 1912

The weather moderated at noon and we made an extra speedy start. What a change! All day the weather improved and we made 5¼ miles, over hard sastrugi polished with drift and wind. At 6.30 p.m. heavy nimbus clouds came rolling up from the south, and we are wondering if it is again going to snow and blow. A halt was made and tents were erected in a dead calm! What a striking contrast to the blizzard's eternal roar. Every sound seems frozen, our voices seem strange in this awesome silence, whilst our ears, so accustomed to continuous din, ache. ...

19 November 1912

Again fortune is with us. The weather is delightfully calm and sunshiny, surface good. As far as eye reach we are girdled by a vast even plain, smooth, monotonous, and devoid of any mark or feature. At noon the sun blazed down upon us, and as yesterday, we divested ourselves of all warm apparel and hauled in our singlets and underpants. How strange it seems with 60 miles of snow and ice between us and the hut and yet we feel the heat as much as an Australian summer. The two parties cut a humorous sight hauling the sledges in this undress regalia, and we are extremely pleased there are none of the fair sex among the party. Took snaps of the party. Turned in dog tired at 10.15 p.m.

21 November 1912

... We have decided to lay our depot at this camp, 67½ miles from the hut. The supports, after assisting to lay the depot, will return tomorrow. As I write in my sleeping bag, I can look out of the tent opening across the great snowfield 11 miles to the northern horizon. The sun has just dipped below the horizon for a few hours and the sky is aglow with delicate prismatic flushings. We spent the afternoon building a large snow mound 10 feet high and about 12 feet in diameter at the base. In the centre of this we fitted a special flag vane about 20 feet high. These two marks should readily enable us to see the depot from a radius of 8 miles. ...

22 November 1912

We stayed all day at the 67½-mile camp which we christened 'Southern Cross Depot'. ...

24 November 1912

A fortnight since we have seen any other object than desolate expanses of snow. Even that has to be observed through goggles to avoid snow blindness. Today has been the most arduous since leaving the hut. We left Southern Cross Depot in a 35 mile per hour wind. The drift cut our faces and the wind split our lips. After a long uphill struggle against this terrible wind, we came into an area of very bad sastrugi and snow ramps. The sledge was frequently overturned and the wind increased but still we plodded on. ... After a great deal of trouble we managed to erect our tent; and ... we decided to build a breakwind of snow blocks ... and it took Bage and myself nearly two hours miserable work to erect it. The wall we have erected is 3 feet thick, 15 feet long and 5 feet high. It is now midnight and, as we lay awake in our sleeping bags, the wind is roaring past at 75 miles per hour! ... Sledging under these conditions is hell.

25 November 1912

... About noon, two snow petrels came hovering around our camp and settled on the snow a few yards away. We hailed these little creatures with joy for they are the only signs of living things we have seen for the past fortnight. From whence they came or whither bound gave us room for discussion. Eighty miles inland on the plateau is the last place in the world we expected to see these beautiful creatures. They allowed me to approach within a few yards of them and secure a photograph. My camera is a bugbear and using it is a nightmare. Every time I have to set the shutter I have to take a number of tiny screws from the front and bend the mechanism into shape, and with frostbitten fingers! ...

29 November 1912

... Today has been the worst day of the journey. Every foot had to be won against a relentless and cruel wind with bowed backs and strained muscles. At 107 miles our troubles increased by having to climb a steep slope: a grade of about 1 in 40 with pitted ice surface and covered with large jagged sastrugi. We became parched and thirsty and tried to quench it by sucking pieces of ice which burnt our tongues and afforded us little relief. At camp time we were dead beat, but the inevitable breakwind had to be erected to save our tent and equipment. ... For the first time this year we have observed the sun at midnight. His rim just skimmed the horizon and then rapidly rose to shine on the toils of another troubled day. ...

2 December 1912

As we were nearing the end of our march we dipped into a curious valley depression, from which rise numerous snow mounds. It is an uncanny place. In the evening light, the sastrugi surface resembles newly tilled land; and the surrounding snow mounds might easily be hills. We have christened the place 'The Nodules'; tomorrow we will investigate. ... My fingers are nearly frozen and writing is painful.

3 December 1912

... Arose at 9.30 a.m. and after 'hooshing', hauled our sledge up the south ridge of the Nodules. Here an amazing field of huge crevasses confronted us. We left the sledge, and linking ourselves together by the alpine rope, went on a tour of exploration. Many of the crevasses were over 70 feet wide and were spanned by great bridges of compressed snow. Webb went down onto one of the bridges which had fallen in and lay jammed 60 feet below the plateau surface. The whole place resembled land cut up into allotments. It was criss-crossed and seared by crevasses in every direction. We went through the snow bridges occasionally and thankful we were for the stoutness of our lifeline. Peering down one of these mantraps, we looked into black nothingness; the walls were delicately festooned and covered with the most beautiful crystals imaginable. The light filtering through the ice walls made the chasms glow with a faint blue light and heightened the effect of these sledging nightmares. To take the sledge over this chaos was our next problem. It was my day leading; so attached to a long rope, I would venture onto the snow bridges, stamping and jumping. If they held me during these manoeuvres, it was fair to surmise they would hold up my two comrades. But I must say I didn't like the 'vocation'. We had to cross over twenty of these bridges, and it was with some relief that we put miles between ourselves and the Nodules. ...

4 December 1912

... [A]t camping time there was not a spot smooth enough on which to erect our tent, so in addition to building our breakwind, we had to chip a site for the camp. It is almost calm, and after hoosh we were able to sit outside our tent in the −4° temperature and feel comfortably warm. I found Bage an ardent motorcyclist, and so we discoursed on this topic, whilst the midnight sun shone down upon us, and then it didn't seem so bad a place after all. The prospect around us looks just as if it were the ocean that in storm had suddenly frozen. The crests of the waves were lit by the golden glow of the midnight sun and the great wild plateau looked inexpressibly beautiful. Total mileage, 150.

6 December 1912

... Sledging was very heavy ... and the light became so bad that we could not discern ridges from hollows, and so we stumbled on, floundering in holes and tripping over sastrugi. As I was leading I had to dispense with my goggles. The drift pelted in my eyes, which are now extremely painful, feeling as though filled with sand. Our mitts and Burberrys are frozen stiff, our feet are wet, cold and tired, yet we must not drop our travelling average below 10 miles per day. We have fifteen days yet to go forward which should take us 350 miles from the hut. Our appetites are terrific, yet we dare not increase our ration by half an ounce. ... Personally, I could do with a good helping of steak and onions.

This sledging ration is excellent and no doubt its calorific value is high, but it leaves one more hungry at the end than at the beginning of the meal. ...

8 December 1912

... [A] 24-hour continuous magnetic observation was carried out. This necessitated giving up our tent, so we set to work to excavate a hole in the plateau surface for ourselves. So we finally found ourselves below the surface of the plateau in an ice cavern. It was much colder and worse in every way than the tent. ...

13 December 1912

Overhauled gear and anything not absolutely essential we ... left at the ... 'Lucky Depot'. ... The depot is marked by a snow mound 9 feet high and 18 feet [in] diameter at base; on the top is set a black canvas flag. We moved off at 8.30 p.m. and are now encamped 4 miles from depot, which is still visible. ...

16 December 1912

... As it was my turn to serve the tea and make the ration, I laid down inside the tent. It was indeed hard to imagine we were on the plateau, with 250 miles away to the hut. There was not enough wind to stir the tent; I dreamt I was in the Australian bush, when the cooker boiled over and brought me back to my whereabouts. ...

17 December 1912

... As we sledged over the plateau, the sun obliquely illuminating the surface changed it to a wonderful tint of grey, the sastrugi that caught the rays full and square, standing up like tombstones. The plateau, under these strange conditions with the absolute calm, resembled a vast necropolis. The temperature continues to fall and when we pitched camp was 50 degrees below freezing point.

19 December 1912

I take back all I said about the harsh weather dealt up to us, for it really does seem as if Antarctica is trying to do the best for us. Today was heavenly – perfectly calm and cloudless. The temperature in the tent when we got out of our bags was 66°! which did indeed astonish us very greatly. The black-bulb thermometer gave a reading of 107.5° in the sun! whilst in the shade, the temperature was 34° below freezing point. I always said this was a humorous country, if you but cared to look on the funny side of things. Sledging was terrifically hot, what with reflection from the snow and sun glare, that we were mightily glad to strip ourselves and haul in our shirts. What characters we looked! Faces nearly black with sunburn and seared with frostbites, begoggled and whiskered. An absolute hush brooded over the plateau, broken only by the creak of our runners as they glided over the wind-polished surface. We all remarked the weather was quite Australian, and we could easily have partaken of and relished ice creams. ...

21 December 1912

Today has been the most momentous since leaving the hut. By 3 p.m. we reached 301 miles. Latitude 70°37′, longitude 148°13′. Ours has been a difficult task, hauling dead in the eye of the wind and under such wretched conditions of surface. Still, it's done and we feel our best has been done. With feelings half glad, half regretful, we turned back. Behind us lay still the interminable ridges and personally I must say I felt regretful to have been compelled to turn back, as the lure of the ridges was strong, and the vacant places seemed to beckon irresistibly. We all felt sad, for beyond the ridges, something seemed to call us back, eager to unfold to a distant world the mysteries of countless ages. Yet it was not to be. The food will run out by the 15th January, when we must be back to the hut. The *Aurora* will be waiting, and then home again to sunny lands and dear faces. Webb calculates our position to be about 45 miles from the south magnetic pole. At Turn Back Camp we hoisted sail on our sledge and in less than an hour had covered the 2½ miles to last night's camp. ...

22 December 1912

We commenced our flight from 298-mile camp at 10 a.m. We hoisted a sail on our sledge, and the wind being favourable, we set off at a great pace. The area of the sail is about 49 square feet, too much for the breeze that was blowing. This necessitated Webb and myself going behind, and holding it back with guy ropes! Bage taking the lead to keep the bows turned homeward. Even then we found it hard to keep the sledge from overrunning Bage. It appears more anxious to get home than we do. Eventually we were compelled to reef sail, so that the load was just balanced. ... Eighteen and a half miles were covered with little more exertion than walking. We felt right proud of our craft as she glided majestically over the polished sastrugi, and very beautiful she looked with white wings outspread – like a tiny barque on a frozen sea. ...

24 December 1912

Christmas eve on the plateau. ... We intend deferring our Christmas feast until 'Lucky Depot' has been reached. ...

27 December 1912

We experienced little difficulty in locating 'Lucky Depot', the big mound we had erected on our outward journey shining out as a white pillar across the grey surface of the plateau. The tent was at once erected and I set about preparing a light lunch. This was to appease our appetites, which are now ravenous for the feast to come. I was 'unanimously' elected cook, and forthwith set about my onerous task. The ... menu was all concocted from a half-dozen ingredients, which had to be tediously separated from the compounded sledging ration. ...

The pudding, about which we were rather dubious, turned out with great satisfaction. We brewed a strange mixture by boiling five raisins in a little of our Primus-methylated spirit – a drink known as 'tanglefoot' and the recipe of one Bob Bage. It was as distasteful as its appearance, and could only be drunk in gulps by holding the nose and breath. It was in truth, as Webb announced, a brew of much 'stingo' and fire. No doubt the King and others would have been greatly amused at the grimaces with which we drank their healths. ... I never knew a happier and more jolly Christmas than this one I spent with Bob Bage and Azzi Webb at 'Lucky Depot' 200 miles on the plateau. ...

28 December 1912

... We left 'Lucky Depot' 'feeling refreshed and strong' as draughthorses. The surface was good and the breeze fair, so that the miles treated us lightly – or rather we treated them so. ...

2 January 1913

Under 100 miles to go. We covered twelve today in the most unfortunate weather imaginable. The heavy nimbus clouds that rolled up last night shut out all bright light, so that the plateau surface and sky were the same slaty tint. Heavy snow fell without intermission. We might just as well have had ground glass before our eyes, for we could discern nothing. The strain told on Bob's eyes so that he became stone blind and we hauled him on the sledge. ...

7 January 1913

Today the light was as bad as ever. It snowed all night and was stagnantly calm. Heaven only knows where the depot lies. I think it must be buried deep by snow. We kept in bags until 5.30 p.m., when we had a quarter-ration hoosh – the first for 17 hours. We struck camp at 6.30 and moved east along latitude 67°57′S. The light was so bad that we could see nothing beyond a slaty expanse of snow and sky. Things are now serious. We have but a day's ration left and have the choice of remaining here to gamble with the weather or make a desperate dash for the hut. If we stay here and the weather does not clear, we starve miserably. (In my opinion, we are as good as dead if we decide on this latter course.) We held a consultation and decided that should the weather be bad on the morrow, we will make a bid for the hut. It will be our desperate yet only chance, for the hut is 70 miles away and the trail runs through blizzard and rough surface to travel over. Still, it is better to peg out fighting than bartering with the weather. We move off at 6 a.m.

8 January 1913

We did not sleep during the night, being anxious and nervy over our ignominious position. We feel like caught in a trap. Early this morning we held another consultation; the remainder of the rations was intimately gone into and Bob and Azzi decided we could not make the hut on them. I was for making the dash, but finally consented, much against my wish, to their ideas. Extending from the coast to 100 miles inland extends an area of fogs, probably brought about by oceanic influence. It is indeed a veritable death trap. We arose at 3.30 a.m. with bright sunshine and Azzi was just about to take a bearing to the 'Ramps' whilst Bage and I walked out to fix the distance peg. Scarcely had this been done when heavy nimbus clouds again rolled up from the south, the harbinger of fog and snow treacherous conditions that might continue indefinitely. We looked at each other and neither spoke; now was the time to make the grand attempt to save our lives. We were all unanimous now that it was the only thing to be done, a dash for the hut. Quickly we went through all our instruments and gear on the sledge and depoted all things not essential to life – excepting our records. ... If the weather would clear, we will pull through. At present, navigation is difficult. The compass needle is useless owing to its proximity to the magnetic pole; there is no sunlight, so we are compelled to take the capricious wind, southerly, as our pilot. Fortunately, we are three hefty and stouthearted individuals.

How we struggled through the day is beyond me. A fierce blizzard raged and whirled up the loose snow that fell during the past two days so that we marched in a river of snow. Oftentimes our leading man was hidden [and] we could not see a yard ahead. We are feeling very weak and another two days of this will about make statues of us. I have been trying to cheer up my companions, but can't say I like our present prospect. If we had but a glimpse of the sun, we could get at least our direction. My comrades are fine men and breathe no pessimism. If we don't reach the hut, I will feel myself to blame, as I was so eager to push off on this hazardous endeavour. Late this evening we observed the ocean ahead of us and the heavens cleared. Although in pitiful plight, I could not but admire the wonderful vista unfolded before us. The distant sea littered with innumerable icebergs – lit by the low evening sun, glowing pink. The ocean a blue mirrory expanse, rippleless; above, a canopy of the most wonderful blue nimbus clouds I have looked on. We three stood together gazing on this profound sight spellbound, but where we are or whether to go east or west we know not. Estimated cover, 20 miles. Another day and we can reach the hut.

9 January 1913

... We found ourselves in badly crevassed and seraced ice, bridged with snow bridges which gave way beneath us and precipitated us at the end of our harness into the abysmal depths. Towards midday we recognised the great ice cliffs of Commonwealth Bay, and a few hours later sighted the Mackellar Islets. It seemed our very eyes were lying to us. In his great excitement, Bage stepped on the lid of a large crevasse, which gave way beneath him, precipitating him into the depths ([he] was attached to sledging harness). With much trouble, we hauled him out and then retraced our steps to get out of this impassable country. At midnight we sighted Five Mile Depot. What touched us most was the handgrip we gave each other and the sight of some dog biscuits, on which we made a hasty start. We crawled into the Five Mile Excavation, and after a hoosh, slept sounder and happier than we had done for many months.

10 January 1913

We left the Five Mile Depot at noon today. Poor Bob's eyes had to be bandaged, as he was stone blind. We hauled him on the sledge and had an exciting time preventing it from capsizing into the crevasses. At 5 p.m. we came down the long ice slope at the back of the hut. Those in the hut came running out cheering. We had a royal reception and were carried into the hut where good old Close had a banquet prepared for us. Although we did not reach the magnetic pole, our records are unique and will comprise some of the most valuable scientific assets of the expedition. ...

2

The Imperial Trans-Antarctic Expedition Diary (November 1914–April 1917)

5 November–4 December 1914

... On the morning of 5 November and our tenth day from leaving Buenos Aires, the obscure outlines of a rugged and mountainous coast was dimly observed through the snow squalls immediately to the south. Unable to accurately determine a harbour entrance in the mist, we were pleasurably surprised to notice, making in our direction, a small craft, which on coming alongside proved to be the *Sitka*, a whaler from Leith Harbour. Captain Michelson her able skipper piloted us into Cumberland Bay, where the *Endurance* laid [at] anchor in a superb miniature haven, King Edward Cove. King Edward Cove is a small basin encircled by noble cliffs that rise precipitously above its sheltered waters some 1500 feet. Apart from the transcending scenery one is at once struck by the pungent effluvium which hangs obscure yet fluid-like over its greasy waters. This is an emanation from the Grytviken Whaling Station at the head of the cove, and from innumerable derelict whale carcasses that float in the vicinity. ... At Grytviken, the carcasses are allowed to go to waste; so polluted are the foreshores of King Edward Cove with grease and decaying carcasses that it is impossible to view the trade with other than loathing. ... South Georgia boasts a magistrate, customs officials, and a post-office and a meteorological station. A pleasing phase of our stay was the insistent hospitality tendered us by the principals – all of whom are Norwegian. A few convivial evenings were heartily enjoyed, they assisting and applauding wholeheartedly our varied vocal efforts. I dined with several other members at Mr. Jacobsen's home and was agreeably surprised with its interior, kept artificially heated at about 'incubating' heat. It sported a billiard table, piano, and real live geraniums blooming in the bow windows. The dinner table was graced with spotless linen so unlike our four-week-old stain absorbers, and tastefully bedecked with a splendid display of blue and gold chinaware, on which basked a tempting and wondrous variety of sliced sausage, dear to the heart – or rather the stomach – of the Norwegian. After regaling ourselves thereon, we were informed that the sausage was manufactured locally. The ingredients being whale-fed pig and whale meat. We epicures were unanimous in praise of the 'wurst'. Next day, however, we observed a herd of the aforesaid 'pig ingredients' emerging from the bowels of a whale, where they had just completed – if grunts are indicatory – a sumptuous gorge.

Afterwards, several of our members did not care to dine at Mr. Jacobsen's. Though for my part, the proof of the sausage is in the eating. I had many pleasant rambles and excursions on the Island, and each time was more deeply impressed by its wild and rugged mountains, its terraced glaciers, and beauteous fjords. Here one can study sub-Antarctic life with all its attendant charm. ... Our good friend Rasmussen took parties of the expedition, self included, to the far reaches of Moraine Fjord, and the Nordenskjold Glacier. Moraine Fjord I mention specially on account of the lasting impression I retain of it. A narrow waterway extending some two miles between jagged and escarped mountains, where nature admires her work in a liquid mirror. At the head of the Fjord are three glaciers that take their rise near the majestic base of Mount Paget (7000 feet) and whose occasional boom and crash precede the dislodgment of icy fragments, the only sound that awakes its echoes. ... We visited Royal Bay, Gold Bay, Hund Bay, and Larsen Harbour. The fifty to sixty miles of coast seen, presented an unbroken chain of rugged mountains and peaks, interspersed with bays and glaciers. Larsen Harbour exceeds in grandeur Moraine Fjord, being almost entirely landlocked, the jagged and pinnacled mountain crests peeping through cloud, look down precipitously on the placid surface of liquid reflections. Larsen Harbour rivals – nay, excels – Milford Sound, New Zealand. ...

We steamed from Cumberland Bay on 5 December 1914, after bidding adieu to our good friends, and Rasmussen highly excited by drowning his sorrows, accompanied us some distance in his motor launch. Aheading, circling, and sterning it, in a most ludicrous and amusing fashion. MacDougall could be seen, the last figure, waving us bon voyage till we rounded Mount Dusie and headed for the open sea and the south.

5 December 1914

Leave Grytviken, South Georgia at 9 a.m. Keep in sight of land till evening. Steering SSE course.

6 December 1914

Passed numerous bergs during the day. Many weatherworn into gorgeous caves, vaults and the multitude of dissipating forms.

7 December 1914

... An easterly course is set, and shortly after 5 p.m. the *Endurance* baptizes her bows in the marginal outskirts of the Weddell Sea pack ice. As we proceed, we discover the field for the most part composed of old weathered floes, and denuded berg fragments growing rapidly denser, as to become almost impenetrable. Accordingly, a course is shaped for the NE and we regain open water. ...

11 December 1914

Glorious morning and being on the 'washdown' watch, have the full benefit of its exhilarating charm (6 a.m. to 8 a.m.).

The sea is dazzling with loose floes scattered over the deep blue, only seen in Antarctic seas. The floes varying in size up to 30 or 40 yards across, are in a high stage of decomposition, the rotten honeycomb section below being clearly visible in the pellucid water; their upper surface presents a smooth snow covering with occasional water pools stained brown by diatom presence. During the afternoon the ice becomes much heavier, and it being my watch at the wheel, have some strenuous exercise whirling the wheel first to port and then to starboard. Our ship steers excellently, responding sensitively to her helm. ...

15 December 1914

Last evening the wind increased to a moderate gale, and not being able to make sufficient speed through the pack to give the vessel steerageway, we hove to. The vessel's head is pressed against the ice, into the eye of the wind, with the engines at half speed. Thus we have been during the past 24 hours, and the position at noon indicates a backward NW drift of 6 miles. No darkness at night now, it being possible to read print at 11 p.m. in one's cabin from the porthole light.

16 December 1914

Wind decreases sufficiently to enable a start to be effected at 3.30 a.m. Considerable patches of open water connected with leads enable fair progress to be made. Beautiful, fine weather. The pack being ineffably charming. The floes are perfectly flat and of enormous area, and tonight it is wondrous calm. The lakes amidst the floes having the calmness and transparency of pools of glycerine – absolutely rippleless. ...

17 December 1914

Very slow progress, having re-entered fields of enormous floes. Many over a square mile in area, and with very little open water. All day we have been utilising the ship as a battering-ram. Backing and then full speed ahead at the barring floes. We admire our sturdy little ship which seems to take a delight in combating our common enemy, shattering the floes in grand style. When the ship comes in contact with the ice, she stops dead, shivering from truck to kelson; then almost immediately a long crack starts from our bows into which we steam, and like a wedge, slowly force the crack sufficiently to enable a passage to be made; and so it has been all day, and I suppose shall be for many days to come. Secure an Emperor Penguin for the larder.

20 December 1914

Held up all day by wind, and enormous area floes. During afternoon indulged in a short game of football on the large floe to which the ship is moored.

21 December 1914

Underway at 2.30 a.m. with improving conditions till at 10 a.m. we entered long leads of ice-free water in which were drifting some fine icebergs of magnificent forms. One, a fine cuneiform mass 200 feet high, I photographed. Passed large hummock, covered floes apparently cemented together by young ice. The season appears too early, as at a later period, segregation would disseminate the floes and there should be considerable open water in this position. In a month, doubtless, the sea would be much more open. ...

24 December 1914

What vicissitudes are awakened. Twelve months ago I was on board the *Aurora*, blown out of Commonwealth Bay, Adelie Land, Christmas Eve, two years ago, on the Plateau, 100 miles from the South Magnetic Pole; three years ago escaped from wrecking on the rocks at Caroline Cove, Macquarie Island. Favourable ice conditions today. The floes, although very extensive, are separated by large stretches of water, so that we are enabled to make a full-speed tortuous course.

27 December 1914

Beset by pack ice, Temperature falls to 21° at 6 a.m. and freezes up the loose brash and water spaces. We will soon have to give up washing down decks as the water congeals a few minutes after swishing down. ...

31 December 1914

Considerable patches of open water enable a run of 51 miles to be accomplished. About midnight we passed the Antarctic Circle with a glorious sunset reflecting in placid waters; and so enter geographic Antarctica with a dawn of the New Year. During the morning we experienced a 'nip', the ship heeling over slightly, which fortunately was of short duration. ...

1 January 1915

Saw the New Year in at the wheel, under snowy conditions. A few enthusiasts joined in an Auld Lang Syne, but the majority were all sound in slumber. During the day had a very gratifying run, passing through vast fields of young ice, or rather recently formed ice in a rapid state of dissipation. The ship cut her way through in noble style, leaving a long wake which could be traced and remained open for a mile or so. I had a platform suspended from the jib boom and secured some fine film. As well as pictures from the foretop yard. ...

5 January 1914

... Was awakened last night towards midnight to take photographs. The midnight sun shining brilliantly, and as its low light tipped the heavy pressure ice and floes, the effect was very beautiful. During the day we have been manoeuvring to find a way south through the heavy and impenetrable coastal ice. After following a lead for a few miles southward, we were called out of bunk to moor the ship at 11 p.m.

6 January 1914

On going on deck we discovered we were in the midst of impenetrable field and heavy pressure ice. It was impossible for the ship to go ahead or astern, so, making fast to a large hummock, it was decided to await favourable conditions. During the day, the dogs were taken for a run on the large floes to which we were anchored. The exercise did them a great deal of good, it being the first they have had for nearly a month. We were forced to change our moorings this evening, owing to the floes drifting together. Fortunately we were able to do so, otherwise the result would have been extremely serious.

7 January 1915

It was decided to retrace our course northward, and look for a more open lead that will enable us to find a way through the belt of heavy coastal ice. This ice, which is at present impeding our way, is the heaviest I have yet seen. It has apparently been subjected to great pressure, and is a consolidated field of hummocks, which in places are higher than our bulwarks. ...

8 January 1915

... The monotony of slow progression I have relieved somewhat by printing a series of prints from my negatives, with the intention of binding them up into a pictorial log of the expedition. ...

9 January 1915

Today is worthy of note, as a week ago our position was latitude 69°49'S, longitude 16°40'W so that our course westward, at the beginning of the week, we passed within a few miles of this identical position. This would indicate that the heavy pack which obstructed our southward progress, has drifted some 30 or 40 miles westward. ...

10 January 1915

A notable day. The first glimpse of Coats Land at 5.20 p.m. after four weeks negotiation in dense pack ice. Seal and penguin life is becoming much more plentiful, while the ocean has altered its tint from a deep blue to a light bottle green ... After a magnificent run in open water, we are again in heavy bay ice which tends to show the close proximity of land.

11 January 1915

The barrier of Coats Land was reached last night towards midnight in latitude 72°10'S, longitude 16°57'W and we have been heading SW in the land-water adjacent thereto ever since. The heights of the ice face varied from 90 to 115 feet. This barrier is evidently a glacier tongue, which was observed this evening away to the south, rising in an undulating slope some 1000 to 1500 feet in height.

15 January 1915

One never knows what is going to happen next in Antarctic circles, for magically, a lead has opened to the south, and we have been following up the land-water by the glacier face, and, as absolutely no pack ice is visible, all sails are set and engines racing as we have not heard them for many weeks.

During the day we witnessed a phenomenal sight. Hundreds of crabeater seals speedily made their way towards the ship, and treated us to a wonderful display, gambolling, sporting, racing and diving under the ship. We marvelled at their sinuous and graceful evolutions, and as they kept with us for over a quarter of an hour, I had a rare opportunity of securing some unique cinema film of this extraordinary sight.

17 January 1915

The freshening wind of yesterday afternoon developed into a strong gale, attaining a velocity of 50 miles per hour. We are compulsorily hove to, weathering in the lee of a large iceberg. Sunday at the best of times is a lazy day, and is especially dismal today on account of the gloomy and fierce weather. I remained on my bunk, reading most of the time. I can glance out of the porthole on to a very dismal prospect of huge great white bergs, rough sea, and lowering nimbus clouds. It is typical of moody Antarctica. I finished reading Marcus Clarke's exquisite book [*His Natural Life* (1874)] which impressed me greatly, especially as I have been to the various places around which his tale is woven.

18 January 1915

... It is now 7 weeks since we first entered the pack, and since then it has been almost an incessant battle with it. It is gratifying to feel that we are only 80 miles from our intended base – Vasel Bucht. We are all keen to reach it, as the monotony is wearying most of us.

21 January 1915

Still held up by the pack. Towards afternoon pressure set in from SE, jamming our helm in a dangerous way. We tried to free it by cutting away the floe, which eventually was done, and the helm freed. Our position, however, is disquieting, as here, with the goal in sight, it looks as though there was a possibility of us freezing in and becoming part of the floes that menace us, and so all our efforts will be for nil. ...

23 January 1915

Midnight. This evening we have been favoured with sunlight. I climbed up into the barrel lookout from where a magnificent panorama was to be observed. From horizon to horizon, and stretching north, south, east, and west, the pack ice extends, dazzling white with the hummocks relieved by long shadows. The sight was very inspiring, and made one feel the tinyness and insignificance of themselves. The shadow of our ship – the only black speck amid this eternal whiteness – was thrown in weird skeleton fashion far across the snows by the midnight sun. ...

25 January 1915

Towards midnight of the 24th, the ice began to break up, and a lead opened only 200 yards ahead of us. All sails were set, and with engines at full speed, an attempt was made to break through the barrier. Our attempt, so far, has only been to free the helm, but as the ice continues to break up ahead, we are hopeful. Crean sustained a nasty bruise to his leg whilst chipping the ice from the ship's side. The ice, suddenly closing in, jammed the ice chisel against his leg and the side of the ship.

27 January 1915

... It appears as though we have stuck fast for this season. ...

31 January 1915

For 15 days we have been immovable, and to say the least of it, our life on board is becoming very trying. The weather is stagnant; there being not even an 'ear' of wind. In striking contrast to Adelie Land where fiendish blizzards rage incessantly, there seems something uncanny about his place, and if I had my choice, I scarcely know which I would select. The calm weather would be very welcome on the plateau out sledging, but we all long for a blizzard to break up the ice, and so free the ship. ...

1 February 1915

There appears to be little prospect of a blizzard breaking up the sea ice and freeing us. The weather today is calm, snowy and overcast. The idea of spending the winter in an ice-bound ship is not altogether pleasant, not only owing to the necessary curtailment of our work, but also the forced association with the sailors, who, although being an amiable crowd, are not altogether partial to the scientific staff.

7 February 1915

Had quite a run of sitters today for portraiture. Took the individual portraits of the shore party, and developed them. Also took cinema pictures of the pups. To bunk at 7 p.m.

10 February 1915

Had splendid view of two killer whales which broke through the young ice astern of us, poking their alligator-like heads through, and blowing arduously. They seem to be regarding the ship with much astonishment, and I must say we felt very pleased to have her stout timbers below. More villainous or rapacious looking creatures I have never seen.

11 February 1915

Engines have been unable to move us out of the soft floe in which we are jammed. At 9 a.m. engines are put full astern, and we 'sally ship' that is, all hands and the cook, at a given signal, double over to port, then to starboard, and so on. This imparts a rolling motion to the ship, and so forces her to split the surrounding young ice. This unsuccessful, all hands muster on the poop, and in rhythmatic [sic] time jump up and down. This sallying provokes much hilarity, but has the desired effect and we re-moored the ship in a position to take advantage of any opening that might occur.

14 February 1915

Land seen faintly to SE about 40 miles off. A decisive effort was made to free the ship, all hands continuing till midnight, and everyone like a Trojan would wield a pick, ice chisel, or any other implement. The ship itself was commissioned as a battering ram. At midnight we had cocoa and wished Sir Ernest many happy returns of the 41st birthday, and all to bunk very tired.

15 February 1915

All hands again attack the ice and we work the ship a third of the way to the lead ahead. All keep hard at it till midnight, when a survey is made of the remaining two-thirds distance, which is some 400 yards. It is reluctantly determined to relinquish the task, as the remainder of the ice is absolutely unworkable, being too deep and a jumble of hummocks and rafted blocks. ...

19 February 1915

During the morning, went for a stroll to the old lead ahead, which is now nearly a foot thick. I was much interested in examining the contexture of the recent young ice formed on the lead and on some pools in our vicinity. The growth commences by the formation of small fish scale-like crystals which accumulate, without definite orientation, in horizontal layers. This formation extends below the surface for about half an inch, when the small plate crystals gradually arrange themselves till they become vertical. This is probably due to the heavier saline solution sinking and so directing automatically the disposition of the plates. The accretion continues by the increments of these vertical scales. This new ice fractures at right angles to its plane. The ice subsequently undergoes further recrystallization, appearing distinctly fibrous in texture.

24 February 1915

Land observable to the SE. Ice conditions unchanged. Hole sawn through the ice around the rudder well to keep the rudder and propeller free. All hands put off ship's routine. We now practically cease being a ship and become a shore station. A night watchman, all taking turns, (except the for'ard hands), in alphabetical order, comes on duty at 8 p.m., remaining thereon till 8 a.m. He is responsible for the safety of the ship during the night, keeping the bogie fires alight and the taking of meteorological observations.

25 February 1915

Fit up the refrigerator as a darkroom and commence developing cinema film, and am gratified to discover the same in excellent condition. Difficulty is experienced in obtaining sufficient water for washing operations. Dry the film by hanging it in the refrigerator, maintaining a temperature equable as possible with Sir Ernest's paraffin heater.

26 February 1915

Dogs all placed on shore, much to their delight. All hands engaged in building igloos, or as the sailors term them, dogloos, from ice blocks and snow. The dogloos are arranged in an extended circle around the ship. The dogs are secured by chain, one end of which is buried in the ice, and frozen therein by the simple action of pouring water on it. ...

27 February 1915

Attempt to receive wireless signals during the evening. After tea, a plenteous supply of winter clothing is issued to all. The clothing is precisely similar to that supplied to the Mawson Expedition.

28 February 1915

... Land still visible to SE and one can distinctly observe the crevasses and details thereon. All leads are now frozen up, and no water is visible anywhere. Preparations are in full swing to encomfort ourselves against the siege of the coming Antarctic winter.

6 March 1915

... During the evening a singing musical competition takes place, the prize being unanimously awarded to Sir Ernest. His voice is quaint, vacillating between sharps and flats in a most unique manner. Wordie, now ex-champion, renders an old favourite, 'The Gambolier', in a voice resembling the shrill tone caused by drawing a rasp smartly across the edge of a sheet of galvanised iron. Clark renders, with much applause, 'My Nut Brown Maiden', in a nasal super tenor, and I render 'Waltzing Matilda', in the melting dulcet tones one often hears a swaggie crooning at sunset when punching his frugal damper. ...

9 March 1915

As no hope can be entertained of freeing ourselves from our icy fastness this season, and as temperatures are rapidly falling, the residential part of the ship is undergoing considerable modifications. The main hold has been discharged, and cubicles are being erected therein along the port and starboard sides. Each cubicle contains two bunks, except the Billabong, two cubicles having been united, resulting in a double-lengther. Dr. Macklin, McIlroy, Hussey and self constitute the occupants. Between the two rows of cubicles, the table is placed where all take meals. Near the after end, the bogie, for keeping up the temperature, is placed. The holders of the various dens or cubicles have assumed various cognomens for their 6 foot 5 inch x 5 foot abodes: 'The Anchorage', 'Auld Reekie', 'The Poison Cupboard', 'The Knuts' and 'The Billabong'. These dwellings are styled the 'Ritz'. The wardroom has undergone a similar alteration, and is known as 'The Stables'. It is tenanted by Wild, Crean, Marston and Worsley. Sir Ernest occupies his original cabin right aft. A bogie has been installed there for roasting purposes.

Wordie, Worsley and self visit the Rampart Berg. It is located some eight miles south of the ship, and on account of its irregular form, is very pictorial. ... This colossal block of ice had a base of some 300 acres, and raised its crenellated towers 180 feet above the surface of the sea. Along its top surface were immense battlemented embrasures – the open ends of crevasses – that gave it the appearance of a titanic fortification. Around its base, the pack ice crunched, rafted and groaned complainingly, being goaded along as the monster ploughed majestically through it. Standing on the rafting pressure, we made its blue caverns echo with three hearty 'coo-ees'. ...

20 March 1915

During the evening I gave an illustrated lantern lecture on Java and across Australia. All hands, afterguard and fo'c'sle, rolled up to a man. It was quite a relief to see some tropical vegetation and flowers, even though they were but shadowgraphs projected on the screen. ...

22 March 1915

Training the dogs. The tuition of canines can only be successfully accomplished by the frequent and judicious application of the whip, assisted by a stringent vocabulary. 'Spare the whip and spoil the dog' is the imperative motto of all dog drivers. The leader is selected for his sagacity and is trained individually in a light bobsledge. ... A good leader will ferret out the best track through rough and broken country, will not allow fights in the team, or indulge in any capricious antics. ... A team of nine dogs can haul about 1000 pounds, while its hauling capacity may be increased considerably by the strength of the team driver's arm, and the impelling vocabulary at his command. (My team is one of the best.) ...

1 April 1915

The engineers strip and oil up engines in order to preserve same during the coming winter, no further hope being entertained of breaking out this season. ...

24 April 1915

Owing to fallen temperature – it being –19° – a heavy condensation develops on cameras when brought aboard. I have made a cupboard on deck where they may be kept at an even lower temperature. Nevertheless, the apparatus needs attention every occasion it is taken out, lubricating with petroleum etc., especially the cinematograph. Under these extreme temperatures, the film becomes extremely brittle and loses about 10 per cent of its sensitiveness.

1 May 1915

Observed the sun today by refraction, probably the last glimpse till the coming Spring. Depth, 175 fathoms.

3 May 1915

Hussey and myself night watch again. During the small hours, we endeavour to cure Lees of his habitual snoring. Asleep on his back, with mouth wide open, the gap seemed to invite a joke. Hussey, refreshing himself on sardines, suggested filling Lees' mouth with the tin, but I, more humanely, dropped in several fish. The sardines disappeared, but the snoring increased and the mouth opened wider, perhaps in anticipation. Lentils, however, being nearby, I emptied a handful into the cavern with satisfactory results. We were able to proceed, without the diversion snores, with our game of chess.

19 May 1915

A form of mid-winter madness has manifested itself, all hands being seized with the desire to have their hair removed. It caused much amusement, and luxuriant curls, bald pates and parted crowns soon become akin. We are likely to be coolheaded in the future, if not neuralgic. We resemble a cargo of convicts, and I did not let the opportunity pass of perpetuating photographically this humorous happening.

27 May 1915

... Had delightful run with team during the morning. The faint daylight mingling with the brilliant moonlight lent a peculiar enchantment to the frozen sea. The northern sky was aflame with the golden glow of the departing sun. The southern sky was more sombre, being delicately prismatic, with a faint blue horizon blending into a pink tint in which stood a silver moon glowing like a halo. One felt quite elated riding on the sledge and driving into the moon's face. Winter, although hoary and blizzard-bowed, is the most beautiful and charming part of the year. ...

7 June 1915

The darkest part of the year. The moon sets at 9 a.m. We have but three hours of dim twilight at noon, and the rest of the twenty-four hours it is dark. Depth, 254 fathoms.

9 June 1915

Take the team out to the lead ahead of ship, and observe the pressure working. Immense blocks of ice are pressed up into high ridges with an irresistible power which makes one think what would the ship's fate be if she encountered one of these.

10 June 1915

... Heavy pressure starts about 500 yards from the ship, and immense blocks of ice, weighing 10 to 15 tons are broken and piled up in a ruin-like chaos. The noise of this working pressure is a continuous din, at times, like the deep boom of distant artillery. Then squeaking, screaming and groaning as huge slab rafts up crushing a smaller one beneath it. Nothing can stop the irresistible pressure wave. Up rises another huge pressure wave, only to continue its work of building up an enormous pile of ice debris some 20 feet high. We are thankful our ship is out of range.

13 June 1915

... From within the cosiness of the Ritz, it is hard to imagine we are drifting, frozen and solid, in a sea of pack ice in the very heart of the Weddell Sea. I often wonder, and I do not suppose I am the only one, what is to become of it all. ...

15 June 1915

Great fancy dress gathering and betting today on the Antarctic Derby Stakes. All available chocolate and cigarettes, the local currency, have been brought into requisition. Sir Ernest is starter, and the line near the ship, is home. All hands are given the day off to see the race. The day opens dull and overcast, and the track is visible only by hurricane lamps. Several of the ABs [Able Seamen] are dressed as bookies, but, as they look a trifle on the crook side, nobody is accepting their odds. The 'Khyber Pass' light flashes the signal, and the teams are off. Great cheering ensues, and the dogs join in by barking. The teams seem to know what is expected of them. Wild's team is seen racing down the 'Pileon' track. Then comes Macklin's and McIlroy's teams, headed by Bony Peter. The drivers urge their teams by shouts and varied vocabularies. Wild wins, covering the distance in two minutes, sixteen seconds. Hurley is next in two minutes, twenty-six seconds.

22 June 1915

Observed as a holiday. The sun begins to return once more and a justifiable merrymaking custom ensues. After an excellent breakfast and lunch of reserved dainties, we partake of a 'feast' dinner, after which all retire to their cubicles to array in stage dress. I erect a stage, illumined with acetylene footlights, and decorated with bunting.

Sir Ernest opens the evening with an egoistic and satiric harangue which is admirably responded to by the Rev. Dr Bubblinglove (Lees). An overture, 'Discord Fantasia' in four flats by the Billabong Band works the audience up to a high pitch, the B.B. opportunely retiring to their retreat. Many humorous sketches and make-ups, interspersed with good-natured persiflage. Rickinsen makes an admirable flapper, whilst McIlroy makes a very good grisette, highly perfumed (betokening oakum and teased-out rope yarn). Greenstreet, the dashing Knut, was a great success. James's humorous brogue dissertation on the calorie was loudly applauded. Marston as a country farmer was superb. The evening, which comprised some thirty items, with an interval, concluded by God Save the King, and Auld Lang Syne. Afterwards we partook of a midnight supper.

27 June 1915

Eerie sounds of distant working pressure are carried on the crispy wintry atmosphere, a faint booming, groaning, and creaking, a sound that to us, the greater the distance, the more the enchantment.

30 June 1915

My turn to night watch. The duties of the night watch are to keep the Ritz bogie glowing, the Stables roasting, and the Boss's, which is right aft, at an equable temperature. The latter is a difficult job, as the Boss's room is but a small cabin. The temperature within is either 90° or well below freezing, according to the vicissitudes of the wind, which greatly influence the bogie draught. Sir Ernest's temper reciprocates with the room temperature. The night watch also arouses his friends, and they sit in quorum around the bogie fire, discoursing in subdued whispers, and partaking of the night watchman's homage, to wit, sardines on toast, (a great favourite) grilled biscuit and cocoa or tea. Frequently, a special 'perk', reserved for the occasion, is produced, and the visitors, termed ghosts, are appreciative. ...

2 July 1915

A typical day. Rise at 8.30 a.m., generally 8.50 a.m., breakfast at 9 a.m. sharp, else woe betide! Sir Ernest's humour in the morning before breakfast is very erratic. Morning, exercise the dogs and 'dinkass' about generally. Lunch, 1 p.m. Afternoon, nil till afternoon tea at 3.30 p.m. till 4 p.m. Nil till 6 p.m., then turn in at own desire after an arduous day endeavouring to make time pass.

7 July 1915

Menial discontent in the fo'c'sle, several hands complaining of the Bosun having called them evil names, and struck them. As harmony is imperative, his promotion to Bosun has been cancelled, and he resumes his former rank as trawling hand. ...

21 July 1915

... Heavy ice pressure is heard in the SW of the ship. Sounds like surf breaking on rocks. During the day one can observe much movement going on amongst the floes ahead of the ship accompanied by a weird creaking and groaning. The ship's deck is cleared and chains secured in readiness to bring the dogs on board at any moment. A diligent watch is maintained; an hourly watch is kept during the night. The crack starts from the lead ahead and runs to within 30 yards of the ship. About 400 yards ahead, on the port bow, the ice has been very active. Crunching and rafting huge fragments, weighing many tons, being forced up and balanced on the top of pressure ridges over 15 feet high.

26 July 1915

> Nor dim, nor red,
> Like God's own Head,
> The glorious sun uprist.
> [from Samuel Taylor Coleridge, *The Rime of the Ancient Mariner*]

For the first time for 79 days Old Jamaica peeped above the horizon, and after winking at us for nearly a minute, set in glowing majesty, firing the sky with crimson and golden tints.

1 August 1915

At 10 a.m., the floe began to move in our vicinity. Eventually it broke up and set the ship free. Shortly afterwards great pressure began working, driving tongues of ice below the ship and heeling us over to starboard. Our position became extremely perilous, as huge blocks were rafting and tumbling over themselves in their apparent eagerness to hurl their force against our walls. An ominous creaking and buckling of the deck manifested the terrific strains being exerted against the ship. The dogs were hurriedly brought on board and gangways raised, and just in time, for shortly afterwards, many of the kennels were overwhelmed by the oncoming tide of ice. Close against our starboard bow we had the unique observation of a big pressure ridge being thrown up. The edges of the floe previously split, came together with such force that the ice was thrown up into a long ridge of crushed debris and huge blocks some 15 to 20 feet high. While we were all feeling in a state of delightful uncertainty, standing by ready at the boats for lowering, and gear equipment ready for quitting, the pressure stopped instantaneously, and all resumed the serene Antarctic quiet once more. ...

5 August 1915

View from the masthead. The ice surface has entirely altered. Away ahead of the ship, it appears as an immense chaos of hummocks and ridges, ice needles and broken blocks piled up in the wildest confusion. Two huge fragments have been launched up on to the surface of the floe, and are several feet thick, and solid ice weighing over 30 tons. The soundings have increased to 1146 fathoms. All dogs are now housed on the ship's deck.

22 August 1915

Beautiful alpengluhen on the pack at sunrise. I walk out to the small lead ahead of the ship. The water is absolutely calm and the pink tinted hummocks and pinnacles bounding the margin are reflected therein. Sir Ernest joins me a little later, and together we walk by the edge of the lead, treading in fairyland. The pack to the Southern horizon reflects the rose pink of early sunrise, and the grotesquely rosy shades. The air is so exhilarating, that one can scarce refrain from bursting into song and singing to thy charms, oh wondrous land! ...

24 August 1915

Took colour camera to lead again this morning amidst the similar gorgeous conditions of yesterday, more glorified perhaps for a fine crop of ice flowers have sprung up on the lead and were illuminated by the morning sun, resembling a field of pink carnations. I secured some fine coloured reproductions. Ice flowers probably owe their origin to the presence, in the surface layers of the newly formed ice, of small inclusions of saline solution, which freezing under the influence of low temperatures, with consequent extrusion of the salt, act as nuclei for the disposition of rime from the relatively humid air adjacent to the ice surface.

27 August 1915

… During the night take flashlight [pictures] of the ship beset by pressure. This necessitated some twenty flashes, one behind each salient pressure hammock, no less than ten of the flashes being required to satisfactorily illuminate the ship herself. Half blinded after the successive flashes, I lost my bearings amidst hummocks, bumping shins against projecting ice points and stumbling into deep snowdrifts. Pack quiet, but away to the distant north clouds of sea smoke arise like a distant fire.

30 August 1915

… Darkroom work rendered extremely difficult by the low temperatures, it being –13° outside. The darkroom is situated abaft the engine room and is raised to above freezing point by a Primus stove. Washing plates is a most troublesome operation, as the tank must be kept warm or the plates become an enclosure in an ice block. After several changes of water, I place them in a rack in Sir Ernest's cabin, which is generally at a fairly equable temperature. The dry plates are all spotted and carefully indexed. Development is a source of much annoyance to the fingers, which crack and split around the nails in a painful manner.

1 September 1915

Heavy pressure set in for the night, and I anticipated the beams alongside my bunk would be splintered. The floor in the Billabong and Ritz buckled in an alarming manner, and the partition between ours and Lees' cubicle sprung tongues from the grooves.

2 September 1915

Heavy pressure all night. One cannot feel but apprehensive when the deck begins moving and opening under one's feet, and you hear the ship groaning and cracking under this awful icy embrace. I do not mind getting out and stretching my legs, although land is over 300 miles away, but I prefer doing it when the temperature is a little warmer, it now being 53° below freezing point.

30 September 1915

Experienced a nip today, the most severe since entering the ice. The ship endures a terrific strain, shivering from stem to stern, when at last it seems that her sides must collapse. The floe splits and, with feelings of relief to us, the strain is alleviated. …

14 October 1915

Uneasiness in the ice ahead of the ship, and shortly after 7 p.m., a rending crash causes all hands to rush up on deck. A crack has opened from the lead ahead of the ship, passed along our starboard to another crack that has formed aft. The ship is free, the first occasion since the 16th February. Through the clear water we can examine the damaged helm ...

15 October 1915

My twenty-eighth birthday. At midnight, the ship drifts from her cradle, where she had been frozen in situ in the floe, and falls astern, leaving her form moulded in the splintered floe behind her. The spanker is hoisted, and we actually sail 100 yards, our first movement since the 15th February. We are now in a narrow lead, double the ship's beam in width, and blocked immediately ahead by a narrow transverse lead. Our position I review with some anxiety, as we inevitably must be severely nipped, should the floes come together.

17 October 1915

The ice seems intent on disturbing our Sunday evening gramophone concerts, for it invariably sets up a whining and 'gets busy' as we are in the midst of musical enjoyment. Punctual to 6 p.m., we hear the dread whining and groaning followed almost immediately by the vessel vibrating and shivering as though she were trembling with fear at the coming conflict. It is a cracky, uneven conflict, receiving all blows and unable to give retaliation. Together came those irresistible vice-like floes, nipping the ship in their terrific grip. She creaks, groans, and shivers in agony, but tighter and relentless is the grip and, when we expect to see her sides stave in, she slowly and gradually rises from the pressure. At this critical junction the pressure fortunately ceased, as suddenly as the stopping of some gigantic mechanism. ...

18 October 1915

The ice remained quiet throughout last night, and up till 4.45 p.m. today, when the ice was again in motion. Standing on the deck watching the grinding of the floes against our sides, one could not but feel apprehensive for the ship's safety. Every timber was straining to rupture. The decks gaped, doors refused to open or shut. The floor coverings buckled, and the iron floor plates in the engine room bulged and sprung from their seatings. ... Shortly after 5 p.m., we began to rise from the ice, much after the manner of a gigantic pip squeezed between the fingers. In the short space of seven seconds, we were shot from the floes and thrown over to port, with a list of 30 degrees. ... During the evening, I took a series of pictures of our ignominious position. We were all fervently thankful when the pressure was relieved again at 9 p.m., and allowed us once more to regain an even keel. ...

24 October 1915

The floes, which have been in motion during the afternoon, set in with great energy about 6 p.m., assailing the ship on the starboard quarter. All hands go down onto the floe with picks, shovels and chisels, and cut trenches to relieve the strain. At 7 p.m., an oncoming floe impinges on the helm, forcing it hard over to port, wrenching the rudderpost. The ship's sternpost is seriously damaged, and the hidden ends of the planking started. Soundings in the well announce the gloomy tidings that we are rapidly making water. The pumps are immediately manned, and steam raised for the engine room pumps. The water is at present easily kept under, and the carpenter immediately set to work constructing a cofferdam in the shaft tunnel. Watches keep the pumps manned vigorously; their clickety-click resounds throughout the night, above the ominous creaking of timbers. The position is serious, as it is evident our old enemy is not going to remain passive at this juncture – the critical period of disintegration.

26 October 1915

... Fine clear day. The ice, which has been in a state of turmoil since this morning, subjected the ship to terrific strains during the afternoon. The menacing pressure ridge on our starboard quarter was in great activity, and a wide crack, extending from our rudder, reunited and was converted into a mass of disrupted blocks and crunched fragments. ... The dogs, instinctively conscious of the imminent peril, set up distressed wails of uneasiness and fear. Sir Ernest, standing on the poop, calmly surveying the movements of the ice and giving an occasional peremptory order. Sledges and all gear are being rapidly accumulated on deck, without the slightest discomposure, as though it were ordinary routine duty. At 6 p.m. the pressure develops an irresistible energy; apparently our vicinity being the focus, as the ice, a short distance off, remains quiescent. The ship groans and quivers, windows splinter, whilst the deck timbers gape and twist. Amidst these profound and overwhelming forces, we are the absolute embodiment of helpless futility. The brunt of the pressure assails our starboard quarter and the damaged stern post, forcing the ship ahead by a series of pulsating jerks, and with such force that the bows are driven wedgewise into the solid floe ahead (4 foot 6 inches thick). This frightful strain is observed to bend the entire hull some 10 inches along its length. At 7 p.m. the order is given to lower the three boats. The boats are hauled some distance away from the *Endurance*, and out of the zone of immediate danger. ...

27 October 1915

... Chips expects to complete the cofferdam tonight, and great hopes are entertained for its success. The dam is being filled with sawdust and cement, which, it is anticipated, will be carried by the flowing water into the interstices of the structure and form a hydraulic seal. During the morning, all hands go down onto the floe and remove an immense embankment of ice debris, which has piled up against our starboard quarter, high above the bulwarks. All, including Sir Ernest, continue turns with the pumps, which are able to keep pace with the inflowing water. We have just finished lunch, and the 'ice mill' is in motion again. Closer and closer approaches the pressure wave on our starboard, like a huge frozen surf. Immense slabs are rafted up to its crest, which topple down and are overridden by a chaos of crunched fragments. Irresistibly, this stupendous power marches onward, grinding its way through the 5-foot floe surrounding us. Now it is within a few yards, and the vessel groans and quivers. I am quickly down on the moving ice with the cinema, expecting every minute to see the sides, which are springing and buckling, stave in. ... Before leaving, I went below into the old winter quarters, the Ritz, and found the water already a foot above the floor. The sound of splintering beams in the darkness was a little too imposing, so that I left in a hurry. Sir Ernest hoists the blue ensign at the mizzen gaff to three lusty cheers, and is last to leave. ... By some curious happening, the emergency light becomes automatically switched on, and an intermittent making and breaking of the circuit, seems to transmit a final signal of farewell.

28 October 1915

... We are approximately 209 miles from Snow Hill and 350 from Paulette Island, the winter quarters of the Nordenskjold Expedition of 1903–4. Here there is a store of provisions, and it is intended that the party should sledge across the sea ice to either of these depots, where the main body will remain, whilst a sledging or boating party will endeavour to communicate with the whaling factories of Wilhelmina Bay or Deception Harbour. The floes are in a state of agitation throughout the day, and in consequence, I had the cinema trained on the ship the whole time. I secured the unique film of the masts collapsing. Towards evening, as though conscious of having achieved its purpose, the floes were quiescent again.

29 October 1915

... The day was spent packing, and lashing sledges, and sorting out gear; the carpenter being very busy constructing sledges for the two boats to be taken. The dump heap is a heterogeneous collection of dress suits, hats, brushes, combs, portmanteaus, books, etc., pleasant though useless refinements of civilization. I even noticed some gold studs, links and sovereigns. After all, I thought, value is but relative, a mere matter of comparison.

During the afternoon, Wild, McIlroy and myself went aboard the *Endurance*. Poor old ship, what a battered wreck she is! The floes, like a mighty vice, have crushed her laterally. The starboard side has been crushed in, and all the cabins along it have been closed up as efficiently as a folding Kodak their broken and splintered walls being forced into the alleyways, which are blocked with an indescribable chaos of debris and ice. The wardroom, too, is a pitiful sight, being crammed to the ceiling with iceblocks and splinters. Without, on the boat deck a veritable 'hummocking' of timbers has gone on, and the supporting beams have been broken amidships, so that the deck falls away to starboard and one can step from it onto the floe. Fore and aft, it is a switchback. The jib boom has snapped off at the gammon iron: the foremast at the crosstrees, the main is splintered six feet above the deck, whilst the mizzen, with the blue ensign still floating at the gaff, is as staunch as ever. With her stern cocked high in the air, and fo'c'sle head overridden by the floe, it would be difficult to recognise, but for the name at her stern – the *Endurance* – the acme of man's ingenuity in shipcraft and constructed specially to combat the strife of the polar seas. The wreck must inevitably sink as soon as the pressure relaxes and the piercing tongues of ice that are at present acting as supports are withdrawn. ... Sir Ernest announces that the march will begin tomorrow.

30 October 1915

... Before leaving, I had a final look at the darkroom wherein is submerged, beneath four feet of water, my treasured negatives and instruments. At 7 p.m., a start is made. ... A pathfinding party of three precedes the advance with a light sledge and demolishes hummocks, bridge cracks, and smooths out the track. This party has a couple of hours lead on the main body. Then follows seven sledges, each drawn by seven dogs, and loaded with an average load of 100 pounds per dog. Five teams then return, and bring up the balance of the gear loaded on five sledges. The remaining two teams, Wild's and my own team, will link together and bring up the light boat. The balance of the party, eighteen members, will man haul the large boat – the *James Caird*. ...

1 November 1915

... Sir Ernest has formed an advisory committee, comprised of Wild, Worsley, and self, and during the morning we scouted ahead for a track. The condition of the surface was atrocious, and the floe is covered with a layer of soft snow into which we sank knee and thigh deep. There appears scarcely a square yard of smooth surface, which is covered by a labyrinth of hummocks and ridges. Owing to this impossible surface, we were of the unanimous opinion that the alternative project of establishing a permanent camp on a piece of heavy old floe, and awaiting the breaking up of the ice pack, should be resorted to. In pursuance of this decision, all the sledges and boats were hauled to a suitable camping floe, and the tents pitched. ...

2 November 1915

The teams ply to and from the wreck, bringing into camp loads of wood and canvas, though very little food. ... During the day, I hacked through the thick walls of the refrigerator to retrieve the negatives stored therein. They were located beneath four feet of mushy ice and, by stripping to the waist and diving under, I hauled them out. Fortunately, they are soldered up in double tin linings, so I am hopeful they may not have suffered by their submersion. On return to camp, my team bolted owing to a killer whale breaking through the ice but 10 yards ahead. Three seals captured during the day. There is at present sufficient food in camp to last the fugitive party 180 days, at the rate of a pound per day.

5 November 1915

... The sailors are busy at work erecting a canvas hut 23 feet x 11 feet from sails and spars, to be used as a galley and shelter. I searched the ship over for a suitable object that could be converted into a cooking range; as the ash chute was the nearest approach to the desideratum, it was conveyed to the camp. ... The stove is designed to consume blubber for fuel, and, when installed in the new shelter, should ameliorate the cook's duties considerably.

7 November 1915

... The canvas erection is completed and is being floored with lining boards from the wreck: it has been christened the Billabong, a tribute to the good luck which rewarded our salvage efforts in the recovery of stores from the original Billabong. During the afternoon, we installed the 'Hash Chute' stove, which proved a great success. It simply roars away like a furnace, generating far more heat than the galley stove on board ship. The cook can now prepare the meals in comfort, and, we hope, cleanliness. The general appearance of the camp reminds one of an Alaskan mining settlement in winter. In the centre, surrounded by the piles of stores, is the eating house, belching from its chimney a trail of brown smoke that has already left its trademark across the snow. The tents are arranged in a row conveniently near, with the huskies pegged out in their respective teams contiguous to the tents. Around us is a vast, illimitable champagne of snow, which not even the most fertile imagination could conceive to be the frozen bosom of the sea. It is beyond conception, even to us, that we are dwelling on a colossal ice raft, with but five feet of ice separating us from 2000 fathoms of ocean and drifting along under the caprices of wind and tides, to heaven knows where.

8 November 1915

Pay the final official visit to the wreck with the Chief and Wild. Yesterday's mild blizzard has put the final touch to the destruction wrought by pressure and the salvage gangs. Large snow ramps have formed around the remains of the hull, almost entirely burying the decks, the fo'c'sle being entirely buried beneath the floe. But for the stump of the foremast and the funnel, one would be sceptical if told that that collection of fragmentary timbers and twisted rails was once a ship. After saluting the ensign, with a detonator fired on the poop, we returned sadly to camp.

9 November 1915

… I spend the day with Sir Ernest, selecting the finest of my negatives from the year's collection. 120 I resoldered up and dumped about 400. …

10 November 1915

… The camp routine is as follows: Camp rise at 8 a.m., breakfast 8.30. Generally fried seal steak with bannock and tea. Routine duties, viz. seal scouting, tidying camp, etc., till 1 p.m. Lunch variable (today boiled suet rolls); the cook was subject to a severe ranting for allowing dirt to contaminate the pudding cloth. Afternoon is spent at individual's discretion, reading, walking, etc. Generally seal or penguin hoosh at 5.30 p.m., and cocoa. Turn into sleeping bags immediately after. Take an hour's watch each alternate night.

13 November 1915

... During the evening, the party congregated in the Billabong, and held a concert. The voices, accompanied by Hussey's indispensable banjo, sounded strangely out of place amidst the profound silence of the hummocks; yet it is gratifying to hear that ring of hearty laughter that betokens contentment and harmony, the attributes of excellent leadership, and good eating.

18 November 1915

... There is very curious attire in the camp; the cook, with a very sooty face and soiled silk dress shirt and a dress suit. Others in varied uniforms and miscellaneous garments. Fortunately, our whiskers are sprouting and hiding some of the dirt on our faces. Have great admiration for the Boss, who is very considerate and kindly disposed and an excellent comrade. Our position is unaltered.

21 November 1915

... At 5 p.m., a movement was discerned in the wreck. The stern rose vertically, and a few minutes later, dived beneath the surface of the floe. We are not sorry to see the last of the wreck, for we have rifled it of everything likely to be of value to us; apart from being an object of depression to all who turned their eyes in that direction, it was becoming more dangerous daily to those visiting it.

27 November 1915

... Crews have been allotted to the three boats, which have been christened the *James Caird*, the *Dudley Docker* and the *Stancombe Wills*, and a list of responsible duties drawn up to be performed by individuals in case of emergency. Since the 21st, a northward advance of 20 miles has been made. ... Little change has taken place in the ice. The present camp has been named Ocean Camp.

5 December 1915

... Lazy day in tent, reading encyclopedia on Borneo, Sumatra and Australia. ...

21 December 1915

Sir Ernest addressed all hands this evening, informing them of his intention to advance. ... The floes were very promising, so that it is decided that a start be made on the 23rd instant. ... It is proposed that the chief will scout out the road with Wild's team. I follow, then six sledges drawn by dogs. The *James Caird* drawn by 18 men, the dogs will return to relay sledges whilst Wild's and mine will take on the *Stancombe Wills*.

25 December 1915

Christmas Day. Today, driving the dog team and hauling the boats for dear life across the Weddell Sea pack ice. ... We had a strenuous time getting through hummocks and filling in small leads. We covered 2½ miles, but the surface was atrocious. The dogs did excellent work. Continuous wet feet for all. Temperature, plus 34°. We spied out a track this evening for two miles ahead for the morrow's march. Wind favourable, and hauling the boats was assisted by hoisting our sails. Seal secured.

27 December 1915

... Reached berg, the terminus of yesterday's scouting, and ascended to survey future prospects. The prospect one might liken to a glimpse of the ice fields of the moon, beautiful in grandeur beyond conception. ...

29 December 1915

... Owing to rotten ice, decide to return ½ mile to solid floe. Turned in again 10 p.m., and slept soundly till 8 a.m. As ice began to break up in the vicinity, again retreated onto large floe, where we lunched yesterday. A decision has been arrived at, to remain camped here so long as the floe is intact, pending the breakup of the ice. Sledges repacked and in readiness, with only essential foods for the boats, should a lead or crack open. Now ten miles from Ocean Camp, in satisfactory position. ...

30 December 1915

Discovered small crack in our floe, during my night watch, which ran through the middle of camp. Called Sir Ernest, and it was decided to strike camp further into centre of floe. ...

31 December 1915

... Many sweet memories crowd on me as I lay in my bag, meditating the last day of the year. Home, faces, places, and our present position that one cannot altogether regard as sweet. Drifting about on the ice floe, 189 miles from the nearest known land. Still, to apply an old sledging motto, 'It might be much worse'. Inside the tents all are comfortable. Sir Ernest is thinking and solving magic squares. We have plenty of food, and with the coming warm season and subsequent dissipation of the ice, are able to greet with cheery aspect the New Year 1916! New Year resolutions. We have none to make as there is nothing to make them for, unless it be to resolve to keep our hoosh pots cleaner – and faces too!

1 January 1916

With the New Year we are imbued with new hopes, for the ice manifests the most satisfactory aspect of breaking up since we entered it a year ago. This morning, Captain Worsley and self rode out on my sledge to Pinnacle Berg ... to investigate the conditions. From the top we observed the floe to be starred and broken in all directions. Radiating everywhere are long narrow leads and pools. The ice is rotting and one is on the alert at all intervals lest he should break through into the Weddell Sea. A lead which has now developed into a lake has opened only a few hundred yards from the camp and we are hopeful of the issue. ...

7 January 1916

... Most notable happening is a change in the direction of the wind, which is now favourable. We are entirely dependent on winds and currents to free us. Long may the wind blow and gain in strength. The surface is untravellable owing to its softness and broken-up nature.

14 January 1916

... During the morning, camp was shifted to an adjacent floe, our present, becoming very limited from splitting and breaking off at the edges. During the afternoon, after the establishment of a new camp, four teams of dogs were shot: Messrs. Wild's, Crean's, McIlroy's and Marston's – (comprising a total of thirty magnificent sledgers). This step has been given lengthy consideration and ... the decision is a wise one. The dogs consuming one seal daily, the same lasting the entire party three days. ...

16 January 1916

Had an easy day in camp, feeling a tiredness after yesterday. Wild shot my team during afternoon – a sad but unfortunate necessity. Hail to thee, old leader Shakespeare, I shall ever remember thee – fearless, faithful, and diligent; ever ready to thy master's bidding. ...

19 January 1916

… Time passes tediously. Eat, read and play cards, and drift with the floe under the guidance of capricious winds and tides. Brighter times are looked forward to, however, and we are cheerfully awaiting the opening up of the ice, that we may take to the boats and so, God willing, reach Paulette Island expeditiously and safely.

30 January 1916

… Came to the end of *Eothen*. I would rather carry this excellent book than six times its weight in rations. Kinglake's magnificent description of the desert, resembles Byron's Ocean – an apostrophe written – not to be excelled. It transported me from the illimitable ice to the interminable desert sands, to the sphinx, to the great pyramids, and dwelt me transiently by the umbrageous olives of far Damascus and the knarled cedars of Lebanon. Alas! the book is finished and round me remains the every unchangeable ice, the same leaden sky, the same existing patience – the same white line that girdles the boundary of vision and acts like a bar to our frigid captivity. But we know that beyond that horizon, lies the great rolling road to freedom and so we look forward. …

2 February 1916

'Rise and Shine' at 1 a.m. and after hooshing, proceed with Crean's team path finding … to 'Ocean Camp'. The object of the 'Sortie' being to rescue the *Stancombe Wills* – the third boat – and bring it on to present camp. … The third boat will enable us to water voyage with considerable comfort and safety, as well as mitigating overcrowding. …

10 February 1916

… During a clear intermission visited the bergs – game scouting. Our blubber supply – the source of fuel – becoming depleted and I, being the Nimrod, have necessarily to take advantage of every opportunity to maintain the reserve heap. In scouting amongst loosening pack, one must needs to be both alert and cautious. Skis are indispensable, cracks 4 and 5 feet have frequently to be crossed and the negotiation of them and brash ice makes one develop a cat-like gentleness of tread. It is astonishing the speed one can travel should a killer poke his head through the thin ice. What curious bosom sensations it excites! Surface today almost unskiable.

18 February 1916

... Strong blizzard with wet snow and headwinds have endured the past 24 hours – the most severe and disappointing setback since encamped on the floe. Summer appears at an end, as the characteristic stormy conditions – the heralds of winter – have harassed us for the past 14 days. It now appears imperative that we shall have to remain another winter in the Antarctic and our hopes are that we may make Paulette Island. ...

23 February 1916

... Necessity hath evolved me from a polar Nimrod to a Nemesis on ski. All things living (other than human) that I discern on the floe from the numerous berg lookouts are as good as in cold storage. Providence is both considerate and kind. It would appear as if the evolution of the penguin and seal species had developed especially along lines calculated to fill the wants of polar castaways. The blubbery layer of subdermal tissue of the seal is sufficient to convert his entire carcass into roasts, boils and hooshes, while the penguin's overcoat – rich also in blubber – is ample to cook all his eatable parts and a little more besides. A seal is consumed by the entire party in five days – just as long as his blubber lasts. Twenty penguins cooked by the fuel of their own skins is a fair daily average. ...

1 March 1916

Wax poetical. ... Magnificent night and morning with crystal-clear atmosphere. The moon almost on the horizon resembled the golden horn of fairy tales pending in a lustrous firmament bespangled with brilliants. One's imagination running riot might conjecture a blast sounded on the golden horn would break the enchantment of the still night and disclose a calm sea of scattered pack. The beau ideal of our dreams. As the horned moon dipped below the horizon, a faint orange blush suffused its path, which broadened and glowed, till dawn spread the sky with tints of pink and blue. The dissipation of night's enchantment disclosed immense pools of still water surrounding our now island floe from which clouds of frost smoke lazily arose – golden in the rising sun – like smoke from a prairie fire. ...

13 March 1916

... Never has time seemed to drag so much as today. Windy (SW) and foggy and the atmosphere very depressing. Even a desert isle would be more acceptable to this drifting imprisonment of mental and physical inertia. Although time hangs on our hands, it is impossible to concentrate one's thoughts for any time reading. Anxiety is felt by all that it is time to be making a move. We seem to be in an icy maze. ...

30 March 1916

... A day of activities. The watchman called an alarm at 5 a.m. to the effect that our floe was cracking up and all hands turned out immediately. All equipage was removed to safety, but shortly before breakfast a recurrence took place, the flow breaking up into a smaller section about 100 yards square. One crack passed under the runners of our large boat, the *James Caird*, and opened so rapidly that we just saved her from falling in. ... The remainder of the dogs shot and skinned, and some steaks cut off the young dogs. ... Hunger brings us all to the level of other species, and our saying, 'That sledge dogs are born for work and bred for food', is but the rationale of experience.

4 April 1916

... By far the most popular of tent topics are talks on 'other lands and unknown places'. I am a frequent raconteur of travel in the East Indies and wanderings in hidden Australia etc., and delight hearing in return the tinkling temple bells of India and all about that dear homeland, from the blasted heaths of bonnie Scotland to London with its 'stream of liquid history' – the Thames. ...

7 April 1916

... Critical point of drift. Anxiety re getting through gap between Elephant Island and King George. ... At daylight, what appeared to be at first an immense berg proved to be an island. ... The way to the land is jammed by treacherous pack moving rapidly by tides, winds and currents so as to be absolutely unsafe and impassable. Would that it would but open up. The pack is bristling with life; seals, penguins and birds of wing, whilst the incessant blowing of blue and killer whales, I may simile to a railway yard chock-full of engines blowing off at high pressure. One may observe killers sporting in the pools, with their triangular dorsal above water or see their alligator-like heads peer above the floe in quest of game. ...

9 April 1916

... Passes under sledges of *Stancombe Wills* and the *James Caird*. Ice behaving under current influence, opening and shutting [with] great rapidity. Crack again splits floe – 11 a.m. tents taken down passes diagonal-wise through ours. Heavy swell. Boats packed, with difficulty get under way by 1.30 p.m. Ice opening from close pack to loose drift ice magically. Wind opportunely changes to S by E and assists greatly. Ice opening well and going satisfactory making, by 6.15 p.m., 7 miles NW true course. Observe phenomenal tide rip and have a race for life. The ice rushing after us at about 2 knots, taking us all energy to escape. Camp for the night on large floe, which feels the heaving motion considerably. Observe whales, fulmars, Antarctic petrels, seals, etc. in great numbers. 156 days life on floe.

10 April 1916

Last night, a night of tension and anxiety – on a par with the night of the ship's destruction. Shortly after 8 p.m., when all the gear was hauled up on to an apparently safe floe, a band was heard, all rush from tents – false alarm – caused by subsidence of surface. Heavy swell running, causing floe to rock dangerously. Floe cracks in halves at midnight, separating *Caird* and our tent from rest of party, and passing through the centre of the sailors' tent. Opens rapidly, and before they have time to struggle out of bags, Holness and Howe fall into the gap, but are speedily rescued. Party reassembled with difficulty. All tents struck in case of further disaster, and all spend rest of the dismal dark night shivering and waiting for morning. ...

Enter what appeared an ice-free sea at 11 a.m. Take hourly shifts at rowing. Hoisted sail on *Caird* and *Dudley Docker* – both doing splendidly. Sea and wind increase and have to draw up on-to an old isolated floe and pray to God it will remain entire throughout the night. No sleep for 48 hours, all wet, cold, and miserable with a NE blizzard raging. ... No sight of land. ...

11 April 1916

Floe remains intact all night and allows our worn-out party to have some rest. Heavy swell sets in from NW, rocking the floe alarmingly with strong surf tearing away masses of our floe. At 8 a.m. an immense field of pack ice came drifting down upon us, surrounding our floe and preventing an escape to open water. From an adjacent hummock heaving like a vessel at sea, one had a transcending view of an infinity of ice-covered ocean berg fragments, shattered floes and brash ice, heaving under the mighty influence of Cape Horn rollers and grinding, crunching, groaning into an indescribable chaos. We viewed with anxiety this profound menace and when it seemed that our floe must split under the rolling motion, the ice opened magically, the boats were launched and loaded, and we were free once more, vowing to remain all night drifting about in the boats, to the vicissitudes of rotten floes. Spend night drifting and rowing along pack margin, the swell having abated for snowing. Cold and wet in boats and welcome sunrise. ...

12 April 1916

... Beautiful sunshiny morning. The pack radiant with the pink flush of sunrise, and resembling the ruins of empyrean marble cities. With fair NW wind, the *James Caird*, *Dudley Docker* and *Stancombe Wills* made SW course, our object being King George Island. ... This position caused grave anxiety, for in spite of strong wind from NE and our sailing SW, we have drifted considerably eastward ... drifting in a sea of loose brash ice and newly formed pancakes. The boats, in order not to lose each other, remained tethered together. ... Everyone was wet and achingly cold. When there was sufficient light to enable safe navigation, the painters were cast adrift and with the SW wind, our destination was changed for Elephant Island. ...

13 April 1916

I am mildly superstitious of numbers, for this day had well nigh made an end to us all. During the morning the three boats were running under sail with a fair SE wind which developed into a half gale by noon, with a treacherous cross sea. The heavily laden boats were driven before it and were forced into the open sea. ... Throughout the night the boats were continually shipping seas, which broke over and froze on to them. The ice had to be chipped away hourly. The *Wills* being in an especially bad way, ice forming on her fo'c'sle head and keeping her down at the bows. ... [A]ll were in sore need of water. Our wet condition, the agonizing cold and the need of sleep, made life well nigh unbearable; furthermore, we were without any definite bearings as to our position. Never was dawn more anxiously awaited, never did night seem so long. Never do I wish to endure such a night. ... Sir E. and self snuggling together for warmth. ...

14 April 1916

Welcome dawn and with it something even more welcome, a glimpse of land! Clarence and Elephant Islands immediately ahead some 30 miles. What a contrast to the terrors of the night. Calm and peaceful the sun rose from out the ocean, with the promised land ahead, tipping the peaks of Clarence Island, till it resembled a vast gilt pyramid, peering through the pink mists of dawn. As Elephant appeared closest, it was decided to make all speed for its shores. With a light fair breeze, the three boats made fair progress, but at noon, the breeze calming, we took to rowing. How anxiously we watched the land gradually loom closer and the details of snowy peaks assume finite detail.

At three p.m. we were but 10 miles from land when it was observed that row as strenuously as we could, we were making no headway. This disheartening circumstance was caused by a strong tidal current. ... As evening drew on, the wind increased to a gale, raising a big cross sea, and taxing to the limit the exhausted capacities of the party. Seas raked the boats and icy sprays hurled by the wind struck one's face like a whip. The carpenter, through exhaustion, fell asleep at the tiller, allowing a big sea to come on board, and Wild, after an unbroken spell of 24 hours, took his place. ... Several times we lost sight of the *Wills*, which we were towing, thinking she had foundered, when she would suddenly emerge from the blackness of the sea on a white crest as we would glide into a deep gulf. I enjoyed the fascination of this wild scene, exulting in our mastery over this savage elemental display. With dawn's first light, land was observed. ...

15 April 1916

... The coast presented a barrier of sheer cliff and glacier faces, wild and savage beyond description. At Cape Valentine, however, a small sheltered beach was observed, which being exploited, was found a capable landing. Whilst the *Caird* and *Wills* were so engaged, the *Dudley Docker* hove in view, she having been driven into an adjacent bay during the night, miraculously escaping foundering. Landing was conducted expeditiously and without accident, the boats being hauled above high water on the shingly beach. Conceive our joy on setting foot on solid earth after 170 days of life on a drifting ice floe. Each day filled with anxiety, patience and watching, and being driven whither to an obscure destination by the vicissitudes of winds and seas. It is sublime to feel solid earth under one's feet, after having trod but heaving decks and transient ice for nearly eighteen months, and feel that on what one is walking is reality – not subject to drifting and gaping caprices that maroon and drop one into the sea.

On landing, a number of seals basking on the beach were immediately stripped of blubber and a long draught of trumilk prepared. Our phenomenal escape was drunk in hot steaming milk that set our frozen nerves tingling. The landing was effected, but just in the eve of time, for so many of the party were emaciated by exhaustion, fatigue and exposure that they could not have survived another 12 hours. Blackborrow had to be carried from the boat, having both feet frostbitten, whilst there were some dozen cases of hands and toes in like condition. Many suffered from temporary aberration, walking aimlessly about, others shivering as with palsy – for the results of five days and nights without sleep or rest in frozen garments, combating the fierce anger of the Southern Ocean in winter, must needs pay its tribute. Tents were hastily erected and after partaking of a meal of delicious seal steaks, all turned in and almost instantly were deep in slumber. How delicious to wake in one's sleep, and listen to the chanting croaks of the penguins mingling with the music of the sea. To fall asleep and awaken again, and feel this is real. We have reached the land; and that our latitude and longitude will remain the same on the morrow.

16 April 1916

Our present 'Happy Camping Ground' being but a narrow beach girt by sheer towering cliffs, affording no shelter from storms, it has been deemed advisable to immediately scout the adjacent coast in the hope of a more propitious haven. Wild and a party of four set out during the morning and returned at 8.30 p.m. with favourable news. Having discovered a suitable landing 7 miles down the north coast. We break camp at dawn tomorrow to take up our refuge there. Scenically, our present environments are some of the grandest I have ever set eye on. Cliffs that throw their serrated scarps a thousand feet into the skies are interspersed with glaciers that tumble in crevassed cascades down to the sea. ... It is a land of nature's moods – inhospitable – angry. ... When the sun, in playful mood, pierces the mists and storm clouds, peaks and sea are glorified with transcending gradation of light and shade and then I miss my cameras and cinematograph.

17 April 1916

... Such a wild and inhospitable coast I have never beheld. Yet there is a profound grandeur about these savage cliffs with the drifting snow and veiling clouds. We sheltered till the other boats came up in the lee of a vast headland, black and menacing, that rose from a seething surf, 1200 feet above our heads, and so sheer as to have the appearance of overhanging. Down the face streamed rivulets of snow that being caught by the hurricane blasts sweeping down an adjacent gorge, were whirled in blinding eddies mingling with the spindrift of the sea. I thought of those lines of [Robert] Service's:-

> A land of savage grandeur
> That measures each man at his worth.

18 April 1916

... The blizzard continued all day. No. 5 tent torn to shreds, its occupants take shelter in the *Caird*. We lay our tent flat on ground, weight the skirting and crawl underneath. The ringed penguins inhabiting the rookery near camp, having had enough of the weather, congregated en masse on the beach and migrated during the morning. Lucky birds! Oh! to be a penguin.

19 April 1916

Atrocious weather ... The *Dudley Docker* is overturned and converted into a shelter for the homeless No. 5 tent, which innovation answers admirably. Now that the party are established at an immovable base, I review their general behaviour during the memorable escape from the ice. The success is due to the admirable and able direction of Sir E., who never for a moment allowed a boat out of sight, did all possible to ameliorate the privations and took no risks. ... It is regrettable to state that many conducted themselves in a manner unworthy of gentlemen and British sailors. Some whom it was anticipated would be the bulwarks of the party, 'stove in'.

In the majority of cases those suffering from severe frostbites could be traced to negligence, whilst the numerous cases of temporary aberration are excusable under the plea of intense privation and suffering. Amongst those that stand meritorious, Sir E. has mentioned: Wild, a tower of strength who appeared as well as ever after 32 hours at the tiller in frozen clothes; Crean, who ably piloted the *Wills*; McNish (Carpenter); Vincent (Able Seaman); McCarthy (Able Seaman); Marston (*Dudley Docker*) and self. Of a fair proportion of the remainder, I am convinced they would starve or freeze if left to their own resources on this island. ... Those who shirk duties, or lack a fair sense of practicability, should not be in these parts. These are harsh places where it takes all one's time and energies to attend to the individual, and so make himself as effective and useful a unit as possible.

21 April 1916

Preparations in active progress for the relief journey. The decking of the *Caird* is nearing completion, and requires but canvassing. The party anticipates departing on Sunday. ...

24 April 1916

... The decking of the *Caird* was completed early this morning, and conditions being reasonably favourable, she was launched at 11 a.m. The launching nearly ended in her destruction, as owing to the heavy surf rolling in, and being unballasted, she rolled almost on to her beam ends. In this unmanageable position she was carried by the rollers to within a foot of the rocks. When it seemed that she must be capsized and dashed to pieces, two of the sailors were thrown into the surf, and so relieved of this top weight, she righted. ... Loading was accomplished by tendering with the *Wills*, which narrowly escaped foundering each journey. ... By 12.30 the *Caird* hoisted sail to three ringing cheers from the shore, and so commenced on one of the most hazardous and arduous voyages that has ever been attempted in a small boat. Great confidence is reposed in her crew (Sir E. H. Shackleton, Captain Worsley, Tom Crean, and three sailors) six proven veterans seasoned by the salt and experience of the sea. The distance to Leith Harbour, South Georgia, is 700 miles, 700 miles of wintry sea, the most tempestuous zone of the oceans. The *Caird* is an excellent sailor, and guided by providence, should make South Georgia in 14 days. It is intended to commission the *Undine* of the Grytviken Whaling Company, and rescue this party immediately. How we shall count the days. ...

28 April 1916

... All hands arduously engaged erecting a shelter by building stone walls and laying the two overturned boats thereon for a roofing, the gaps around the wall being filled with canvas. The floor is covered with gravel from the beach. The whole promises to be a reasonably dry shelter. ...

30 April 1916

Fingers nearly frostbitten, writing with difficulty. ... We take up residence in the boat shelter this evening on which all have been at work during the day. We pray that the *Caird* may reach South Georgia safely and bring relief without delay. Life here without a hut and equipment is almost beyond endurance.

1 May 1916

... The shelter is decidedly comfortable compared with tents and will ameliorate our existence considerably. The size of ground space enclosed is 18 feet x 12 feet. The roof is formed by two overturned boats resting on two low walls fore and aft, and to the boat's keel is 7 feet high. The walls are covered in with canvas taken from the tents. The small blubber bogie is installed, which radiates a pleasant warmth, does the cooking and so fills the place with soot and smoke that our eyes run and lungs nigh choke. Still, it is a decided improvement and a step in the direction of making life more endurable under such severe climatic conditions. The entire party of twenty-two sleep in this small space, and snugly, though sardiniously, stretchers are arranged between the thwarts, six sleeping in each boat, the remainder boding on the floor. Boxes of rations are arranged in a circle around the bogie during the day for seats. ... The climate producing prodigious appetites. Impossible to write coherently owing to the jabble and impossible light and smoke.

2 May 1916

I make this entry on the highest point of our camping spit which has been named Cape Wild ... a narrow neck of land jutting out from the mainland some 200 to 250 yards. ... To the east – the coast stretches in glorious vistas of perpendicular peaks, terminating at the exquisitely castellated Cornwallis Island, heavily capped with glaciers that hang and cascade to the sea like frozen cataracts. Looking west, there is a gorgeous blue glacier, down which the interior roars its SW blizzards, and debouches incessant avalanches. ... From my elevated lookout, seaward, there is a view beautiful beyond imagination, yet unwelcome, over an ocean obscured by pack ice. ... On the eastern side of the spit, there is a fine gravelly beach on which we secure seals and penguins. ... Such is our home, and its environment. Transcending in scenic charm and given cameras and plates, one could spend the year in aesthetic contentment. ...

8 May 1916

... I can imagine the look of surprise and bewilderment with which any visitor would regard this grizzly, bearded and unkempt assemblage should he be suddenly thrown among us. Bewilderment would speedily become aversion; for our blubbery emanations and the odours from twenty-two crowded and 'seven month unwashed', coupled with the blue liquid tobacco smoke 'fug' must be productive of an atmosphere distinctly unsavoury. ... After 'smoke O' the decks are again cleared by stowing the 'box seats' to form the cook's bunk, the tenants of the attic bunks swing into their repose with monkey-like agility and the 'ground plan' is spread with sleeping bags into which the owners retreat like gigantic snails. Hussey generally treats us to a half hour's banjo serenade in which our choristers join their voices. The dim rays from the blubber night light sheds its feeble glow over a catacomb-like scene of objects resembling mummies. These objects are us, in reindeer sleeping bags, mingling our snores with the roar of the blizzard. ...

15 May 1916

... The weather falls calm early this morning and lights NE. Airs spring up later. Pack is to be seen along the horizon evidently coming up from the east. A remarkable feature of yesterday's blizzard was the blowing about of ice sheets about the size of windowpanes. This was brought about by the previous day's warm NE producing a surface thaw, the subsequent cold SW freezing this surface into a brittle layer ¼ inch thick. The terrific winds carried these slabs about like splintered glass. ...

30 May 1916

Cold raw day, with heavy mist, freezing as it came into contact with one. The surrounding country presents the most wintry, bleak, and inhospitable prospect conceivable. The landscape is buried deep in snow, only occasional rocky outcrops being visible, it being difficult to determine where the land ends and pack-covered ocean begins. ...

31 May 1916

... I hope never again to be in such a filthy unkempt condition as at present. All faces and hands are black with blubber soot and grime. As for our garments, I shudder to look at them. Reindeer hairs from moulting sleeping bags and penguin feathers find their way into our food, but are unheeded. Food is eaten out of the mugs by the fingers, knives, forks, etc., being lost during our escape in the boats. As for the atmosphere, even our hardened blubber-saturated selves say phew! and are glad to escape into God's own fresh air, blizzard or bleak though it be. ...

1 June 1916

... Heated argument being at present indulged in over the encroachment of an inch of space; it has been going on for the past half hour, but has arrived at a deadlock. Wild arbitrates and halves the alleged encroachment and the dispute is settled.

8 June 1916

... Have had ample opportunity of forming our opinion of our sailors, having now lived together under the same confined roof since landing at Cape Wild. In my estimation, with a few exceptions they are a very meagre set, ignorant and illiterate, and of far more complaining disposition than the shore party. Their sole conversation is their stomach capacity – being grossly incapable of discoursing on even the most commonplace subjects. Even as regards endurance, the genteel born has proved himself far more capable of sustaining prolonged exertion under arduous circumstances and hardships.

15 June 1916

... Dr McIlroy's patient, Blackborrow, who has been treated for a frostbitten foot since the boat journey – eight weeks ago – had to be operated on today, the toes of the left foot having to be amputated at their junction with the foot. All hands, except Wild, self, and Howe were sent out during the performance to take 'fresh air'.... Never perhaps was anaesthetic administered under more extraordinary circumstances. The operating table was built from a number of nut food boxes covered with blankets, the temperature of the 'Theatre' (our murky interior) being maintained at 79° by ardently stoking the bogie with penguin skins. In spite of the extremely unfavourable conditions, the operation was eminently successful. ...

3 July 1916

... 10 weeks since departure of *Caird*. ...

5 July 1916

... Wild has devised an ingenious arrangement for the cure of chronic snorers. Lees, who continually disturbs our peaceful slumbers by his habitual trumpeting, was the first offender for the experiment. A slip noose is attached to his arm, which is [then] led by a series of eyelets across the bunks in his vicinity. As the various sleepers are disturbed, they vigorously haul on the line – much as one would do to stop a taxi – it might do the latter, but Lees is incorrigible, scarcely heeding our signals. It has been suggested that the noose might be tried round his neck. ...

15 July 1916

... The glacier in West Bay has been extremely active, debouching avalanches. Its forward movement can be distinctly heard by a low cracking followed by the dislodgement of immense fragments. The vast section precipitated this afternoon gave rise to an enormous wave, that had it not been for the pack in the bay damping the swell, we had well nigh been washed off the spit. ...

26 July 1916

A little zest was lent to the monotony of our immutable existence last night; when turning over in my bag, I plunged my hand into water. This induced dreams of falling through cracked floes into the sea, and I awoke precipitately with feelings of apprehension. The reassuring gruntings of miscellaneous snorers dispelled my fears, and an investigation of the wet hand revealed 'floors awash'. ...

1 August 1916

Two years since the *Endurance* left London and twelve months ago since she experienced her first severe nipping from the pressure. ... Surely the old *Aurora* will come this month, and so the watching day by day and the anxiety for the safety of our comrades of the *Caird* lay a holding hand on the already retarded passage of time. ...

10 August 1916

... About thirty gentoo penguins came ashore and I am pleased the weather was too bad to slay them. We are heartily sick of being compelled to kill every bird that comes ashore for food, and will be pleased when the sea elephants return that this unfortunately essential slaughter may cease. ...

20 August 1916

... Today sees the last of the nut food rations. ... All are becoming anxious for the safety of the *Caird*, as allowing a fair margin of time for contingencies, the *Aurora* should have made her appearance by now. The weather is wretched. A stagnant calm of air and ocean alike, the latter obscured by heavy pack, and a dense wet mist hangs like a pall over land and sea. The silence is extremely oppressive. ...

30 August 1916

Day of Wonders.

During morning collect limpets along foreshores E. Bay and return to hut at noon. Whilst the party were in at lunch, Marston and I were without shelling limpets, when I called Marston's attention to a curious piece of ice on the horizon which bore a striking resemblance to a ship. Whilst we were so engaged a ship rounded the Gnomon Island. We immediately called out 'ship O', which was instantly followed by a general exodus of cheering (semi-hysterical) of the inmates. The hoosh was left to burn and the meal forgotten. A beacon was kindled and attention attracted to which the vessel signalled response. She came within safe distance and lowered a boat. On coming alongside we recognised the Boss and heartily thanked God for his safety. All gear was hurriedly rowed to the vessel in just under the hour (1 p.m. to 2 p.m.). (The *Yelcho*, under command [of] Captain Pardo.) We subsequently learned that this was the fourth attempt made to effect our rescue. Had a musical evening and heard all the news of the war of the world etc., etc., on board.

31 August 1916

Now that the initial excitement has subsided, I append a more rational entry of the preceding day. After the general exodus from the hut, all gear, which consisted of notes, photographic negatives and a few personal sundries, was carried to a suitable embarking rock together with the invalid Blackborrow (who had been confined to the hut since its erection), by this time the boat was alongside, manned by a Chilean crew with Sir E. in charge. Fortunately, the sea was calm and all the gear and personnel were transferred to the *Yelcho* without mishap and amidst salvos of cheering on either side. I am not very susceptible to emotions, but this happy reunion with our comrades whom we had almost given up for lost, and our happy release, with these lonely peaks like mute sentinels witnessing our departure, has left an indelible impression. Two boatloads sufficed to carry all our worldly belongings and ourselves on board. At 2 p.m. we were under way, with engines at full speed, racing for the open sea and freedom. Oh! the bliss of once more feeling the motion of the sea; the music of fresh, though foreign, voices and to sense at last that our anxieties and privations are ended and will soon be reunited with home and civilization. Yet as those noble peaks faded away in the mist, I could scarce repress feelings of sadness to leave perhaps forever the land that has rained on us its bounty and been our salvation. ... After taking a photograph, our first thoughts were to wash, this novel sensation rejuvenated and gave us something of the appearance of our fellows. Then followed a meal. ... The excitement of the night did not enable many to secure sleep. I lay on the floor wrapped in a blanket, meditating and thinking how ineffably more pleasing to be kept awake by the throb of the engines, that are hurrying us back to life, than lie like smouldering logs on Elephant Isle, harking to the stertorous snores that ebbed away our existence. There was so much news to be told, of the wonderful adventures of the Boss and his companions on the *Caird*, of their crossing those blizzard-swept ranges of South Georgia and how after three unsuccessful attempts, and miraculous escapes, to rescue us from the besetting ice, was rewarded by his fourth effort. Good old Boss! The war news and multitudinous magazines and cablegrams furnish us with a profusion of data that will acquaint us with all the world's doings to which we have been strangers.

1 September 1916

We have learned further details of the remarkable efforts and hairbreadth escapes of Sir E. and his party. ... Three times he endeavoured to relieve us, each time compelled to retreat from an impenetrable ice barrier; undaunted, his fourth attempt has been successful and stands as one of the most brilliant achievements in the annals of exploration. ... After sixteen days of unspeakable privations in the *Caird*, the party reached the west coast of South Georgia. 800 miles of turbulent sub-Antarctic ocean had been crossed in a small whale boat but 23 feet long. The whole time shivering from cold and being soaked with water, they landed six emaciated individuals more dead than alive, just in the nick of time. Several days were spent recuperating in a small cave before crossing the incognita and supposed unpassable interior of South Georgia to the whaling station. Sir E., Worsley and Crean set out on this hazardous enterprise, and were rewarded after a 36-hours march across mountains and crevassed glaciers by sighting the Stromness Whaling Station. Of the perils encountered I am not going to discuss, suffice to say, ... it is typical of the man 'To endeavour – and To succeed'. ...

3 September 1916

Beautiful sunrise, with fine mist effects over the hills and distant mountains surrounding Punta Arenas. Shortly after 7 a.m. Sir E. rowed ashore and telephoned our arrival on to Punta Arenas, so that the populace might roll up and greet us after church, we being due to arrive at 12 noon. The *Yelcho* was bedecked with flags, and we moved off from moorings in order in arrive punctually. ... On nearing the town, we observed displayed everywhere the flag of welcome, the Chilean Ensign. On nearing the jetty we were deafened by the tooting of whistles and cheering motor craft, which was taken up by the vast gathering on the piers and waterfronts. All introduced to the governor. On landing from the motor launch, we were welcomed by an immense crowd frantically cheering and by the naval band. We march through the street in our filthy Elephant Island togs, followed by the band, through packed streets bedecked with flags. ... I shall ever remember this kindness and goodwill. ... Immediately on taking up residence at the Royal Hotel, had a glorious scrub and bath, the first for ten months! ...

4 September 1916

... During the day, Mr. Vega, the leading photographer of the town, placed his fine darkrooms at my disposal and I spent most of the time in developing. All the plates which were exposed on the wreck nearly twelve months ago turned out excellently. The small Kodak film suffered through the protracted keeping, but will be printable. Mr. Dixon, Chief

Engineer, Chilean Navy, is having constructed a developing machine in order that I might run through my film (cine).

6 September 1916

Spent the day between the hotel and Vega's darkroom, developing cinema film. The film exposed twelve months ago has lost nothing of its excellent quality. ...

7 September 1916

Most of the influential citizens of Punta Arenas will be suffering from the results of the magnificent welcome given us last night at the Magellanes Club. This affair was practically the official welcome by the Chilean nation. The banqueting hall was splendidly decorated with festoons of evergreens and blazed with electric light, no curb being laid on the expenditure to render the function a success. ... Social positions were eliminated in this overwhelming wave of national hospitality, and I had the unique experience of observing a greaser (one of the Expedition engineers) drinking champagne familiarly with millionaires, and puffing luxuriously the best of cigars, with the complacency of a magnate. Then there were a few others, the guests of the wealthy, flashing diamond pins and wearing fur-lined overcoats. What a change from filthy, blubber-reeking garb, and how amusing to observe the 'inflation' and growth of head. ... The magnificence of the welcome, apart from ourselves, must play favorably in the minds of all Britishers, and intimated the feeling of friendship existing with the Empire. Punta Arenas was a town of expensive living, dominating in wealth, and where champagne was drunk like soda water, and cash was but the fuel of enjoyment. ...

8 September 1916

The splendid studio and darkroom of Senor Vega have been placed at my disposal unreservedly, and I have made the utmost use of them. The fine shop contains the latest in photographic equipment, and the assortment of delicate mountings, albums, plates, papers and sundries exceeds those purchaseable in Sydney. ... Entertainments continue to be given, afternoon levees and 'midnight' receptions, which I skillfully yet determinedly evade. One grew heartily sick of this prolonged revellery, and had it not been for my photographic work, I should have immediately make my exit to the Camp – (country) to study country life and sheep-farming methods. I met Wild today wearing a fur overcoat worth over 200 guineas. I suppose the owner considered its value increased by being worn by this distinguished explorer.

5 November 1916

... It will be with some feeling of relief when we set foot in Old England, after this gauntlet running and submarine dodging.

11 November 1916

About 6 a.m. we entered the Port of Liverpool and anchored in the Channel, being delayed entering the docks by several transports with Canadian troops. Here the war is brought very cogently home to one, as the huge transports swarming like bees with khaki-clad and cheering men, drew up alongside the docks. The way being clear, at 1 p.m. we moved up to the berth through a maze of docks and waterways, active and crammed with shipping. Huge vessels were coming and going – discharging or loading, like ferryboats. The customs occupied considerable time, especially with the film, which was weighed – a method of estimating the length – and charged an import duty of 5 pennies per foot. The entire film netted a customs revenue of £120. ... The voyage from Buenos Aires was thoroughly enjoyable, and a welcome relax after our bumping from pillar to post through Chile and the Argentine. ... We arrived in London at 8.30 p.m. and straightaway to the *Chronicle*, where I had a lengthy talk with Mr. Perris on expedition affairs, and handed over the film. I subsequently took up residence at the Imperial Hotel, Russell Square.

15 November 1916

Deeply considered film affair, and arrived at the decision that it would be inadvisable to have it projected or marketed in any way whatsoever until an addition of suitable animal life, in which the film is lacking, be secured. I have suggested to Perris that for the mutual benefit of all concerned, I return to South Georgia and take the necessary subjects. I believe that by this means, the film value would be increased tenfold. Perris appears pleased with the project, and is endeavouring to secure all rights from the ITA film syndicate for £10 000. During the morning visited the *Daily Chronicle*. Lunch with Sir Douglas Mawson and Mr. Gent. Afternoon, *Daily Chronicle*. Mr. Wilkins of the Stefansson Expedition dined with me this evening at the Imperial. We subsequently viewed the Battle of the Somme at the Scala Theatre, and later exchanged views on the respective expeditions. Mawson returns to Liverpool.

16 November 1916

Working at *Daily Chronicle* darkroom on Elephant Island negatives. ... London is bad enough to find one's location in daytime and physically impossible at night when the lights are subdued. Add to this an occasional dense fog. Even policemen and motorbuses get lost.

18 November 1916

... London is the gloomiest place on earth in the wet. A thin layer of liquid mud covers the roadways, which are rendered extremely slippery thereby. ... At night with Perris to view Ponting's pictures. They are the acme of photographic perfection. Ponting's patter is splendid and gives one the impression the penguins were actually performing to his words. The show well deserves its worldwide merit. Ponting's manner and delivery is excellent.

21 November 1916

Up early and to Watford to the Paget Company and put in hand the colour pictures of the expedition. ... During afternoon to Raines at Ealing, and started them on making slides and albums, one of which is for the King. ...

23 November 1916

During morning, through courtesy of my old friend, Mr. Gent, I was able to witness the first official showing of the Salonika films at the West End Cinema, Piccadilly. The show and films were quite good. I was introduced to Lady Scott and her charming young son, Peter. Mr. Wilkins of the Stefansson Expedition was with us also. I lunched with Wilkins and then to the *Daily Chronicle* on expedition photographs. ...

28 November 1916

All London is excitement on account of a zepellin raid which took place in the small hours of this morning. Four zeppelins participated and two were brought down. Late at noon, a German seaplane dropped a bomb just in front of Harrods. ...

2 December 1916

Had our photographs taken during the morning (Webb and self) thence to *Chronicle* and commenced the first stages of a contract in conjunction with the coming visit to South Georgia. ... At evening we met Sir Douglas Mawson, who is staying at the same hotel with us, having come down from Liverpool to see Webb. With Lieutenant Ireland we all went round to the various theatres, which we found full, and ended up by going to the Marble Arch Picture Hall. ...

4 December 1916

To *Chronicle* during the day, compiling a list for the coming South Georgia expedition. Mawson and Webb visited Dr. Chree at Kew, so I did not meet them till dinner, after which we all assembled in the lounge and talked of old times. Azzie's conversation is rife and brilliant with vivid descriptions of work at the front. He has been in the thick of it. ...

6 December 1916

... Afternoon with Azzie to Ponting's magnificent lecture 'With Captain Scott in the Antarctic'. This is my third visit to the show, and it is to me as fresh as ever. ... I received a very kind tribute from Ponting to my work in the Antarctic, a copy of his beautifully illustrated work *In Lotus Land*. This is one of the highest tributes that could be paid to a brother artist of the trail, as Ponting is looked upon as being the leader in Antarctic photography.

7 December 1916

... Afternoon, went to the great universal store of Gamages, where I purchased equipment for my coming expedition, from rubber boots to an ice axe. As a Christmas bazaar is in full swing, the stores were more or less congested with people, which despite the cry of war economy, seemed to be making all sorts of worthless and unnecessary purchases. At night with Lieutenant Ireland to the 'Bing Boys are Here' at the Alhambra. The house was packed, only standing room being available. The audience appeared mostly to be officers and soldiers on leave with lady companions. Both music and acting were superb and kept the house in a continual state of hilarity. No doubt these shows are an essential relax to the returned soldiers and helps all for the time being to forget the horrors of this war.

15 December 1916

The *Sphere* published their second series of the Shackleton pictures today. It is a fine tribute and exceptional advertisement for the expedition, to be given such attention with practically unlimited space in the leading press when its pages could be out-crowded with war and ministerial photographs. We could not have wished for more notoriety or salience even in times of peace. ...

16 December 1916

... Morning with Blake around the city. Afternoon to Madame Tussauds. This huge waxworks display I found very disappointing. The terrors of the Chamber of Horrors are absurdly overrated. ... Blake is woman-mad and gives me the pip.

27 December 1916

... A dense fog obscures the city so that it is almost impossible to see across the road. At evening, vehicular road traffic was practically suspended, and were it not for the tubes, everything would be hopelessly disorganised. At the principal corners, powerful kerosene pressure vaporisers shed a feeble glow that illumines their immediate surroundings like a flame seen through a smoking fire. The pedestrians carry electric torches which keep up an intermittent flashing like glowworms. ...

28 December 1916

... London is at present a hotbed of infamy and immorals. This of course, has developed through the war, which has stirred the dormant animal passions of man. Prostitutes appear to have flocked to the city, where in powder and attire, no doubt they present meretricious attractions to those who have returned from the thunder of battle. It is a deplorable state of affairs. So hard is it to discriminate between the respectable and the irresponsible, that I find it more satisfactory to keep aloof. I am not nevertheless a wowser – but one can hardly associate with 'demurely forward' wenches without being talked about and 'blowing in quids', so I am not having any. London appears to be thriving under the influences of war. This is occasioned of course by the vast number of Colonials and Imperials, who spend their 10 days' leave here. Their accumulated back money burns and quickly goes, so that one sees no demonstrations of poverty, but overstocked and busy shops. Rarely even does one hear the war talked of – generally it is theatres. The purchasing value of a sovereign has decreased during the past two years to about 13 shillings.

7 January 1917

... Afternoon at *Daily Chronicle* actively engaged piecing together film and writing up lecture for it. Evening to bed early. The best way to pass a Sunday evening.

24 January 1917

Had display of the Paget color plates in the Polytechnic Hall. The pictures were projected 75 feet onto a screen about 18 feet square, though the size of the picture was 25 feet. The size of the slides is ½ plate with a current consumption of 60 amperes. The projected image was magnificent. ...

3 February 1917

… Everyone is in a state of excitement and tension regarding the position the [United] States will assume in regard to Germany threatening to wage submarine warfare on all neutral shipping. This evening I learned from Perris that diplomatic relations have been severed with Germany and the States, and that a declaration of war appears inevitable. All are of the opinion it is the only course the States could pursue. This undoubtedly means the defeat of Germany and the conclusion of the war at what is hoped no very distant date. Great excitement prevails and nothing else is spoken of.

3

The Great War Diary
(August 1917–August 1918)

21 August 1917

The day has at last arrived and I have left London. After an early morning's packing and visiting administration offices, I caught the staff train from Charing Cross at 12.50 p.m. Never had I dreamt there were so many generals, colonels and majors engaged on staff work. The train was packed with them. ... A couple of hours brought us to Folkestone where the *Princess Victoria*, laden with returning troops, and the staff steamer were waiting. The large amount of equipage carried by myself, gave me an anxious time keeping it from getting mixed with the ponderous amount of baggage dumped promiscuously in the vessel's hold. Whilst waiting, several aeroplane scouts treated us to a magnificent display of diving, turning and manoeuvring. So apparently easy and graceful were their movements, that there appeared no more danger in their evolutions than if they had been birds on the wing. I met Wilkins on board; and so we left the shores of dear old England for the grim duties of France. The weather was beautiful, and our vessel, convoyed by two destroyers, did her 17 knots without a movement. Soon the French coast came in sight and the details of Boulogne gradually became more distinct. We had a particularly fine view just before entering the port of the beach, where great numbers of folk were bathing. Nothing seemed more distant than war and had it not been for the great number of troops embarking and disembarking, everything was serenely peaceful.

At Boulogne, Captain Bean was awaiting us with two cars and we conveyed all our goods to safe storage. After an excellent meal ... we left for Headquarters, which are situated at Hazebrouck. Even here one is scarcely conscious of a war, except for the great numbers of transports and khaki men. ... Everywhere, tiny villages were surrounded by closely cultivated lands, and the golden grain, partly mowed, lay in long rows of sheaves, with here and there great conical ricks. The roads were in excellent order and planted on each side with long rows of poplar and other trees. Darkness soon came on ... and as we wended our way towards Hazebrouck, the sky gradually grew brighter with the flickering quiver of hundreds of guns in action. It was the most awesome sight I have ever seen. As we neared Hazebrouck the guns could be heard – almost synchronising with the flashing. We took up our quarters with a number of the headquarters staff beneath canvas.

23 August 1917

So much passes, so much seen, and such unprecedented happenings that to enter them at length would take hours. ...

I will never forget the beauty and glorious colour contained in this country. The tents surrounded by wheat fields and great hayricks, with occasional gay-tiled cottages set in their midst and everything just alive with khaki-clad figures.

The roads too are thronged with transports (motor) teams and riders. A feverish activity strangely out of contrast with the country and the leisurely methods of the peasantry, husbanding the grain with a sickle or making tiny furrows with a small push plough. Tedious and slow as are their methods, the entire country is closely under agriculture. ...

We called for Bean at his office at 2.30 p.m. Bean, who is the Australian Official War Correspondent, has a remarkable knowledge of the maze of roads and is a veritable walking dictionary of events, an excellent fellow and not afraid to be in any of the stunts in which our fellows take part. The road runs through Kemmel, near where we viewed the battle from yesterday, thence through Dickebusch to Voormezeele. The way was an endless procession of vehicles, transports, horses and men, which were keeping up the supply to the front line or relieving. The village of Voormezeele is a mass of ruins and stumps of houses, and here the luxuriance of vegetation ceases and the shell-swept battlefield properly begins. Trees, villages and even contours of the landscape have been altered by the incessant bombardment of three years. Around this area the enemy have been forced back but two or three miles!

Putting on our shrapnel helmets and carrying our gasmasks, we walked across this desert, whose outskirts are already becoming green with grass, past myriad sandbagged dugouts to Lock 7, once an old canal, but now just a swampy depression. Here the awfulness of the battlefield burst on one. The great howitzer batteries were in full operation and the ear-splitting din was followed by the scream of a hail of shell which swept over our heads to the enemy lines. Things were very quiet, however, and our harassing fire was only lightly replied to. We plodded through shell craters and shell-torn ground littered with fragments of burst shell and shrapnel, torn equipment and smashed entanglements over the blood-drenched battlefield till we arrived at the famous Hill 60. Here the Australian batteries were in full operation, bombarding the enemy lines at 4000 yards. Captain Bean, Wilkins and myself were hospitably received by Colonel Shelshire at the headquarters, situated in a series of dugouts linked together by a series of underground tunnels not unlike catacombs. Soakage trickled in through the roof or oozed through the walls and the blackness seemed to be made blacker still by a few spluttering candles. These candles gave a convulsive jump as the reverberating shock of a near heavy gun was fired. The continual rumble and boom of artillery shook the ground violently, so that one might liken it to an earthquake sensation. ... The whole place is just a network of telephone wires, which are constantly being destroyed by shellfire and almost just as speedily repaired.

...After, we climbed to the crest of Hill 60, where we had an awesome view over the battlefield to the German lines. What an awful scene of desolation! Everything has been swept away; only stumps of trees stick up here and there and the whole field has the appearance of having been recently ploughed. Hill 60 long delayed our infantry advance owing to its commanding position and the almost impregnable concrete emplacements and shelters constructed by the Boche. We eventually won it by tunnelling underground and then exploding three enormous mines, which practically blew the whole hill away and killed all the enemy on it. It's the most awful and appalling sight I have ever seen. The exaggerated machinations of hell are here typified. Everywhere the ground is littered with bits of guns, bayonets, shells and men.

Way down in one of these mine craters was an awful sight. There lay three hideous, almost skeleton, decomposed fragments of corpses of German gunners. Oh, the frightfulness of it all. To think that these fragments were once sweethearts, maybe husbands or loved sons, and this was the end. Almost back again to their native element, but terrible. Until my dying day, I shall never forget this haunting glimpse down into the mine crater on Hill 60 – and this is but one tragedy of similar thousands and we who are civilised have still to continue this hellish murder against the wreckers of humanity and Christianity. ... Looking across this vast extent of desolation and horror, it appeared as though some mighty cataclysm had swept it off and blighted the vegetation, then peppered it with millions of lightning stabs. It might be the end of the world where two irresistible forces are slowly wearing each other away. ...

In the dusk of the evening, we began our return, feeling the way in dark, as we dare not show lights owing to hostile aircraft. The battlefield in the night was a wonderful sight of star shells and flashes. The whole sky seemed a crescent of shimmering sheet lightning-like illumination. It was all very beautiful, yet awesome and terrible. We returned to tents in Hazebrouck at 11.30 p.m., dog-tired and wiser men.

24 August 1917

During morning Bean, Wilkins and self motored out to see the St Omer Aerodrome of the Royal Flying Corps. This great aerodrome consisted of many large hangars and more resembled the extensive edifices of a great central railway station. ... In the afternoon I visited my new prospective quarters at Steenvoorde. Here I am having a darkroom erected with living quarters. ... Steenvoorde is about eight miles from Hazebrouck and in a much more central position to the various fronts. ...

25 August 1917

... My contempt and disgust for army administration increases with every trifling matter I have to see headquarters about. Things that could be settled in five minutes take usually ten days! And why? Because it has to pass through a score of unnecessary channels that seem to have been created to find soft jobs for 'string pullers'. ...

26 August 1917

... Afternoon Bean, Dyson, Lindsay, Wilkins, self (and batman) motored out in the two cars to Voormezeele (about 20 miles) and with my rather too numerous equipage made our way up to Hill 60 on foot. ... During the afternoon Blake and I strolled out to an advanced position in front of Hill 60 over the recently won ground. What a devilish sight it was. Everything to the horizon has been shot away.

Took picture interior dressing station on Hill 60. This has been excavated in the famous tunnel excavated by the 1st Australian Tunnelling Company for the mining of Hill 60. Also photographed the interior of the Elephant Iron dugout of the O/C [Officer Commanding] Major Morris of the 105th Howitzer Battery. Blake on left, Ikin centre and Major Morris right. Blake was a member of the Mawson expedition: went right through the war with the artillery and was killed the morning the armistice was signed.

29 August 1917

With Bean, Murdoch and Gullett, I went to Campagne (near Renescure) to photograph the 2nd Division Australian Infantry being reviewed by Sir Douglas Haig. The event took place in an uncultivated farm and looked a trifle incongruous with the surrounding haystacks and quaint rustic spectators. These men are in great condition, having been out on furlough for three months. The review, doubtless, is the preceding inspection to these men being placed in the active line. ...

Later, I also attended the inspection of the 5th Division, which took place in a recently harvested wheat field. It is hellish to look on this flower of our country as just so much food for the guns. How many of these brave fellows will survive the privations of the coming winter, or impending battles in which they will very shortly be engaged? ...

1 September 1917

... My new quarters lay about ¾ mile from the picturesque little village of Steenvoorde. ... The construction is of curved iron known as the Nissen hut, a type which is housing many of the staff and administration officers. The length is 23 feet by 15 feet and comprises a darkroom, two living rooms and a workroom. ... The room is lined with matchboard and is as comfortable a little bungalow as I could wish for. I have my own Ford car and driver with the garage at the doorstep; my other assistants sleep in the tent. We draw our rations and cook on the premises in a little cookhouse we have erected. My assistants are Lieutenant Wilkins, who has charge of record work; Sergeant Harrison, field assistant; Martin, darkroom and generally useful; Dick, my driver; and Harvey, the batman. They are all an excellent crowd of fellows and enthusiastic. I am learning Sergeant Harrison to act, should occasion so arise, to take my place. Without the car it would be absolutely impossible to move about over the country as I cover some 80 miles per day. This morning I went and photographed some anti-aircraft guns near Hazebrouck. ...

2 September 1917

... The weather promising favourable, Wilkins and self went to Bailleul and visited the 11th Brigade, 4th Division Artillery. The roadways were crammed with artillery and transports. The former was partly made up of the 54th Battery Australian Artillery, evidently migrating to another part of the line; these heavy 9.2-inch howitzers were drawn by curious tractors which were impelled forward by an endless belt arrangement. ... On the main roads there are frequently as many as three lines of traffic; troops, motorcycles, cars, ambulances, huge motor transports and an occasional mule. These vast masses and conveyances produce many glorious effects as they move along the cobbled roadways which are avenued by beautiful long, slender trees and poplars. ...

In the afternoon, we continued our way to Voormezeele and visited the advanced dressing station of the Red Cross in the bowels of a cellar. There is no lack of darkrooms in these dingy abodes and here we changed plates. Voormezeele is a chaos of ruins absolutely blown to fragments. A beautiful moonlit night favoured us, so that we had no difficulty in arranging our gear amidst the ruins of the church, which we intended to flashlight. Whilst waiting for the darkness, 'Fritz' began shelling the batteries immediately on our right and left, ... the shells burst only a few hundred paces away, sending up high columns of mud, stones and shell fragments. The waiting seemed an interminable time under these circumstances, but as a fair number of Fritz's shells were 'duds' we got off scot-free. I, however, got rather badly burned by my own flash powder prematurely exploding.

... Aeroplanes are far more numerous here than birds. They fly the skies at all times. In gale, rain, day and night, the buzz of the engines can be heard like the buzzing of innumerable beehives. Above this buzzing one hears the occasional crackle, crackle, crackle, of their Lewis gun[s] and looking up, is spellbound, watching a duel between a Boche and [a] British plane. ...

3 September 1917

It is evidently a pretty warm corner we have had our darkroom erected in, being kept awake most of the night by the enemy's machines raiding and bombing the town. ... We left at 9.30 a.m. for Ypres, but an hour later found us advanced only a mile! ... Eventually we succeeded in eluding the congestion by taking diverse obscure roads and joined into the main Ypres road near Poperinghe. ... The country peasantry were making hay and ploughing, heedless of the rush and roar of transport traffic or the not-far-distant voice of heavy artillery. After leaving Poperinghe, the main road to Ypres runs through charming country, which now is absorbed by military camps and dumps. A mile before entering Ypres one enters a magnificent avenue of fine old trees, which bear the scars of shells and shrapnel, many being shot away altogether. It is a noble approach to Ypres. Here and there on either side are small hamlets – the outskirts of the town – demolished by shellfire. Up high in the sky is the line of sausage balloons which 'spot' on our artillery fire and report its effect. They trail in a long line across the sky, parallel with the front line and out of range of Fritz's shrapnel. Like great horseflies circling and flashing in the sun are numbers of our scouting aeroplanes.

On the road, toiling through the dust, march on the endless procession of men and munition transports. But here we are at Ypres, and the traffic sentry warns you to put on your 'Tin Hat' (steel helmet) and have your gasmask slung at the ready position. He sees our camera gear in the car and we produce our passes. It was a good move insisting on securing a captain's rank, for had I not done so, it would have been practically impossible to move with freedom. Now, however, my three stars are an introduction everywhere, whilst the rankers are amusingly obsequious. It has its drawbacks, for one is ever saluting and looking for salutes. But this is by the way, and we are in Ypres. ...

Wilkins, myself and Sergeant Harrison wandered through the ruins, pathetic though awesome in their demolition. The main roads have been cleared of most of the debris and instead of the fine buildings that were, hideous gapings and breaches in shot-away remnants remain. In many cases the roofs and top storeys have been blown away and the fronts shorn off, so that the smashed-up rooms gape into the street. ... Roaming amongst the domestic ruins made me sad. Here and there were fragments of toys. ... Bedsteads broken and twisted almost into knots lay about, almost hidden with brick dust. A stove riddled with shrapnel. Roofs poised on almost shot-away walls, and walls balanced in every possible fashion, that seemed to defy all laws of equilibrium and gravitation. ...

But most regrettable of all is the ruin of the famous Cloth Hall. This magnificent old church is now a remnant of torn walls and rubbish. The fine tower is a pitiable apology of a brick dump, scarred and riddled with shell holes. Its beautifully carved facades are 'smallpoxed' with shell splinters, not a vestige of the carving having escaped. The figures are headless and the wonderful columns and carved pillars lay like fallen giants across the mangled remnants of roofs and other superstructures. Oh! It's too terrible for words. Returning to the car in the evening over the shell-cratered roads, we came upon an enormous crater – God knows what did it, but pacing round the lip, it measured 75 yards round, its depth about 25 to 30 feet! Then we came to a tiny courtyard, which had escaped for some time the ravages of bombardment. The strafed trees were coming back to life and budding, and there beside a great shell crater blossomed a single rose. How out of place it seemed amidst all this ravage. I took compassion on it and plucked it – the last rose of Ypres. ...

4 September 1917

I'm afraid that I'm becoming callous to many of the extraordinary sights and sounds that take place around me, and things which astounded me when I landed now seem quite commonplace. ...

At Ypres ... we again took the cameras through the ruins out by the Menin Gate and along the ramparts. In bygone days, the city was surrounded by immense ramparts and a deep moat. Even the great brickwork wall has withstood remarkably well the battering of the shellfire. Here and there, however, great breaches ... have been made in the wall, and the Menin Gate absolutely demolished. The surroundings are very unhealthy as regards shellfire, the Boche sending over a great many of the famous 5.9s. We returned through laneways heaped with fallen walls and debris, over places where houses once stood, through gaping walls, till we came to the post office. This once fine edifice remains still five storeys high. The roof has gone and one entire corner has been blown in from top to bottom by a single shell. The fine oak ceilings have been ripped to matchwood and the walls deeply pitted by shell splinters. It is just recognisable as a building. Climbing to the topmost storey through torn floors and shot-away walls, we had a transcending view of the ruined city. Not a building stands intact; most are just brick heaps and unrecognisable dumps of debris. Behind us, one of our 12-inch guns fired with such a boom, that it seemed the building must give way under the concussion. ... It is a weird, awful and terrible sight, yet somehow wildly beautiful. For my part, Ypres as it now is has a curious fascination and aesthetically is far more interesting than the Ypres that was.

I took some photographs. ... There is a touch of pathos and sadness in these new ruins; little patches of clothing and domestic things; each speaks its own tale of suffering, of homes wrecked, of death and ruination. Many walls are blood-splashed and tell the most pitiful tragedy of peaceful folk swept into eternity during their sleep time. Everything tells of the horrors of war, of unspeakable agonies and wanton murder. People of Ypres, may you one day be revenged upon those who have demolished your city and filled your lives with agony and suffering. ... Whilst looking at the ruins of the Cloth Hall, I noticed a flock of pigeons rise from the ruins and, after circling around for some time, returned to their homes in the lofty ruins. ...

5 September 1917

Remained in camp all day, except for a short trip to Cassel to see the censor. ... Martin I have placed in the darkroom to look out after printing and titling. Wilkins will attend to the records and I myself to publicity, pictures and aesthetic results. ...

Our infantry and artillery are active and it looks as though they will be going into action. ... When there is any objective which other troops cannot take, the Australians are sent in to do it. I must say that although our fellows have the reputation of being unkempt and undisciplined, they always achieve their object, have the dash and resource and are unsurpassed.

6 September 1917

I had a long talk today with Captain Bean over affairs generally and the best method of running this department. Wilkins will be operating practically separately, and will be at headquarters most of the time. It is therefore necessary he should have separate equipment and so I have advised that he go to London and have gear overhauled and lay in a stock of materials. ...

10 September 1917

... I met Captain Bean ... and thence to Warlencourt, where we interviewed the photographic censor. His duty is to examine all photographs likely to convey any information to the enemy – seemingly in most cases a most absurd proceeding as the enemy is already aware of most if not all the negatives held up. I shuddered when I saw the careless manner in which negatives are handled and shuffled like packs of cards – to think that mine must go through the same procedure! ... Bean and I then motored on to Montreuil – to the general headquarters. I have never seen any country so heavenly and well tended as northern France. ... the elms and poplars are taking on their autumn tints, the hay is being stacked in big conical ricks, mostly by women and old men, for every eligible man is fighting for La Belle France or has died for his country. And it is a country for a patriot to die for. ... I left Bean at Fauquembergues. ... As we neared Steenvoorde we noticed a great bunch of searchlights converging on one spot and at the apex glittered something like a great moth – a Boche Gotha aeroplane. The sky was bright with bursting stars of shrapnel, but evidently unsuccessful, for we noticed them following him away to the horizon.

13 September 1917

The roads from Steenvoorde right up to Dickebusch are almost one continuous line of Australian troops, marching on to take over the front line, which they will do tomorrow. I followed them along in the car, photographing and cineing. Fiendish dust at times almost obscured the men, who, laden with full equipment and sweat and dust begrimed, marched on cheerfully as only Anzacs can. I received a great amount of banter from the troops and retaliated in equally cheerful way, which the men approved of. ...

14 September 1917

... I took a number of route and cinema films along the Poperinghe–Ypres road of the endless streams of men going and coming. ... We followed along the Ypres road, which is being metalled and corduroyed in places for the coming winter, and visited Ypres, where Wilkins and I had a potter about the ruins and took a few pictures. We left the city by the Menin Gate, or rather where it used to be, and I left Wilkins and proceeded on foot along the Menin Road to our advanced batteries ... the liveliest two miles I have ever walked. It is along this way that all our supplies and ammunition must go to the Ypres front. ... The way is strewn with dead horses – the effect of last night's shelling – and battered men's helmets that tell of the fate of the drivers. The Boche was very active around Hellfire Corner and his 5.9s were bursting around there in rare style. His spotting balloons could be very clearly observed and doubtless his remarkable precision was due to their observation. The trees along the Menin Road are avenues of shot-away stumps and the surrounding lands, ploughed up with shells like a sieve. The stench is frightful and even the old stagers dodge this charnel-like thoroughfare. I saw the Boche put out of action one of our batteries and explode the ammunition dump by a direct hit; I had to seek shelter in an adjacent dugout owing to him barraging the road, shells dropping along it in a long trail-like succession. ... One lives every moment in anticipation of being blown skywards ...

15 September 1917

Suitable weather again prompted me to visit our 54th Battery of 8-inch howitzers ... between Zillebeke and Voormezeele. I was just in time to film them sending down a practice barrage. All the guns in the vicinity, hundreds in number, opened fire precisely on the stroke of 4 p.m. The effect was terrific; with simultaneous bursts, hundreds of shells went screaming and hissing away to the enemy's line. Then independent firing continued for half an hour. The din and roar kept up of the concentrated fire from the massed cannon and screaming projectiles is beyond me to describe. Our aeroplanes hovered by circling over the battery groups, and sent down wireless reports of the results and also directed the fire and ranges. The Boche returned the fire on one of the heavy batteries with wonderful precision. Our artillerymen speak in high terms of the enemy's gunnery; while though we send over much greater quantities of projectiles, his precision is admittedly superior. A number of Gotha machines came over our lines and did some serious bombing whilst I was there. ...

17 September 1917

... At sunrise we were in Ypres. I never saw ruins look so majestic or imposing as when silhouetted against the beautiful sunrise this morning. We visited Lille Gate, particularly beautiful in the calmness of the new day, with the torn trees and ruins reflected in the placid mirror-like moat. ... The Menin Road is like passing through the Valley of Death, for one never knows when a shell will lob in front of him. It is the most gruesome shambles I have ever seen, with the exception of the South Georgia whaling stations, but here it is terrible, for the dead things are men and horses.

We arrived at Hooge, where the tunnellers are excavating a series of underground dugouts, which will be occupied by the headquarters of our infantry. It is a wretched job as they are working 25 feet below the surface level and most of the time knee-deep in mud. From the roof trickles water and mud, which they jocularly term 'hero juice', on account of it percolating through tiers and tiers of buried corpses. ...

19 September 1917

Headquarters acquainted me late last night that the battle will take place tomorrow. So Bean, Wilkins and self, set off at 1 p.m. to take up suitable positions for the great event tomorrow. Bean, who learns all information at headquarters, informed me that we are undertaking a new system of attack. At 5 a.m. the artillery will all simultaneously open a barrage on the front Boche lines for a period of an hour or so. This is intended to engage his artillery and demoralise them; the machine guns will play on his infantry. At a specified time the barrage will be lifted and our troops will dash over into the enemy's lines. This objective secured, a second barrage will take place, and the second wave of infantry will again move forward over the area controlled by this barrage. The third and final barrage will take place about 9.30 a.m. It will isolate the third section of the enemy's lines and our infantry will advance at 10 a.m. The barrage will be maintained for some time so that our position may be consolidated. Altogether we expect to advance 1500 yards over a frontage of about 15 miles. ... We all anxiously await the morrow.

20 September 1917

It has been a glorious and frightful day. The battle is over and we have achieved our objectives. ... All last night a heavy bombardment was maintained on the enemy's lines; and from where we were at the dressing station, we had a magnificent view of it. The whole country, viewed from the third storey of an old ruin, was so alive with gun flashes that I can only liken them to looking over the twinkling lights of a city, and during a violent thunderstorm. The flash of the heavies in our immediate vicinity lit the landscape up, and moving masses of troops, with the fitful gleam of a continuous succession of lightning bursts. ... A large number of casualties were coming in when we left, as the Boche artillery, instead of duelling with our artillery, opened up on our storming infantry. Those that came in and were not over-seriously wounded expressed their pleasure of having escaped the horrors of another battle. ... We were just walking along the Menin Road in the twilight, near Hellfire Corner, when our barrage began. ... Nothing I have heard in this world, or can in the next, could possibly approach its equal. The firing was so continuous that it resembled the beating of an army of great drums. No sight could be more impressive than walking along this infamous shell-swept road to the chorus of the deep bass booming of the drum fire and the screaming shriek of thousands of shells. It was great, stupendous and awesome. We were glad, notwithstanding, to reach the more or less sheltered site of the mine crater at Hooge, wherein are the excavated dugouts of the brigade headquarters some 25 feet below the level of the ground. Here we met Bean, who introduced me to General Bennet, the director of operations on this front. Last night's rain had made things frightfully sloppy and muddy, the dugouts being no exception, as the soakage percolated through the roof and oozed through the walls. This filthy liquid had to be incessantly pumped out, but even then it left the passageways deep in slime. Anyhow, it was shell proof and I was grateful to be inside for a brief lull from the frightful din without.

At 7.30 a.m. a message came over the wire that the first objectives had been won with very slight casualty. A large number of prisoners were captured and sent in. This body of men, which came into the crater a little later, were in extremely poor condition, haggard, emaciated and dejected. Many were mere boys and shadows of men. One could not help feeling regret for these wretched prisoners, forced into the front line no doubt on account of their inferiority and intended merely as buffers, whilst the finer troops were held in reserve. It was one of the most pitiful sights to see the wounded coming in, many of our men being carried on stretchers by the Hun prisoners, others with their arms around each others' necks, being assisted whether by friend or foe, and all eager to get away from the horrors of the combat. Bitterness and hatred were forgotten; for after all, we are all but men, and this frightful scene of carnage seemed to bring each other back to the realities of humanity and to hold them spellbound by the horror and terribleness of their own doings.

We learned the second objective was also gained and more prisoners and wounded followed. The artillery duel raged fiercer than ever, but as the daylight began to improve, I decided to push on and reach the infantry in the advanced position. Whilst leaving the crater, a 5.9 shell landed six or seven paces away from us; fortunately it failed to explode. I pushed on up the duckboard track to Stirling Castle – a mound of powdered brick, from where there is to be had a magnificent panorama of the battlefield. The way was gruesome and awful beyond words. The ground had been recently heavily shelled by the Boche, and the dead and wounded lay about everywhere. About here the ground had the appearance of having been ploughed by a great canal excavator, and then reploughed and turned over and over again. Last night's shower, too, made it a quagmire, and through this the wounded had to drag themselves and those mortally wounded pass out their young lives.

The shells shrieked in an ecstasy overhead and the deep boom of artillery sounded like a triumphant drum roll. Those murderous weapons, the machine guns, maintained their endless clatter, as if a million hands were encoring and applauding the brilliant victory of our countrymen. It was ineffably grand and terrible, and yet one felt subconsciously safe in spite of the shellburst and splinters and the ungodly wanton carnage going on around.

I saw a horrible sight take place within about 20 yards of me. Five Boche prisoners were carrying one of our wounded into the dressing station, when one of the enemy's own shells struck the group. All were almost instantly killed, three being blown to atoms. Another shell killed four and I saw them die, frightfully mutilated in the deep slime of a shell crater. However anyone escapes being hit by the showers of flying metal is incomprehensible. The battlefield on which we won an advance of 1500 yards was littered with bits of men, our own and Boche, and literally drenched with blood. It almost makes one doubt the very existence of a deity – that such things can go on beneath the omnipotent eye. I greatly admire the magnificent work of the stretcher bearers who go out in the thick of the strife to succour the wounded.

... We were mighty glad to return to the crater and home via the Menin Road, which was, for a wonder, free of shelling. ... In place of the transport bringing up rations and ammunition, the Red Cross coaches were returning packed with wounded. The Menin Road was a wondrous sight, with stretchers packed on either side awaiting transport and the centre crowded with walking wounded and prisoners.

... I saw a large number of these latter enjoying a great meal of white bread and cheese. The poor devils were ravenous and I am pleased to say our fellows treated them kindly – not as enemies, but as fallen heroes; for indeed, these men were. ... We returned to Steenvoorde at 7 p.m., but it was nearly one o'clock before we had developed our records of this glorious day, a day that shall never die in the annals of our history.

21 September 1917

Yesterday I should have made mention of the magnificent work done by our aeroplanes, which kept on bombing and harassing the enemy and preventing him from coming over our lines. Returning home, I saw one of our machines catch fire, and like a great streaming rocket, come to earth. It was evidently shot down by a Boche tracer bullet. Wilkins and I went out over the newly won field, taking Hooge crater (at the top of Menin Road) as the starting point. ... It was wondrously quiet. Only an occasional shell was fired – the aftermath of the storm – and it sounded for all the world like the occasional boom of a roller on a peaceful beach, with the swish of the water corresponding to the scream of the shell.

Westhoek was alive with men, digging in gun positions for the 18-pounders, running up communication cables, restoring and remaking the roads and all the other industries of war. Wounded and prisoners continued to occasionally come in, but the dead were unburied. I went along a trench communicating with a pillbox lookout and there I found several partly buried, their feet protruding through into the open trench. Actually, several dead lay in front of a captured pillbox in which a number of our men were living, and though they had to pass in and out over them, they took no more notice of these dead than if they had been but earth itself. ...

26 September 1917

Yesterday we damn near succeeded in having an end made to ourselves. In spite of heavy shelling by the Boche, we made an endeavour to secure a number of shellburst pictures. Many of them broke only a few score of paces away, so that we had to throw ourselves into shell holes to avoid splinters. A barrage fire he also concentrated on the head of the Menin Road, and there, about eight motor transports, ammunition dumps, timber for corduroying the roads etc. were in flames. I took two pictures by hiding in a dugout and then rushing out and snapping. We eluded shells until just about 150 yards away, when a terrific, angry rocket-like shriek warned us to duck. This we did by throwing ourselves flat in a shell hole half filled with mud. A fortunate precaution, for immediately a terrific roar made us squeeze ourselves into as little bulk as possible, and up went timber, stones, shells and everything else in the vicinity. A dump of 4.5 shells had received a direct hit. The splinters rained on our helmets and the debris and mud came down in a cloud. The frightful concussion absolutely winded us, but we escaped injury and made off through mud and water as fast as we possibly could. ...

I'm sick of being amongst killed and wounded and hearing that hellish din of cannonade and dodging shells. One becomes a fatalist and I am convinced it's no good shell-dodging. We have even a worse time than the infantry, for to get pictures one must go into the hottest and even then, come out disappointed. To get war pictures of striking interest and sensation is like attempting the impossible. ... Had a great argument with Bean about combination pictures. Am thoroughly convinced that it is impossible to secure effects without resorting to composite pictures.

28 September 1917

Went with Wilkins again over our advanced positions. ... I had the questionable excitement of being potted at by a sniper, the ping of his shot whizzing past only a few yards away. ... I also came across a weird individual, whose sole mania is collecting souvenirs. He goes into all positions and dives with a whoop on new prisoners and 'acquires' the proprietorship of all their unprisoner-like trinkets and possessions. I took a photograph of him surrounded by a heap of watches, chains and innumerable miscellanies. ...

29 September 1917

After the gruelling of the past week, I decided to stay away from the front and clear affairs up with the censor. With this end in view, I took Wilkins with me and we went to Warlencourt. Later we motored on to Albert. ... I went and took a combination moonlight/flashlight study of the Leaning Madonna. The unexpected explosion of half a pound of flashlight powder quite 'put the wind up' the near inhabitants, who anticipated a bombardment – they were much relieved to discover a camera enthusiast to be the sole cause.

30 September 1917

Wilkins and I pottered around various ruins in the vicinity of the church ... to fossick out unique standpoints from which to take photographs. We found no scarcity of vantage points, as the entire surroundings, dominated by the fine spire and famous Leaning Madonna, compose one vast picture from any outlook. I took half a dozen from various ruins, and vistas through shell-holed walls. As the church is out of bounds to troops, we had some difficulty forcing a way through a meshing of barbed wire and finally entering the building. This latter we accomplished through a shell hole. The interior is a very pitiable sight. The roof in most places has been shot away and many of the great supporting columns. The rest are so torn and mutilated by shell fragments as to be irreparable. ... After completing my work at Albert, we ran down to Amiens to view the cathedral there. ... Its pure Gothic gracefulness and elegance surpass anything I have yet seen in architecture. The interior, unlike most other similar edifices, is exquisitely lighted. The light filtering through harmoniously coloured windows at once fills one with a pleasant sense of peace, rest and quietude. ...

1 October 1917

... I dined with Generals Birdwood, White and Carruthers this evening. Had a lengthy discussion with Bean re pictures for exhibition and publicity purposes. Our authorities here will not permit me to pose any pictures, or indulge in any original means to secure them. They will not allow composite printing of any description, even though such be accurately titled, nor will they permit clouds to be inserted in a picture. As this absolutely takes all possibilities of producing pictures from me, I have decided to tender my resignation at once. I conscientiously consider it but right to illustrate to the public the things our fellows do and how war is conducted. They can only be got by printing a result from a number of negatives or reenactment. This is out of reason and they prefer to let all these interesting episodes pass. This is unfair to our boys and I conscientiously could not undertake to continue the work.

2 October 1917

I sent in my resignation this morning and await the result of igniting the fuse. It is disheartening, after striving to secure the impossible and running all hazards, to meet with little encouragement. I am unwilling and will not make a display of war pictures unless the military people see their way clear to give me a free hand. Canada has made a great advertisement out of their pictures and I must beat them. ...

3 October 1917

Went to headquarters and photographed the 1st Anzac Staff. I met General Birdwood who spoke with me re my resignation and he said he hoped to fix matters up. I am, however, inflexible, and if my end be not obtained, under no consideration will I retain office. I remained at Steenvoorde all day taking a rest cure. The battle is to come off tomorrow when we intend taking the ridge in front of Zonnebeke. ...

4 October 1917

Punctually at 6 a.m. our infantry attacked along an 8-mile front after first it had been battered by our artillery barrage. ... Our infantry followed up in three waves, the barrage being lifted for each attack, and carried all objectives. We penetrated his line over 1000 yards ahead of Zonnebeke and gained the commanding ridge, which places us in a very gratifying position. The enemy are now on the slope of the ridge immediately ahead and we look down on him. About 3000 prisoners were captured and several machine guns. Our casualties regrettably were higher than usual. ... The battle was fought in a misty rain – heavier falls having taken place overnight, so that the entire battlefield was a great quagmire of mud. It is marvellous what conditions our fellows can and will fight under. There are no troops in the whole fighting force equal to the Australians for storming troops.

I went to Zonnebeke during the day to try and get pictures, but it was being so heavily shelled that we ... were fortunate to escape injury. ... I don't know whether one becomes callous or turns a fatalist, for the wounded and dead scarce make any impression, and one is absolutely heedless of the fact that his turn might be next instant. It's a damnable business. I wake up in the morning as though I had passed through some weird wild dream. It's impossible to realise that men are just murdering each other around you, and that you are in the heart of a great battle. The frightful roar of artillery and scream of shell, though, brings one to reality; but even it passes off as soon as you leave the scene of battle, and when I am back again in my cosy room at Steenvoorde, I quickly forget the horrible doings of the day and, after a good dinner, develop my plates and then turn in with no more thoughts for the day than if I had been at business all the while and had just returned from a late evening working overtime!

5 October 1917

Morning, visited a 15-inch howitzer battery near Hellfire Corner. (Captain Cummins in charge.) This ponderous weapon fires a projectile weighing 1400 pounds. It has a range of 11 000 yards! ... The guns were being brought up under frightful conditions. Sometimes they would sink to the axles in mud, and the mules would be hidden from sight in the depths of the treacherous shell craters. But still we do it, and the same work goes on, but the men work in deep mud and even then hail a cheerful persiflage at the photographer. Our fellows are superb. ...

Early morning I visited the 'birdcage' at Hoograaf, where about 600 prisoners are interned from yesterday's battle. Mostly they are [of] mediocre physique, though one notices an occasional fine specimen. They appear right glad to be in our hands, and their general opinion is that Germany is done. ... I took a number of photographs amongst them and they willingly submitted, except a brigadier, who turned his back on the camera. I did not press the point out of courtesy.

6 October 1917

... Headquarters have given me permission to make six combination enlargements in the exhibition! so I withdrew my resignation. They must at least appreciate my efforts, as they were dead against this being done. However, it will be no delusion on the public as they will be distinctly titled, setting forth the number of negatives used etc. All the elements will be taken in action. ...

10 October 1917

... The weather is turning out extremely cold and it is evident the winter is with us. God help the poor devils in the trenches.

11 October 1917

... I found myself 'lured' back to the battlefield (great emphasis on the 'lured', for there is no place in eternity that is more hellish). My enthusiasm and keenness, however, to record the hideous things men have to endure urges me on. No monetary considerations or very few others in fact would induce any man to flounder in mud to his knees to try and take pictures. The past rains have made the place a great slough. One dares not venture off the duckboard or he will surely become bogged, or sink in the quicksand-like slime of rain-filled shell craters. Add to this frightful walking a harassing shellfire and soaking to the skin and you curse the day that you were induced to put foot on this polluted damned ground. A few bursts of sunlight allowed me to make a few pictures in the trenches on the Broodseinde Ridge; a heavy barrage of 5.9s were coming over at the time, so that I had a devilish tight time for an hour or so. Then the six and a half-mile tramp back through the slush and mud to Ypres, where the car has to be left, just about beat me. Soaked through and mud to the thighs, I fervently thanked God when I was aboard the Ford and bound back for Steenvoorde.

12 October 1917

Last night I found a letter awaiting me from Captain Bean telling me of another battle which is to come off tomorrow. Our objective is Poelcappelle, about 800 yards advance. God knows how those red-tabbed blighters at headquarters (60 miles from the front) expect our men to gain such a strong position when they have to drag themselves through mud. Curse them! ...

Owing to Joyce (my camera lumper) funking it, Wilkins and I set out in the car for Hellfire Corner. ... Here we got onto the Zonnebeke railroad which has been shelled and blown to fragments during the past two years of strafing. It is now a raised bank of mud and bits of scrap iron rails. ... It is littered with bodies, both of our own men and Boche. Things were reasonably quiet till we got near to Zonnebeke – but the mud! trudge, trudge, sometimes to the knee in sucking, tenacious slime – a fair hell of a job under ordinary conditions, but with a heavy camera up and being shelled, I hardly thought 'the game worth the candle'. ... Shells lobbed all around and sent their splinters whizzing everywhere – God knows how anybody can escape them; and the spitting ping of machine-gun bullets that played on certain points made one wish he was a microbe. ...

This shelled embankment of mud was a terrible sight. Every twenty paces or less lay a body. Some frightfully mutilated, without legs, arms and heads and half covered in mud and slime. ... We pushed on through the old Zonnebeke Station (now absolutely swept away), up Broodseinde and entered the railway cutting near the ridge crest. Shells began to fall just about a hundred paces ahead and ... induced us to retire. The light, too, failed and rain set in. We got no pictures but whips of fun. ... I noticed one awful sight: a party of ten or so telephone men all blown to bits. Under a questionably sheltered bank lay a group of dead men; sitting by them in little scooped-out recesses sat a few living, but so emaciated by fatigue and shell shock that it was hard to differentiate. Still the whole way was just another of the many byways to hell one sees out here... We left the embankment near Zonnebeke Station and took to the duckboards for home. ...

13 October 1917

... Today I am setting out on an unpleasant task. Shackleton has not met his obligation to me for £530, an amount he promised faithfully to meet already several times. He also ignored my letter concerning it, and as he is leaving for South America in a few days, I see his intention is to take advantage of me being in France to slip off. This has compelled me to go to London, drop important events here where every day counts and pursue him. It is my intention to make the unprincipled blighter sweat for this, and if he has not already eloped with my cash, I guess I'll collect it or stop his trip.

... The passage was fairly rough, last night's gale having stirred up a nasty cross sea. At Folkestone we caught the usual waiting train, and arrived at Charing Cross 7.15 p.m. ... put up at the Imperial Hotel, Russell Square. It is quite like home being here again. ...

15 October 1917

... Afternoon to *Chronicle*, where I met Perris and Shackleton. The latter has agreed to pay me the amount due in the morning. Met Azzi Webb who is over on leave, dined together, and afternoon at Australia House. Lieutenant Smart is giving all attention to the preservation of my negatives, and am pleased to see my pictures are receiving a great publicity in the press at present and I am receiving many congratulations. Evening with Webb and several friends to see *The Boy* at the Adelphi. It was delightfully funny and a pleasant relaxation.

16 October 1917

Met Shackleton and he paid up like a man. I might say, though, that had I not been over to collect the amount, I would have been a poorer and wiser person. ...

17 October 1917

Running around after a panorama camera and other materials for winter. ...

19 October 1917

Lunched with Sir Douglas Mawson and Lady Mawson at their flat. ... During the evening, a raid warning was given and most of the folk made for the tubes and basements. With a large party of visitors, I remained in the dining room of the Imperial Hotel and had a very pleasant concert. ... [A] number of enemy Zeppelins bombed the East End and also Piccadilly way. A number were killed.

20 October 1917

This morning I saw from the train several of the places where the bombs had fallen. The houses were blown to heaps of broken bricks. It looks as if London is going to pass through a severe time during this moon, and it is sincerely to be hoped that a retaliation will be made in the form of overwhelming and indiscriminate bombing reprisals. ...

Left Charing Cross Station at 11.50 a.m. and joined at Folkestone the channel ferry. Arrived at Boulogne at 4.30 p.m. where I found Wilkins waiting with the car. ...

27 October 1917

I went with Joyce and Wilkins on an ambulance lorry to the Hooge crater and had considerable excitement on account of the Boche shelling the road. Afterwards, we went through the infamous Chateau Wood and up the enfiladed road to Westhoek Ridge. This region always suffers heavy shelling and we passed through nearly a mile of strafed limbers and wagons and dead horses. I have never seen a more terrible scene of desolation, waste and destruction than hereabouts on Westhoek. The Boche observation on his area is superb, and the least congestion invariably brings shelling. We returned over the duckboards by a safer route to Hellfire Corner, and thence on to Ypres. A fine sunset beautified these solemn ruins that awakened feeling[s] of awe and made one sorrow for the things which war has done. Took eighteen plates.

28 October 1917

... We succeeded in reaching the infamous Chateau Wood without incident, when a fleet of 14 Taubs and Gothas came over us. They dropped their bombs vigorously a few hundred yards away and peppered the roads with machine gun fire. We took refuge close beside a big tree stump and escaped the machine gun fire, the bullets pelting a few yards off. Our safety was but momentary, however, for a 5.9 shell lobbed only fifteen paces off and showered us with mud. A narrow squeak.

Chateau Wood must have been a glorious spot, with its lake on one side and heavily foliaged timber. It is now so lonely and desolate that one feels as if death alone dwells there. The trees are smashed and splintered and only stumps; the ground is heaved up into wave-like ridges with shelling, and here and there along the lonely duckboard track lies a stricken soldier. One does not linger more than necessary in this place over which hangs the pall of gloom and death. Guns boom all around, yet everyone dodges the awful loneliness and hazards of Chateau Wood. ...

29 October 1917

... Having had a fair share of excitement yesterday, I decided not to go into the actual fighting front, but remained in Ypres. I enjoyed the pottering about amidst ruins and cellars, composing a picture here and there in (an unknown recently) a pleasant leisurely way. Passing over the levelled ruins, one sees here and there smoking orifices, which appear like innumerable fumaroles. There is quite a piquant odour to the smoke, which needs no telling that the occupants in the cellars are preparing grub. Large numbers are now billeted in these subterranean rooms, which are reasonably safe. The enemy, however, is sending over much fire into Ypres, and I visited a room where twenty-six were laid out yesterday by one shell. ... Ypres is also subject to Gotha visits and cellar dwellers are busy reinforcing their roofs. There is an observation balloon near the Lille Gate in which I made an ascent to 1000 feet. I had a transcending view of the ruins and over the whole salient. The effect of millions of shell craters, now filled with water, was weird in the extreme. The atmosphere, unfortunately, was hazy and useless for photography. I intend, however, doing considerable work from this balloon, as it will be of extreme record value, every detail of country being visible. In the distance, Passchendaele was visible. The scene, with the flickering gun flashes and pall of haze which overhang the battlefield, was impressive beyond words. ...

31 October 1917

... The mist lifted a trifle during the afternoon and I made another balloon ascent to 3500 feet. From this altitude I had a superb view of Ypres, the fragmentary walls looking like innumerable tombstones. In fact Ypres viewed from that height looks like a vast necropolis. The view over the battlefield was inexpressibly wondrous and grand. ... Although the visibility was bad, the misty atmosphere enhanced the terrible desolation and reality of this artificial hell, whereon thousands of lives are being expended and the resources of the world thrown. Imagine one's feelings suspended in a tiny rocking cradle, with the ruins of Ypres 3500 feet below; in front, a vast stretch of smoky and misty flat desolation, crisscrossed with familiar tracks and scintillating with innumerable red flashes. Looking back, was a wondrous bird's eye over more peaceful landscapes, but peppered with little round white dots and almost equal-sized circular pools of water. The little white dots were an army in bivouac, and the pools, shell craters brimming with the recent rains. Over this vista rolled banks of heavy woolpack cumulus clouds and a veil of smoke from thousands of smoking chimneys.

Scarcely had we been in the air more than half an hour, when a fleet of seventeen Gothas came over. They came down from the north and were heavily laden with bombs. When two miles off they began releasing them on battery positions and roadways. We had a wonderful view of the results. As they flew over the landscape, they left a trail of bursting bombs behind them. The ground rose in vast columns and resembled the effect produced by dropping huge stones in a calm pool. The whole fleet came directly over us, [and] as we could not see them on account of our gas bag, we had a few minutes of anxiety. Expecting to be shot down or ignited by tracer bullets, we stood on the rim of the basket ready to leap into space in a moment. ...

We joined the car which was waiting in the square in front of the Cloth Hall, and after a skidding drive, got home to Steenvoorde, 6 p.m. Finished developing, 1 a.m.

9 November 1917

... Received orders from headquarters to proceed to Egypt. An active campaign is there in progress and it has been thought a good opportunity for me to secure historic pictures. At present there is no official photographer with the forces. ...

10 November 1917

... Retrospecting on my work done in the [Ypres] salient, I conscientiously feel it has been successful and is practically complete in all details. With Wilkins' record work, practically every branch has been dealt with. We have both applied ourselves diligently to the work and now sense the reward of our endeavours. Wilkins is an excellent fellow. Enthusiastic, conscientious and diligent. The innumerable hair's-breadth escapes and our marvellous good luck I only hope may continue. And we return our thanks for it.

11 November 1917

Left France. Bean called for me with his car at 11 a.m. and we ran through to Boulogne. ... We had an uneventful trip to London ... where we arrived at 7 p.m. I put up at my usual quarters in the Imperial Hotel, Russell Square.

13 November 1917

Busy as blazes collecting materials and arranging up generally. Have managed to induce headquarters to send me by P&O steamer to Port Said. Smart gave me a fine office in Australia House, where I will arrange the pictures for the forthcoming exhibition which will take place March 1918.

19 November 1917

Left by train at 11.25 a.m. for Tilbury and after passing through the usual formalities, finally boarded the *Malta*. Towards evening we slowly dropped downstream and in the morning anchored off Deal.

20 November 1917

Here we lay all day and at dark crept out to Plymouth. The view shoreward was particularly fine, the silhouette of the land being broken up by a number of powerful searchlights scouring the skies for hostile aircraft.

21 November 1917

Steaming along with the land dimly on our starboard, a patrol came alongside and ordered us into Weymouth. Evidently submarines were active outside, for all shipping was deflected into this port. Our cargo consists of guncotton and other explosives for Palestine, so every precaution is being taken to evade submarines with this valuable shipment. At dusk an order enabled us to proceed to Plymouth where we arrived at 4 a.m. and dropped anchor outside the port.

22 November 1917

The port is enclosed by a steel net and mines, the entrance being guarded by a mined boom. At evening the boom is closed and vessels are compelled to remain outside. ... A large number of ships are riding at anchor, and evidently will be part of the convoy of which we are to form a unit. ...

24 November 1917

At 10 a.m. an order was sent out for the convoy to proceed to sea and the line of great ships hauled up their anchors and proceeded through the channel way to the open sea. We are made up of twenty merchantmen, averaging from 4000 tons upward; our escort is a large auxiliary cruiser (the *Armadale Castle*) and six destroyers. All the merchant vessels are armed with guns varying from 4.2 up to 8 inch. One of the most impressive sights I have yet seen was this great line of fine vessels proceeding to sea, past the Eddystone [Lighthouse], in majestic file, that even must have terrorised the most audacious submarine lurker. It thrilled one to see old England's might still proudly ploughing the seas in dignified defiance, and one's admiration warmed for these skippers and men, who play their great share in their country's work.

Great deeds are done here on the seas, and the greater the deeds because they are so little known and so little rewarded. It is to these men of the merchant service that the country and army should take off their caps, for their dauntless courage and unselfish effort. Their unceasing vigilance and indifference to personal risk has kept open the gateway of commerce, and made possible the duration of the war by carrying on the vital overseas transport, and keeping united our island home and scattered empire. It is in such men that the power of the British nation lies; for the Boche with all his 'Wilhelms' and military Germany with her military dogma can never breed such men as the British sailors. ...

30 November 1917

As we steam through the Strait of Gibraltar, I make this entry in my diary on the last day of the month. Glorious calm weather is now with us and our fleet of sixteen large vessels and escorts, scarcely seem to be moving through the calm seas. We sighted the Spanish coast, a blue misty line down on the horizon, just before 9 a.m., and at 2 p.m. were off the entrance to Gibraltar. Our great convoy smoking up and making the passage of the Strait, with the rugged coasts of Spain to the north and the barren jagged outlines of Africa to the south, thrilled every Britisher aboard. ...we are now in the hottest submarine area in the Mediterranean. ...

15 December 1917

At 2 p.m. we sighted Port Said and by 4 p.m. dropped anchor inside the breakwater. Almost immediately, a large number of native boats put off, clamouring for fares. After passing through the usual examining of passports, I had all my great quantity of paraphernalia transferred to the Customs. Here I deposited instruments and materials, taking only immediate necessities on to Cairo. I never in all my life saw such a multitude of clamouring useless beings as the porters at Port Said. Each tries to outdo the other in noise and apparent effort, so that nothing is accomplished and everything hopelessly mixed up. With my twenty pieces of baggage, I felt helpless. I finally managed, however, to unravel the tangle, and caught 6.30 p.m. train for Cairo. ... Unnecessary to say, I felt damnably lonely, an utter stranger in these parts, and especially as I had many friends on the *Malta*. I had the good fortune also to make the acquaintance of a Nurse Locke, who was a charming companion during the voyage and from whom I was very sorry to part.

On arrival at Cairo I took up residence at the Continental Hotel.

16 December 1917

... I reported to headquarters during the morning and set about preparing a plan of campaign. The object of my visit is to secure a series of publicity and record pictures and also to appoint photographers to carry on this work when I leave. I do not intend remaining longer than six weeks in Palestine. ...

17 December 1917

Morning to headquarters and arrange for assistants. I have secured two, both promising young fellows, one Sergeant Major Edmunds and the other, who will act as my batman pro tem, Bugler Johnson. ...

During the early afternoon I went by tram to the pyramids at Gizeh. I received the services of a guide by the name of 'Mozes', an entirely unnecessary person. Still, one has to pay for experience, and the £1 it cost me to look over the pyramids I did not grudge. If it had cost me a hundred, I would have paid it unhesitatingly. The tram run was most enjoyable. Mozes discoursing on all sorts of superfluous and uninteresting subjects rather disturbed my meditations, and when I told him to shut up, he apologised profusely and was quiescent for about three minutes. Then he would burst into other eruptions of verbiage, so I threatened to dismiss him, which threat had the desired effect. The way to Gizeh is very delightful, with the overflow waters of the Nile on the left and the shaded road on the right. This road itself is a study; a diorama of native life, of donkeys and camels laden with produce and sugarcane, of ragged Arabs and noisy children and an occasional misplaced motor. Before one realises it, he is there stepping from the tram ... [H]ere the pyramids stand, untouched by time, and as indestructible as the very sands which surround them. And there is the Sphinx, gazing in solemn silence into the future. ... Surely such objects as these can alone convey some slight impression to the senses of time and space. Kingdoms rise and fall, nations become but names, but still the Sphinx gazes on, heedless, inscrutable and unwrinkled.

... From the summit of Cheops, there is an awe-inspiring outlook across the rolling illimitable sands of the Libyan desert, and east, far over the agricultural lowlands to the Nile Delta, which calls to mind a tracery of silver threads. I had a great inclination to visit the interior of the great Pyramid 'Cheops', and having secured the three guides necessary, satisfied myself. With one of the guides leading, and bearing an absurd toy Christmas candle, another holding a hand in the front and the third, my remaining hand in the rear (thank heavens I had no more), we descended a very slippery stairway, thence along a narrow tunnel way (bent double), up stairways and through various chambers alleged to have been the burial places of famous Egyptian queens etc. ... One of the guides offered to tell me my fortune from a design he drew in the sand on the floor. ... I wonder if the ghost of old Cheops still haunts his den, and how he appreciates his vault being turned into a house of fortune?

As my guides neared the entrance they asked me for baksheesh for their magnesium ribbon and fortune telling. I gave them a couple of bob for their entertainment (which was certainly worth it). They evidently then anticipated me a good mark, no doubt thinking I would be induced by their number and environment to yield up more of the shining perquisite. 'Not so thou'. James Francis did quite a remarkable high-kicking performance, which so impressed his guides that it was not long before the narrow point of light at the entrance grew larger and larger, and we emerged into God's own sunshine again. ...

18 December 1917

At headquarters morning, and arranged to leave Cairo by train tomorrow evening. Afterwards visited that treasury of the Ancient Egypt, the Museum of Egyptian Antiquities. ... Afternoon, I drove to the citadel, from which lofty outlook one has a magnificent view of Cairo. From this aspect one sees little of the European Cairo, but looks out over the old town with its flat roofs, mosques and thousand spires. Away in the distant west the pyramids loom up like four volcanic cones.

On my return I wandered through the narrow streets of the native quarter and had a rare enjoyable time watching the workmen fashioning their wares. ... Every turn a new picture is presented; every shop is a picture, every face a study ... How quaint and beautifully oriental it all is. ... What a beautiful study in colour that fruit vendor presents. The golden oranges, figs and other fruits harmoniously arranged on coloured papers invite you to buy. And the moving population! What a variety of tints and colour they are bedecked in. ... The women alone are dressed in black. Their big flashing eyes sparkling above their yashmaks; and their shapely ankles fettered with silver anklets. They are not only enchanting themselves, but they assist in producing that air of mystery which is the lure of the East.

19 December 1917

... Left Cairo at 6.30 p.m. Dined onboard the train and arrived at Port Said 11.30 p.m. Put up at the Eastern Exchange Hotel.

21 December 1917

Damned cold night spent on Kantara Station, which we left at 6.30 a.m. in a train made up of all sorts of army stores and niggers. Almost immediately after leaving Kantara (which by the way is an important railhead, being used as a landing depot for ships coming up by way of the canal) the line runs through dismal desert covered with a sparse scrub. The outlook, however, across the desert to Sinai was remarkably beautiful, on account of the fine sunrise ... At El Arish we had to change over our goods to a troop train on account of congestion delays. This was the most exciting part of the journey as we had to shift out two truckloads of niggers, which was only accomplished by the aid of the boot and sticks. We arrived at Kelab 6.30 p.m. and I straightaway reported to GHQ. ...

22 December 1917

Went to Gaza by car and had a look over the ruins of the town which has been practically demolished by shellfire and by the Turks looting every scrap of timber. ... Roads are in frightful condition beyond Gaza on account of recent rains. ... As GHQ are now more than 50 miles behind the lines, I have decided to push on to Australian headquarters tomorrow evening. Transport is my most difficult problem, there being great scarcity of cars and the railways are decidedly erratic. Owing to the bulk of my equipment and distances to be covered, camel or horse travelling is almost out of question.

23 December 1917

... I left GHQ at 10 p.m. and embarked onboard the goods train with all my impedimenta at 11 p.m., bound for Deir Suneid.

24 December 1917

Very unpleasant ride last night on the 'goods', as we were compelled to camp under a number of water carts and the weather blew up frightfully cold and windy. We had alternate snatches of sleep and nightmares owing to the innumerable bumpings, buffetings and stoppages. We finally succeeded in reaching Deir Suneid about 2 a.m. and were bumped into a siding to await the pleasure of the unloading gangs. ... Deir Suneid is an important railhead and distributing point and there are immense stores of rations and fodder and army requirements. ...

The goods train in which I was to entrain for Esdud, 20 miles distant, was timed to leave Deir Suneid at 9 a.m., but after making countless false starts, left at 7 p.m.!! We with our burden were camped in an open troop truck, and I thought what a curiously fitting place to be spending Xmas eve in contrast to others I have spent under circumstances equally as incongruous. It was damnably cold and windy and the arrival at Esdud was welcomed heartily. Esdud is at present the 'existing' railhead. ...

27 December 1917

... During the morning I had a great surprise, for Gullet came down to meet me. We both visited General Cox of the 1st Brigade Light Horse and afternoon went over the sand dunes to the sea about two miles away. ... The sand compacted by the recent rains was good walking; its moving dunes, assuming quaint shapes by wind action, rolled in great golden billows to the distant horizon. Down on the beach, the blue waters of the Levant were making their music amongst the millions of shells that carpet the strand. The beach is deep with them, their varied colours sparkling in the sunshine like innumerable prisms. Gee! it was beautiful. Along the beach they were unloading a large steamer. She was laying out to sea and scores of surfboats were busy plying to and fro. It was a scene of indescribable bustle and noise, thousands of natives were there, unloading, manning the boats and packing the camels or stowing the cargo in great dumps. It is a great boon that we have the ocean so close, as the line is still held up and communication with supply sources would otherwise be severed. Returned across the desert, there being a wonderful sunset of which I took a number of colour plates.

28 December 1917

A limber from headquarters (now at Deiran) came down to convey myself and equipment from Esdud to thither last night, and at 10 a.m. this morning we were en route. The road is frightfully cut up and muddy from the recent rains, through which the springless limbers bumped and ploughed a foot deep. Nevertheless, the journey was filled with interest at every turn. No conception or comparison can be formed between the campaigns of Egypt and France. In the former, transport presents the greatest difficulty and the maintaining of lines of communication generally. Disregarding the magnificent engineering feats of the railroad, horse, camel, mule and donkey are the means of locomotion. One sees very few motor lorries. Stores and ammunition are dumped by the railway at various distributing railheads, from where they are conveyed by quadruped transport to the various units. At intervals along the coast, supplies are also landed from vessels anchored about half a mile out to sea, and the dumps are distributed generally by camels. This means that we keep up thousands of these animals for transport and during the journey we passed endless trains on the move. ...

Almost every object one sees has some biblical history or recent association. ... We passed through the interesting village of Yebna, built on the top of a lofty rise, its mud huts and walls looking from the plain like a swallow rookery. The prickly pear bounded roadway that leaves the village is alive with the inhabitants; women bearing water beakers on their heads as they did from the times of history, the men with their asses carrying immense loads, and the noisy children crying for baksheesh. Just at the foot of the village is the well, a quaint wooden construction that creakingly raises the water, actuated by a number of 'gyppos' walking in a circle and pushing a beam around. This in turn causes a chain of wooden buckets to lift and empty the water into a trough, from which it is drawn by the women. The whole scene is a riot of colour, and the chanting shanty of the labourers as they did their rounds, harmonising with the babbling of the womenfolk, gave just the right touch of life to this interesting little picture.

About 5 miles from Yebna we drew into Deiran, where the Desert Mounted Corps at present have their headquarters. There is an extraordinary contrast between this pretty little village and the native villages through which we have been passing. Its inhabitants are principally Jews, and their clean, well-built houses at once transported me to the outlying areas of Mosman Bay, Sydney. The walls are of stone, generally painted white, and roofed with red tiles. The streets are well kept and avenued with Australian gumtrees; Australian troops wander in the streets. It is all so Australian and so very incongruous for Palestine. ... Desert Mounted Corps are billeted in the various residences and I admire their selection, for not only have they selected the best of the villages, but they have settled in the finest residences. I took up my residence with a Captain Bruce. We jointly occupy a room which is part of the residence occupied by an old rabbi. ...

30 December 1917

Messed 7.30 a.m. and proceeded by motor to Latron. Thence by Ford car to our front-line position called Khurbetha Ibn Harith. The ride in the Ford car greatly reminded me of my 'cross Australia ride' being frightfully rough and stony. ... I stayed with the 3rd Brigade Headquarters' General Wilson, everybody living in tiny bivouacs beneath the olive trees. During the afternoon I visited, with the General, the front-line positions. The country is a series of great limestone hills, terribly rough and impassable but for the bridle tracks we have made. These hills are terraced off so as to hold the soil from being washed away, and give to the hills a curious effect of concentric ridges. The terraces are planted with olive trees, with here and there the fig. As we walked over the country I was surprised to see daisies, narcissus and cyclamen in bloom; the atmosphere was scented with the perfume of the herbs which carpeted the ground and which I recognised as good old thyme etc. The opposite ridge I was told was in the occupation of the Turks; I didn't see any and judging by the numbers of our men holding our position, the enemy forces must indeed be feeble. It all reminded me of a great picnic. It seemed impossible that hostilities could extend to these quiet gorges and ranges. Now and again the clatter of a machine gun echoed down the valley, and an occasional sniper's rifle rang out, but this was all. What enjoyment after the hell of France! ...

After dinner the boys invited me to their campfire and asked me to give them a few words about my Antarctic expedition business. ... It is not everybody who is privileged to sit amongst his own countrymen away out on the Judean hills, with the 'Star of Bethlehem' bright in the heavens recounting his adventures. ...

Turned in to our tiny bivouac with my Sergeants Edmunds and Johnson, which recalled life under the boats on Elephant Island, tightly packed, but warm and contented.

31 December 1917

... I have been out most of the day with General Wilson, taking pictures around the front-line positions. My heavy equipment took six men to carry it, owing to the rocky country and the difficulty in climbing over these rocky slopes. The country in which we are now fighting is very mountainous and composed of limestone. It affords the most exquisite shelter for defence, and if the enemy had but the morale and supplies behind him, the country might be held for 'the duration'. ... During the evening the boys had a very enjoyable concert, which was held in an old tomb mosque. There was much talent amongst them, mostly the songs and recitations being of Australian origin. Here I would contrast the Australian out here with his brother of France. Here a life more nearer to home is lived. Most of these men are from Western Australia, bushmen and cattlemen. They have not lost any of the traits of our country lands. Hospitable, warm-hearted and ingenuous they remain. Every man a horseman. The general and his officers have not assumed that rigid militarism which is so obvious in France, and so one finds more harmony, sympathy and kinship. ... Life here is more Australian, open air and expansive. There is not the strain of war nor the eternal fear of death. It would be a man's bad luck to be killed here in action, whilst in France, he might consider himself fortunate to escape with life. France is hell, Palestine more or less a holiday. ... The Australian in France has lost much of his charm due to association and intermingling with society. He is comparatively a few hours from London and Paris and so has assumed in some degree the mannerisms of the people.

2 January 1918

The camel transport arrived at camp at 7.30 a.m. and all gear was packed up for a move. The roads are quagmires and extremely bad for camels, their padded feet slipping and sliding, so that with the regulation load of 300 pounds up, the poor brutes are absolutely helpless. Scarcely better off are their native drivers. These absolutely destitute beings have little or no shelter during the rains, with the results that numbers perish through cold and exposure.

The entire brigade left El Burj at noon and moved off in sections. The long column winding its way like a great serpent over rocky defiles and plain made a very impressive spectacle. ...

3 January 1918

General Wilson had the Brigade (3rd) paraded in column formation for the cine. The column with transports extended over two miles. It made a magnificent sight, stretching over and winding across the undulating plain like a great serpent. ... Tomorrow morning I intend leaving for Desert Mounted Corps headquarters at Deiran.

4 January 1918

... We were at Corps at 11.30 a.m. and I took up my residence again in billets with the old rabbi. It was just like returning home. I met Gullett at 'headquarters' and we had an enjoyable afternoon chat over comparisons of Palestine and Campagne in France. ...

5 January 1918

I left with my staff sergeant and batman, accompanied with my vast amount of equipment, in a box Ford car for Esdud. ... Just outside the village of Mughar we had magneto troubles which prevented us going further until a reserve car came to our assistance. In the interim we visited the native village of Mughar and secured a series of plates. The village is built on a steep hill which rises from the plain and is by far the most pictorial I have visited. The houses, if I might so dignify them by the word, are built entirely of mud and stone – very little of the latter. They are invariably hedged in by high walls, flat roofed and squalid. In the small courtyards are kept considerable numbers of fowl, and here the numerous children indulge in the same pranks as our own offsprings. The women, too, arrayed in their multicoloured dresses, may be seen prattling away on the steps, or carrying water in the characteristic earthenware bowls on their head, [or] house-building, or farming; for here woman takes her share with man. ...

The gyppos ... put us on the road to Esdud where ... I visited the 1st Brigade headquarters and joined their mess. ... I intend staying at Esdud for about a week.

8 January 1918

Improvement in weather, which enabled the 1st Brigade to parade for the cinema. The horses and men, which have been in rest camp now for several weeks, are all in fine fettle. The riding was admirable and all seemed to enjoy the exercise and turnout.

The immediate neighbourhood is the centre of a number of camps, so that the sandhills are always abustle with horses and men and the unending streams of accompanying camel transport. Our headquarters have their tents pitched in what was once an old 'figgery'. ...

9 January 1918

Morning enacted a cinema scene of sinking for water in the desert. Water is plentiful in the vicinity, as a sump had only to be sunken 12 feet. The water is pumped up by means of a Downton pump into canvas troughs. The whole of the brigade horses were watered and the effect produced was very fine. ...

11 January 1918

Glorious weather. Visited the 2nd Brigade, and by appointment with General Ryrie, the brigade paraded for pictures. A finer body of men it would be well nigh impossible to find. They sat in the saddles as though part of their horses, the discipline excellent and the manoeuvres even excited the General's admiration. ... The 1st and 2nd Brigades are moving towards Deiran tomorrow and I have decided to travel with them.

12 January 1918

Reveille at 6 a.m., early breakfast out in the open under an old fig tree. Tents struck, limbers packed and the column moved off at 10 a.m. The seeming endless stream of men and horses winding their way across the plains recalled to mind the great columns of the African fighting ants on their way to battle. Far away to the horizon, the stream moved slowly along; over rises, into valleys, across streams it pushed impressively. The men were in high spirits, and the horses in good fettle. ...

The brigade went into a wet bivouac about a mile from Deiran ... where we put up for the night at 'Harlap's', a comfortable little hotel where we were able to dry our clothes and secure a good meal.

14 January 1918

... There appears to be considerable conflict between the Imperial and Australian heads at Corps, which I can only attribute to jealousy on the part of the former. Desert Corps, which administers the entire mounted forces, is composed of a theoretical representative selection of Imperial and Australian officers. For unexplainable reasons, there is a great preponderance of the former. General Chauvel commands the Australians – General Trew, the Yeomanry (Imperial). Unfortunately, the former is rather weak and has not sufficient 'push' to secure the full privileges due his men. This leads to much dissension and dissatisfaction, and there exists a decidedly unfriendly attitude between the 'Imps' and 'Aussies'. I have experienced an unwillingness to assist on [the] part of the former, but have succeeded in securing my needs by appealing direct to our heads.

My new workrooms are part of a house occupied by a Yiddish family and are clean and convenient. ... Developed a number of colour plates, which I found excellently exposed (F/11 – 1 sec.). The actinic value of the light is about equivalent to that of English summer. ...

16 January 1918

Went to Zernukah – a native village a few miles from headquarters. ... Zernukah like many other similar villages is built on a hill slope, its approach being hedged by fine avenues of cacti. The sheik gave us all assistance possible, and all the rest of the indolent ragged population, and the ever-accompanying crowd of small boys joined in. I had the 2nd Regiment paraded through the narrow laneways and in many other pictorial settings. It is amusing what the troops will do for the camera. The various brigades have been marshalled and all in turn have passed before the cinema. They have all keenly participated. ... But the most interesting sight of Zernukah, and in fact most other villages, is the waterwheel. ... Around the valve of the reservoir, the 'bynts' (women) collect with their big terracotta water jars, and discuss, no doubt, the gossip of the village. ... But the colours are the greatest charm. ... I secured a very interesting series of pictures of the Light Horse amidst these quaint surroundings and returned to Deiran [at] 5 p.m. ...

18 January 1918

... I met General Chauvel and requested that twenty men with officers be sent to Jerusalem to take part in the photographic visit I am making there in a few days. ... My idea is to include a number of Light Horsemen in my pictures for historic records, and though they did not actually take part in the capture, it was undoubtedly due to their speedy advance in the direction of Jaffa and their threat to outflank the enemy, which greatly facilitated the fall of Jerusalem into our hands: furthermore, pictures of Jerusalem are of no military or public interest unless some of our troops are included.

21 January 1918

Left Deiran at 7 a.m. with Captain Rhodes in a Ford for Jerusalem, my two men following in a boxcar with equipage. With a wonderful morning favouring, we had a fine, though bumpy, run to Latron which is at the foot of the hills. The plain abruptly terminates, and we began the ascent of the foothills along a passably good road which bends and winds amongst the steep inclines of Judea. The scenery is very fine. As one passes along, ever upward, through the narrow gorges of limestone, there are transcending glimpses into deep valleys, blue-grey with weathered limestone and cultivated here and there, wherever there is sufficient soil, with gnarled old olive trees. And close inspection shows the mountain slopes to be ablossom with narcissus, anemones and the beautiful little cyclamen. ... Halfway up the pass we met Lieutenant Hardy (in charge of the twenty men I had asked for) with his troop and limbers. I took a series of pictures. ... As we neared the first summit, a short halt was made to enjoy the magnificent panorama which opened up. Looking back westward over the great round waves of limestone which characterise these hills, one could see over 25 miles of plains, to Jaffa in the distance and the sea beyond. ... On the eastern slopes immediately below us, began a series of sharp hairpin-bend descents which led into the valley. Immediately in front, perched on a hill crest, lay Kulonieh, near where the Turks destroyed the fine bridge over the Wady Surar when they retired on Jerusalem. ... Only a mile away on the hilltop lay Jerusalem. Every inch of the ground was interesting with some biblical association. ... The entry into Jerusalem is as disappointing as entering a mansion by way of the scullery door. The way is through modern buildings and a densely peopled thoroughfare, dusty and commonplace, that quite disappointed me. ...

30 January 1918

It is amusing the keenness of the staff and brigades to have their photos taken. I have had three brigades turned out! Generals coming from distant parts of the country! and all the impossible stunts enacted for the cinema. Fancy taking a party of troops to Jerusalem for the sole object of taking part in a cine performance! Flying stunts and bombing raids! Every department solicits my presence, even to the GOC [General Operational Command]. This unbounded vanity and desire for publicity, I regret, is absorbing much time and I shall be glad to be on the move again. Gullett returned, and we have been going into the matter of the appointment of an official photographer. At present I am having difficulty in securing a suitable man to carry on. The Kodak appears to be part of the equipment of the Light Horse, but all are raw amateurs and unsuited to carry on serious record work. ...

1 February 1918

Left Desert Corps at 10 a.m. with Colonel Farr in his Vauxhall for Jerusalem. Although I have been over the same route previously, it was as interesting as ever and filled me with anticipations at every turn. Farr was in raptures and enjoyed every inch of the journey. We put up at the Fast Hotel – where, considering the great scarcity of foodstuffs, quite excellent meals are served and a good clean bed. It is amusing to see the guests (military) arrive, each with his bread ration under arm or other rations. During the afternoon, we visited the city within the walls and went [by the] Via Dolorosa to the Mosque of Omar, thence to the Jews' wailing place. A number of them were indeed crying bitterly and we were astounded at their religious fervour. They wail for the destruction of their temple, and no doubt it is part of the routine of their religious beliefs; but to see young children sitting by the wall, praying and evidently deep in sorrow and penance, impressed me with great admiration. ... We visited also the Church of the Holy Sepulchre, wherein tradition hath it, that our Saviour was buried. The church is a fine old rambling place composed of a number of courts, of the various denominations, all grouped around the supposed sepulchre. The sepulchre itself has been faced with marble, but unfortunately, so many of the sights are imaginary that one even doubts the fallibility of this one. We spent some time at the American store purchasing souvenirs, every description of useless articles being manufactured from the local woods or executed in metalwork, which has developed with some degree of art. ...

4 February 1918

Left Desert Corps 8.30 a.m. for the 4th Brigade at Belah, about 65 miles south. I intend putting in a few days with the 67th Flying Squadron. Altogether I anticipate being away a week. ...

5 February 1918

Made out a programme of intended 'stunts' which I require doing and prospected the surrounding country for position. ...

6 February 1918

I had two squadrons sent to Gaza to participate in my pictures. The weather turned out excellent and I did some excellent work. ... We wandered all over Gaza, which once must have been a very fine town, but nowhere did I see an intact building, not even a room. Gaza is the Ypres of Palestine. ...

7 February 1918

Photographed various stunts – battery going into action, machine-gun drill and ambulance turnout. Afternoon, two regiments turned out and reenacted their famous charge at Beersheba. The scene was filled with excitement, and I can well imagine the demoralising effect on the enemy of two regiments with bayonets drawn, sweeping down onto them. In some small degree, I sensed the excitement myself, for the charge was directed against the position which I occupied. ... Evening, visited the 4th Regiment and gave them lecturette on Antarctica.

11 February 1918

Left 4th Brigade at 7.30 a.m. with Gullett in the box Ford, the road having improved sufficiently. ... We arrived at the Camel Brigade Headquarters (General Smith) in time for lunch. During the afternoon interviewed battalion commanders and arranged the ... programme for tomorrow.

12 February 1918

The busiest day I have had so far, and by far the most unique performances. The events opened with a battalion in attack, a reenactment of the battle of Rafa and on the very grounds. The battalion, mounted on camels, came into action at a fast trot. In the cover of some big hills, they halted and dismounted. The men rapidly formed up and so the attack opened. Small parties worked round the cover of the hills, taking advantage of every rise and screen, until a point of vantage was reached immediately under the supposed enemy position. Here the men, under the cover of a small declivity, formed up and at the signal, rushed the position at the bayonet point. The whole affair was most realistically done and I quite found myself the nucleus of a fearsome bayonet charge. ...

13 February 1918

Left Rafa 10 a.m. and arrived at Majdal at 4 p.m. (Lunched with 4th Brigade at Belah) ... and arranged a programme with Major Williams for taking a series of photographs of the 67th Flying Squadron from the ground and air. Looked over the aerodrome, which is the most complete I have visited. Every branch of craft essential to a flying squadron has its separate shop. I anticipate the results will be the most spectacular I am likely to take here. ...

14 February 1918

... I intend carrying out and producing a film that will include the whole incidents connected with a bombing raid, and started on this intention during the morning. ... I intend securing my cinema to the machine and taking film therefrom. With this object I made experiments to ascertain the points of minimum vibration and have decided to clamp the machine across the gun cockpit, insulating it by means of flat rubber sponges under compression. ... The squadron fly Bristol Fighters and Martinsydes.

15 February 1918

... Morning examined some old ruins a little distance from hangars. Some excavations have been carried out by several of the men and fragments of a magnificent mosaic have been unearthed, together with several broken slabs; coins and pieces of exquisitely stained glass have also been dug up in the near vicinity, and judging by the position of the extensive amount of fragmentary pottery and eroded building material, the site must have been covered with a considerable city.

Just before lunch, we observed a machine land with smoke rising from near the pilot's seat. He had only time to jump out when the machine burst into flame and was speedily demolished. Fortunately, I had both cinema and camera at hand and secured some unique pictures. During the afternoon, ten machines loaded with bombs took off from the aerodrome and flew so as to just pass over the top of the cine. The effect was extremely impressive. I went up in Captain Smith's Bristol Fighter (a 190 horsepower machine) and doing over 90 miles per hour, we rapidly came up with the formation. We went down nearly to Beersheba, our machine circling round the flat whilst I took cinema; at 7000 feet we looked down onto banks of cumulus and through the fleeting openings, down onto the old Turkish trenches. Captain Addison did a series of manoeuvres, looping, diving and rolling, etc., which showed the admirable control of the pilot with modern machines. At 4.30 a spiral nosedive dropped us from 5000 to 2500 feet in a few seconds. We returned to the aerodrome without mishap, after a delightful run, which I can only compare with the ride of old Elijah when he went up in his heavenly chariot.

16 February 1918

I had a new fitting made for my cinema to absorb the vibration of the engine on our 190-horsepower Bristol Fighter, and Major Williams arranged a flight for me to try it out. With Captain Ross Smith piloting, we left the hangars at 9.30 a.m. Oh, the exhilaration of that upward climb! The powerful throb of the engine whilst on the ground now resolved itself into a whirr, and the hangars rapidly decreased in size until they became mere specks. Up, up, we go – 1000, 2000, 3000, 4000 are indicated on the gauge and still we climb heavenward. The earth below is assuming the appearance of a patchwork. Here and there numerous villages are scattered ... the roads radiate from them like white ribbons, the streams and wadies might be arteries with networks of veins. Long since, traffic on the road has converted itself into mote-like specks and still we climb heavenward.

Almost before one realises – the flat plain is gone, and the country looks rough and broken. From our great height it appears as if some mighty thumb has pressed into the earth and impressed it with its markings. ... We are crossing the hills of Judea at 90 miles per hour and yet from our great height we appear stationary. Away on the horizon lays a dark streak which is rapidly enlarging. It is the Dead Sea. In a few minutes we are over it and gliding down in volplane (at 100 miles an hour). I am powerless and utterly incapable of describing the wild and tremendous grandeur of the view now stretched before us. We are over enemy territory and they are firing at us with their 'archies'. Wretched shooting, to which we pay no attention. One is too absorbed in contemplation, in fact intoxicated by the mighty works of nature, to heed the vile endeavours of Turkish rabble to shoot us down. From the ground, we appear as a tiny humming bird flitting through the infinity of cloudless blue; from my seat, we are hurtling along on the wings of a tornado, poised over the deep blue waters of the Mystic Sea! Still we glide down and fly over the stagnant waters only 1000 feet above their surface. We are flying 200 feet below sea level, for the Dead Sea and the valley of the Jordan are 1200 feet below sea level.

Just in front of us lays the valley of the Jordan. ... Like a great serpent, its convolutions wind and double back on themselves in the most fantastic and irregular manner conceivable. The valley of the Jordan is as flat as the surface of the Dead Sea. I was living every moment of this wonderful flight, fascinated by the miracle of nature which was unfolded below us. Our great bird even seemed to appreciate it and moved along purring and cleaving the Jordan atmosphere with felicity and joy. Near the Jordan Bridge, we turn back and speedily find ourselves over Jericho... Again the archies greet us, but the shooting is bad. Then we followed the winding course of the Jericho–Jerusalem road, which winds and twists amongst the hills... I was lost, enraptured by the ineffable beauty of the scenery below, and knew this flight to be the most interesting and grandest, from a spectacular aspect, that I have ever, or ever will gaze on. It was a glimpse of another world, a peep into the realm of the infinite. We flew along, following the course of the roadway at 8000 feet until the Holy City lay below us and I felt I had realised a dream in my existence. We glided slowly down to 2000 feet above Jerusalem, but unfortunately, the weather became dull and rendered it bad for photography. Borne on the wings of our great bird, which circled over the city like a great albatross, one scarcely seemed to be of this world... I could easily recognise the familiar streets and buildings within the walls and even discern pedestrians and traffic on the highways.

The clouds continuing to gain in intensity, Smith piloted his machine up to 17 000 to 18 000 feet. At this elevation it was extremely cold. The fleeting glimpses we had of the earth through rifts in the clouds reminded me of the hazy impressions one has of places during a dream. Beautiful and wondrous as it was below the clouds, the effect was now glorified a hundredfold. We flew over a billowy sea of silver mist thrown into fantastic forms by the wind and sun shadows, and one could quite easily have fancied themselves floating over icy mountains and snowy plateaux. I took some wonderful film and when we descended below the clouds, I could pick out Jerusalem and Bethlehem and the road winding away to Jericho to the east like a white ribbon. We landed at the hangars at 2 p.m. just in time to witness Major Williams reviewing his squadron. This day ranks as one of the [most] salient in my life, for I feel I have travelled and seen the most fascinating and wondrous area of our globe. At evening I gave a lecture to 200 men, which was well received, on Antarctica.

17 February 1918

General Chauvel rang me up a few days previously to return to Desert Corps (Deiran) and take a group of the administrative officers of the AIF forces, who are all on a visit, to corps. I regretfully bid adieu to my very kind friends at the Flying Corps, and I hope to return in a few days to complete their programme. ... Great activity is noticeable in the transport section and I hear rumours a 'stunt' is shortly to come off near Jerusalem.

18 February 1918

Up ere break of day and away to Jerusalem by box Ford car. With me are my batman, Johnson, and an excellent driver, Mackenzie. ... The operations, which likely will be of great public interest and also spectacular, are to be directed against the Turkish positions just north of Jerusalem, and also to force them across the Jordan, leaving Jericho in our hands. ...

19 February 1918

... The brigade left camp at 10 a.m. and threaded its way through the winding narrow ways of Bethlehem, and a noble sight they made. ... Every step was filled with interest and I felt a glow of pride, as I rode alongside the general, to see that long thin endless line of my own countrymen, riding this sacred ground and bent on the mission of freeing it from the Turkish oppression. ... Camp was pitched close to Solomon's Well, a (half-made) great cavern hewn from the limestone cliffs in which channels are cut to drain and conduit the rainwater. What a contrast to biblical times; amidst these sacred surroundings lay an army in bivouac, and the soldiers in great swarms were filling their water bottles at the well. ... High up amongst the hills, the Bedouins were shepherding their flocks of goats amongst the wildflowers, which draped the mountainsides and carpeted our very path. After tea, a start was made for Muntar where we were to camp for the evening. ...

20 February 1918

At 3.30 a.m., the brigade moved off again, intending to carry the strongly entrenched Turkish position of Nebi Musa. ... At daybreak we entered upon much more open country, undulating and covered with low hills. ... Already the fighting for the heights was going on and from our position, everything could be observed as if it were a great stage play. The cavalry (New Zealand Rifles) advanced their horses to the nearest safe cover, where they dismounted and advanced in battle array on foot to the base of the precipitous heights. The enemy were clearly observable on the crest, strongly entrenched and well equipped with machine guns. Our brigade (under Brigadier General Cox) was ordered to remain under cover until called upon. ... [W]ith the 'Brig' and staff, I climbed to the top of a nearby eminence and watched the whole battle. I hold in contempt the Turk, as a soldier, for allowing our men to even reach the base of his stronghold, which, with a few machine guns, might defy an army who were without artillery support! In the face of the impossible, the New Zealanders and 60th Division Infantry slowly gained their way up the hill, though the Turk had the mastery of the position and artillery supporting. ... During the afternoon, we took possession of three Bedouins who informed us of an unprotected pathway by means of which we might gain the Jordan Valley and so attack the enemy's rear. General Chaytor (in charge division) agreed to Brigadier Cox's suggestion to take his brigade by this route. We started off in single-file formation, guided by the Arabs at 5 p.m. The enemy's rear was to be attacked at daybreak.

21 February 1918

... The descent into the Jordan Valley was indeed exciting and awesome. At times the horses slid more than walked down the steep rocky faces, and the only guide was the dim outline of the horseman ahead or the trail of sparks from the horseshoes. As the daybreak advanced, we were near the foot of the great hills and entering the plains of the Jordan Valley. ... Being curious of investigating Jericho, I rode through it, and must say I was disgusted with its filthiness and squalor. The Turks, during their residence, had not improved the cleanliness or sanitation of the village, and which, by way of showing their appreciation for hospitality received from the dwellers, pillaged them the night before we took possession. Jericho is just a small uninteresting dirty little village and but for the biblical interest and romantic situation, is a place to avoid. ...

22 February 1918

... At early morning I desired to visit the Jordan and secure a series of photographs of our front line. According to reliable information, the Turks had absconded to the western bank of the river and our front line lay directly along the eastern bank, being patrolled by the New Zealanders; accordingly, I set out in the Ford, accompanied by Drs Ahearn and Wybird. We ran along the excellent road which runs in a direct line from Jericho to the Jordan Bridge for a distance of four miles. Anticipating this road to be enfiladed by enemy artillery, I ordered the car to be secreted in some nearby bushes and turned about, ready for home. ... In the dim light of daybreak I noticed a patrol of some twelve to fifteen cavalry on our right, with about six on the left; naturally thinking they were our own patrols, we leisurely walked in their direction. When only 400 yards distant, we were speedily disillusioned by a volley of rifle fire. ...[W]e had all but run into a patrol of Turkish cavalry. As the distance between us and the car was too great to make, and as I did not wish the whole of the rifle fire to be directed against us. ... I gave the order for the car to immediately get out of range. ... the batteries enfilading the road from the Turkish bank of the Jordan, opened up and sniped its retreat with 10-pounders.

... Our own position now was highly hazardous. We dodged from cover to cover amongst the sparse and stunted sage bush, evading the fusillade of rifle fire and sniping. ...they made no attempt to advance, but were content to snipe at increasing range. When we became winded, we crawled into a large bush and lay there perfectly quiet until the little sandy spurts and feu de joys ended. Evidently thinking we still kept in hiding, the enemy vigorously shelled our position. The small 10-pounder shells, however, were as effective as his rifle fire and we still kept our cover. After an hour and a half in this cramped attitude, I decided to make shift to return. ... By cutting a quantity of saltbush and binding it into bundles so as to imitate a couple of bushes ... we wriggled on our stomachs back to safety, taking advantage of every little bit of cover. Through the screen we could distinctly see enemy horsemen still alert for our reappearance.

After covering half a mile in this ignominious position, the cover became sufficiently thick to allow us to crawl, which we did for nearly a mile. ... I could not help laughing at the absurdity of it all. Here were we, apparently sane men, crawling away from a foe whom we never met nor bore grudge against, with God's own blue sky above, and the warm sun, and the beautiful flowers offering up their sweet perfume. ...

We were now on safe ground and reasonably away from observation, so that we got up and walked away like men. We met a body of Light Horse coming to our rescue, but fortunately, we were able to carry out my maxim of 'He who gets himself into trouble should have the resource to extricate himself'. ... The objective of Jericho had been gained, and as it was only our intention to hold it for twenty-four hours so that a new line might be established on the hills controlling the valley, the brigade evacuated the position at 7 p.m. In the little Ford, we made a hurried return towards Jerusalem. ...

23 February 1918

... Arrived at Deiran 12.30 p.m. Afternoon, I set about packing up for my return to the Flying Corps.

25 February 1918

At 10.30 a.m. seven machines set out on a bombing raid to El Kerak and El Kutrani. The former town is about 70 miles distant and therein are quartered a large number of Turkish cavalry. El Kutrani is an important railway siding on the Hejaz railway, another 20 miles further east. The clear weather became very gusty as we crossed the Judean hills at 8000 feet and very cold. The wonderful scenery of the ranges viewed from this elevation beggars description; the mountains appear to be great piles of limestone covered with stunted growth and around their bases, the wadies, now dry, have cut deep channels. These ramify like a great system of arteries and veins, and bear some testimony to the force of water which rushes down the precipitous slopes during the torrential rains of January–April. We crossed the Dead Sea at Point Molyneux. There, the sea is constricted into a narrow waist by a curious peninsular of flat land and is only about four miles wide about the middle of the sea. It lay below us like a great stagnant blue pool, rippleless and dead. From our height, we could look from end to end of its abyssal basin, the high ranges surrounding the waveless shores like the walls of a mighty dam. Below us, the fleet of bombing planes soared like great birds, making the desolation echo with the hum of power.

... Across the narrows of the sea we passed, and up over the great mountains and chasms that line the eastern shore. Clouds rolled by and the chaos of mountains and valleys was chequered with sunshine and shadows. Just in front of us lay the large village of El Kerak. Built on the crest of a high hill, it seemed impregnable enough, and its only vulnerable point from above. At the southern end, built on the precipice edge, lay the citadel, which we noticed to be swarming with Turkish troops. This was one of the objectives of our raid. (El Kerak was the most eastern point reached by the Crusaders and probably the citadel is a relic of those times.)

The machines circled like great vultures over the doomed citadel, and I could distinctly see the large 100-pound bombs drop through the air. With a great detonation, one fell directly in the courtyard. God knows what heinous damage it wrought, but the whole place lay obscured by the dust of crunched masonry and smoke. We then fled on our mission of destruction to El Kutrani. At the station lay a train under full steam and about 100 rolling stock. Close by we observed a new Hun aerodrome with five hangars and a number of machines out on the flying ground. We bombed them lustily, and returned with all speed, fearing pursuit by hostile aircraft, nor were we left alone by the archies. They fired at us until outranged, but the shooting was 'rotten'. Returning home, we encountered squally winds, so that the machine went through all the evolutions of a small boat in a sea. It was with relief that the home hangars came in sight and we glided down to mother earth, which we touched as a feather and taxied up to the big hangars where the machines were quickly housed. After a wash, we went across to lunch, where the topic naturally was the raid and we all wondered how many we had killed and wounded!

1 March 1918

The looked-for fine day arrived at last and enabled me to complete my film with the Australian Flying Squadron. We left the hangars in a Bristol at 10 a.m. and in 20 minutes were once more climbing in the blue sky over the Judean summit; another 15 minutes and Jerusalem lay below us. ... We circled around the city a number of times and I took both films and 'still' pictures from heights 8000 to 1000 feet. We returned to the aerodrome 12 o'clock and after lunch, I bid adieu to my very fine friends of the Flying Corps and returned to Desert Corps at Deiran, 35 miles.

4 March 1918

Spent morning in packing up and left Desert Corps, Deiran, at 5 p.m. to join 7 p.m. train from Ludd to Cairo.

The last ride through the orchards to Ramleh, along the red, narrow, cactus-hedged lanes made on me a deep impression of sadness for leaving this place of sunshine, freedom and flowers. The Judean hills that I shall never forget were just turning purple in the sunset; every landmark, village or well-known place I left as if I were parting with friends. Oh Palestine – Garden of Eden, home of bounteous nature, may I live to come back to you again, for thou art indeed a dreamland of beauty and happiness. ...

5 March 1918

Quite a comfortable run through the night, during which I slept most of the time, landed us at Kantara at 5.30 a.m. ... and left by train for Cairo 9.15 a.m. ... I anticipate being in Cairo for at least ten days, as all my work has to be submitted to censorship. Have arranged that Sergeant Campbell should take over the official photographic work on this front.

7 March 1918

In order to further safeguard against submarining risks, I have arranged that a good glossy print be produced from each negative and kept at our Cairo war records department, and that the cinema film be duplicated. ...

6 May 1918

At high tide, steamed up the Thames and by means of lighter, landed at Tilbury 5 p.m. Put up at the Imperial Hotel, Russell Square. Evening, went to *Daily Chronicle* and saw Perris. He informed me the rights of the Shackleton film have been sold on the Continent for £5000 and the British for another £5000. The film is now free of all encumbrances and any further sales of rights will be distributed.

7 May 1918

... The big exhibition of Australian war pictures opens in the Grafton Galleries on the 25th May, when the whole results of my ten months work will be exhibited. Visited Australia House and met Captain Smart who has had the show in hand and arranged for offices in the building in which I am to work.

8 May 1918

Visited the Grafton Galleries and looked over the wall space; also went to Raines and Company of Ealing who are doing the enlargements. Many of the pictures are being enlarged up to 20 feet by 12 feet; the work is well in hand and looks magnificent.

9 May 1918

Selecting negatives and arranging pictures with Lieutenant Leist. Leist has been for some time assisting in producing the pictures whilst I was away in Palestine. ...

10 May 1918

To Australia House where I now have an office and with Leist arranging prints for the coming exhibition. The work is extremely tedious, as I have such an abundance of subjects and find great difficulty in selection. ...

15–16 May 1918

On exhibition work. During my visit to Palestine, affairs have been frightfully muddled. Pictures were made from wretched subjects, indiscriminately and without consideration to size. The result has been a waste of time endeavouring to make pictures fit. Double the amount of work has therefore been thrust on me.

17 May 1918

Today I received a batch of colour reproductions from the Paget Plate Company. The Palestine results are far beyond my expectations. The colours such as one only sees in Palestine have been rendered perfectly and should be one of the main features of the exhibition.

20 May 1918

... Went into office and writing up a lecture for the colour plates. Time is passing very quickly and I am seriously perturbed the exhibition will not be ready by its official opening date.

22 May 1918

... Not a picture is yet hung and the show is to open on 24th!

24 May 1918

Worked until 1 a.m. this morning and we managed to cover the walls, chiefly with substitute pictures. I was particularly disgusted with the arrangements. Captain Smart, who has them in hand, utterly lacks powers of organisation and I have to thank him for more or less presenting the exhibition in an extemporised and unfinished condition. I was so disgusted that I did not appear at the official opening and I believe things were more or less mixed up by the projecting man, for the colour work being missing. Here again, Smart showed his incompetence by discovering at the last minute that the hall for projecting purposes had been previously engaged. Everything was left until the last minute and had I not returned from Palestine in the nick of time, the whole fruits of my work would have been so much wasted time. I expect to have things complete and in satisfactory order in a week's time.

25 May 1918

The exhibition was well patronised today. The colour lantern is working excellently, but I regret the best of my pictures have yet to be hung. There are about 130 exhibits, exclusive of the artists' room. The largest picture, an episode during the battle of Zonnebeke, measures about 21 feet by 15 feet. It is a combination of twelve negatives. The colour slides depict scenes on the West Front, Flanders, and also Palestine. They are gems, and elicit applause at every showing. A military band plays throughout the day.

26–28 May 1918

Time occupied in completing the exhibition. Our largest picture, 'The Raid', depicting an episode at the Battle of Zonnebeke, measures over 20 feet in length by 15 feet 6 inches high. Two waves of infantry are leaving the trenches in the thick of a Boche barrage of shells and shrapnel. A flight of bombing aeroplanes accompanies them. An enemy plane is burning in the foreground. The whole picture is realistic of battle; the atmospheric effects of battle smoke are particularly fine. Another sensational picture is 'Death the Reaper'. This remarkable effect is made up of two negatives. One, the foreground, shows the mud-splashed corpse of a Boche floating in a shell crater. The second is an extraordinary shellburst, the form of which resembles Death. The Palestine series are magnificent. Collectively, it is a rare exhibition and from the point of view of art and from the criticism I have heard, is ahead of anything which has been shown in this country. It is some recompense to see one's work shown to the masses, and to receive favourable criticism after the risks and hardship I have taken and endured to secure the negatives. The pictures represent ten months active fieldwork.

29 May 1918

Still busy on picture making and hanging. The exhibition is at last assuming shape and looks truly magnificent. The colour slides are wonders. The daily attendance numbers 600. I receive notices almost daily and also a great many letters of congratulations.

30 May–2 June 1918

… The exhibition is a magnificent display of photographic technique. … I am asking that this set of pictures be sent to Australia and retained for the national collection of war pictures. …

4 June 1918

Wilkins came over from France. He was awarded the MC [Military Cross]. I received nothing. I feel very much receiving no recognition as I took equal share and risks. I worked day and night to secure the results and have made the entire exhibition. There has been string pulling. Wilkins certainly deserved the MC but there should have been no distinction. I have prepared everything in the exhibition and have no acknowledgment, financial or otherwise.

5 June 1918

Captain Bean, whom we directly come under, came over today and visited the exhibition. I am urging that the present set of enlargements be sent to Australia for propaganda. No better medium could we possibly have. The exhibition has been pronounced by experts to be the best since the beginning of the war.

6–8 June 1918

At Galleries. Have great difficulty in securing capable lecturers for the colour slides. The attendance is rapidly on the increase. I am having a great fight to secure the pictures for Australia. It makes me lose patience when I see all my efforts over which I spent all my time and risked my life thrown to the winds. I am so sick and fed up with the whole affair that I don't care what happens, whether the pictures are ruined by touring provincial towns or whether they ever reach Australia. After all, it is my own fault for not making proper arrangements at the beginning.

14–21 June 1918

I have omitted a week from my diary, having been so disgusted with the treatment I have received from the High Commissioner's office and the AIF. It has worried me considerably. A deadlock has been arrived at which excludes me from taking the exhibition of my own pictures to Australia. Unfortunately, I have absolutely no say whatsoever in what is to be done with my own negatives and results. The injustice done me has embittered me greatly against the AIF. Fortunately, I made certain arrangements at the beginning which enable me to resign and I have unhesitatingly done so. The only reason Australia House subscribes to their attitude is because I am soliciting publicity. They accuse me of making a Hurley show of the exhibition, which is an infernal lie. I have contended that all photographs, by whomsoever they are taken, should bear the name in the corner of the taker and he should be mentioned in conjunction with them wherever possible. I also had in the colour pictures a slide of a pile of shells. I appeared in this picture and it was removed from the collection! The treatment has been so mean, unnecessary and unjustifiable that I have washed my hands absolutely with the AIF and will not be identified with [them], nor give any further efforts on their behalf.

Here is twelve months of my life thrown away. All my experience, enthusiasm (for the work was my hobby), my colour slides, films and results I consider fruitless. It seems beyond conception that a government can assume such an attitude, which is nothing but the outcome of personal jealousy. I do not intend to let the matter drop here, but will have it taken up further by the Australian press. The wretched management of the exhibition, the absurd lecturers and the indolent manner in which everything was conducted gave a stigma to the whole show that was decidedly derogatory. Officially, the show closes on the 22nd instant.

I have fought hard to take all the pictures to Australia for propaganda purposes, but am up against a stone wall. They are being sent around the provincial towns, starting with Blackall and Brighton! In conclusion, I offered to produce a duplicate set of pictures, but was also turned down. I cannot understand at all the attitude of the AIF in the matter. All the photographers, British, Canadian and even my own section, have received recognition for their services and I have been conspicuously turned down. ... The time will surely come when I shall be able to repay the ... injustices.

21 June–10 July 1918

As this gap indicates, very little of change or importance has transpired. I have neither visited nor taken further interest in the exhibition and am so embittered against the High Commissioner's office that relations have been entirely broken off.

I am now negotiating with a Mr Martin, late of the Fraser Film of Sydney, and my old friend Fred Gent, of the same firm London, to form a small syndicate to exploit the Mawson, Shackleton and Scott films throughout Australasia. We have succeeded in securing the Scott film and the others are well on the way. It is my intention to leave Martin, who has an unsurpassed knowledge of the film business throughout Australasia, to handle the commercial side, whilst I will attend to all producing and lecturing matters. Gent will act as London agent.

11 July 1918

I have officially resigned today from the AIF and have been gazetted to the Reserve List. It is good to be free once more and to be untrammelled by military dogma and discipline.

17 July 1918

Have been endeavouring for some time past to secure the rights for Australasia of the Shackleton, Mawson and Scott films. This latter has been secured. Mawson is favourably inclined, but a deadlock has been arrived at with Perris, who is endeavouring to drive a hard bargain. This work is holding me up in London. I am keenly anxious to leave and join my wife, but the securing of these films should enable me to form the nucleus of a considerable business in Australia. So I am doing my utmost to drive a bargain.

18 July 1918

... Martin, who will be my partner, has secured the Australasian rights to the Scott film, on a profit-sharing arrangement with Herbert Ponting (the Scott photographer), viz., each takes 50 per cent of the profits. Sir Douglas Mawson also appears willing.

19 July 1918

After over a month's negotiations, I have at last secured the Australasian rights of the Shackleton pictures. For these I had to rescind my one-fifth share in the rest of the world's rights (the British and Continental being already sold). I received 400 lantern slides, two copies of the film and £250. As these will realise immediately on exhibition in Australia, I think the deal reasonable. ...

20 July 1918

Saw Mawson during morning with Martin and Gent and projected the Mawson film, which I consider superior to either Shackleton or Scott. Dined with Sir Douglas and his lady and then went through his lantern slides and pictures of the expedition. He has a magnificent collection and unsurpassed. We definitely agreed on the showing of the film throughout Australasia. I consider we have scored an achievement, as we now have the rights of the Scott, Mawson and Shackleton films. The three films and expeditions over here are antagonistic and to have secured the entire three in one mutual interest is indeed something to be proud of. We intend showing the films throughout Australasia; I will lecture to the three. Afterwards, if affairs and profits justify, I will start a photographic works.

24 July 1918

All day with Ponting on his lecture. Ponting is quite a charming character, honourable and a man to be relied upon. I like him immensely. He is, however, pernickety, with too much regard for trifles, which he is prone to magnify to the extent of worrying himself. His work I cannot speak too highly in praise of and I set him up as an ideal. Evening with Martin discussing business affairs till near midnight.

25 July 1918

Morning sorting out Shackleton's negatives for slides. Afternoon at Will Day's establishment. Day is one of the cinema pioneers, extremely interesting, and more so, as he has a fine collection of machines of deep historical interest which show the development of the cinema and moving pictures from the first stages up till today. I left with him to dispose of for me one Pathé camera – with six boxes in all, a turntable (tilting top and stand). Signed contract with Shackleton which gives me the entire Australasian right of the film and 'stills'. Night at Mawson's flat sorting out slides for his lecture. An endless job finished at 12 midnight.

26 July 1918

Morning, promenading London to try and purchase a 5x4 reflex [camera], a typewriter and a pair prism binoculars. I visited practically every house worth visiting. Cameras are impossible. It is nearly two years since any were made and they are all sold out. The few second-hand instruments are extortionate in price. Typewriters are worse. The import is forbidden, with the result that almost any instrument fetches double or treble its original price. 'Coronas', which were £11 10s prewar are now unpurchaseable. I saw only one, a miserable second-hander for £25. Yosts and Smiths are as high, second-hand, at £40 and I heard of a brand-new machine being sold for £100. Decent glasses are unobtainable without an order and then the prices are beyond reason. ... Afternoon to Ponting's flat setting lantern slides.

27 July 1918

Have extremely little spare time at present. The preparation of the expedition films and slides needs my own personal selection, care and attention.

Left Hotel at 8 a.m. and to Raines and Company at Ealing. Put in hand Shackleton slides. Afternoon to Sir Douglas Mawson's and with him through the expedition films and slides. Sir Douglas and his lady are the embodiment of kindness and hospitality, and in proportion as my esteem for him increases, so does it wane for Shackleton. The latter is inclined to forget his obligations, and is purely on the lookout for gain.

To hotel at midnight dog tired.

28 July 1918

With Martin to the *Daily Chronicle* and put in the day selecting sections of the Shackleton film for Australia. Feeling pretty fed up and anxious to get away and join the wife in Egypt and then home. ...

The Shackleton lecture shows 100 slides
The Mawson   ”   ”   150   ”
The Scott   ”   ”   80   ”

And as five sets of each are being made it means about 1600 slides in all! Quite a tall order to make each one perfect. In addition, two copies of 5000 feet [of] film each have to be made for each expedition, 30 000 feet film in all to be carefully toned and stained.

29 July 1918

With Mawson morning, with Ponting on Scott film afternoon, with Mawson again evening till midnight. Shackleton film and lecture bridging in spare intervals. Am tired of the sight of films and lectures. Was paid my outstanding account with military after some four months. A balance of £22 still owing will be paid in November by paymaster, Victoria Barracks, Sydney.

1 August 1918

My quick decision to depart for Egypt has plunged me into a whirl of confusions. The different expedition lectures and pictures are but started, the agreements partly completed. ...

2 August 1918

Up at 7 a.m. and every minute filled with interviewing and completing contracts. ... Mr Tod Martin of Sydney, who has the Scott film rights, and myself entered into partnership today, to exploit the Mawson, Scott and Shackleton films throughout Australasia. I like Martin very much indeed and whilst he has the commercial knowledge, I have the technical. I will do the lecturing to these films, which I anticipate will take me nearly twelve months. ...

3 August 1918

Up at 6 a.m. Wretched wet morning, a million things to do and every second fleeting. Taxi cab impossible to secure – just got one in time to catch the train leaving Fenchurch Street Station. Ponting and Martin came down to see me off as far as Tilbury in a train packed like a tin of sardines. So infernally tired, almost impossible to walk. Did not have time to feel the regrets with which I leave London, which has become a home city to me. Dear old city. I love it and all the friends there – shall I ever see them again? I arrived at Tilbury with my endless luggage and just in time to board the *Nore* before the gangway was hauled up. After all, it is worthwhile having applied myself to getting away, for a bright future opens up beyond the seas and soon I will be reunited with the two best women in all the world – my wife and my dear old Mater. ... But now I am going to apply myself wholeheartedly to the business ahead, which must be a success. ...

5 August 1918

Proceed to sea at 8 a.m., damp foggy weather; several other of the vessels accompanying us and all escorted by a torpedo boat. When off Dungeness, we heard a loud report and on going on deck discovered that the vessel immediately ahead of us had been torpedoed. She was at the time barely three-quarters of a mile away. She was slowly settling down by the head, and when we came up, her crew were already in the boats. ...

1. Sledging Diary, the Australasian Antarctic Expedition (November 1912–January 1913)

Figure 1.1 Frank Hurley. The *Aurora* (Australasian Antarctic Expedition). 1911–1913. nla.pic-vn3125706

Figure 1.2 Frank Hurley. Midwinter dinner, Adelie Land. 21 June 1912. ML Home and Away – 36078

Figure 1.3 Frank Hurley. A Blizzard (Antarctica). 1912. nla.pic-an24615776

Figure 1.4 Frank Hurley. 301 Mile Camp: Eric 'Azzi' Webb and Robert Bage in view, southern sledge party. December 1912. ML Home and Away – 37836

Figure 1.5 Frank Hurley. Frank Hurley in Burberrys. November–December 1912. ML Home and Away – 37849

2. The Imperial Trans-Antarctic Expedition Diary
(November 1914–April 1917)

Figure 2.1 Frank Hurley. Grytviken Whaling Station, Prince Edward Cove, South Georgia. 5 November–4 December 1914. nla.pic-an23478495

Figure 2.2 Frank Hurley. The wake of the *Endurance* through the thin ice in the Weddell Sea. 1 January 1915. nla.pic-an23478078

Figure 2.3 Frank Hurley. Frank Hurley with camera on ice in front of the bow of the trapped *Endurance* in the Weddell Sea. Winter 1915. nla.pic-an23478309

Figure 2.4 Frank Hurley. The *Endurance* in the Antarctic winter darkness, trapped in the Weddell Sea. 27 August 1915. nla.pic-an23478503

Figure 2.5 Frank Hurley. Frank Hurley left, and Sir Ernest Shackleton right, in front of their small tent at Patience or Ocean Camp, Weddell Sea. November – December 1915. nla.pic-an24039565

Figure 2.6 Frank Hurley. The Landing on Elephant Island. 15 April 1916. nla.pic-an24039590

Figure 3.1 Frank Hurley. The First Australian Siege Battery near Comines Canal, Ypres. 12 September 1917. AWM E01918

Figure 3.2 Unknown photographer. Frank Hurley, Australian official photographer with his 35 mm cinecamera, probably a Debrie, and assistant. 14 September 1917. AWM E01995

Figure 3.3 Frank Hurley. Ruins of the Cloth Hall and the Cathedral at Ypres. 8 October 1917. AWM E01117

Figure 3.4 Frank Hurley. Members of an Australian field artillery brigade, Chateau Wood, Ypres salient. 27 October 1917. AWM E01220

Figure 3.5 Frank Hurley. The First Australian Light Horse Brigade passing over the steep sand hills at Esdud. 10 January 1918. AWM B01510P

Figure 3.6 Frank Hurley. Australian Light Horse on the march in Jerusalem. January 1918. AWM B01619

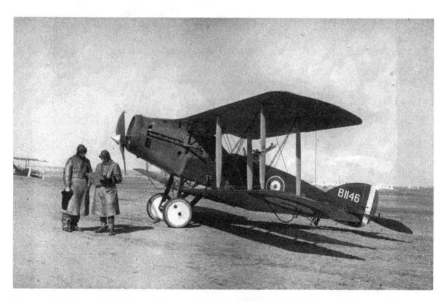

Figure 3.7 Frank Hurley. Observer, pilot and Bristol Fighter F2B aircraft No 1 Squadron AFC. Pilot left is Captain Ross McPherson Smith. 25–28 February 1918. AWM P03631.013

Figure 3.8 Frank Hurley. 'The Raid', also titled 'Over the Top' and 'A Hop Over'. Composite photograph. May 1918. AWM E05988A

5. The Torres Strait and Papua Expedition Diaries (December 1920–August 1921)

Figure 5.1 Frank Hurley. Torres Strait types. 1921. nla.pic-vn3313709

Figure 5.2 Frank Hurley. Murray Island dancers. December 1920–January 1921. nla.pic-vn3313864

Figure 5.3 Frank Hurley. Mabuiag. January–February 1921. nla.pic-vn3314129

Figure 5.4 Frank Hurley. On the Opi river. 21–22 April 1921. nla.pic-vn3359871

Figure 5.5 Frank Hurley. Mission Road extension beyond Ononge. 1921. 8 July 1921. nla.pic-vn3355927

Figure 5.6 Frank Hurley. Scenes at Ononge. 16 July 1921. nla.pic-vn3356000

Figure 6.1 Frank Hurley. Captain Frank Hurley's *Pearls and Savages* title. n.d. nla.pic-an23381987

Figure 6.2 Frank Hurley. The two seaplanes at anchor at Elavala Village, Port Morseby. 11 September 1922. AM VV3108

Figure 6.3 Frank Hurley. A glimpse of the holy of holies Kau Ravi, Kaimare. 8 October 1922. nla.pic-an23382005

Figure 6.4 Frank Hurley. Presentation of pig to the *Seagull*, Kaimare. 11 October 1922. AM VV3137

Figure 6.5 Frank Hurley. Sailing up the Fly River. November 1922.
nla.pic-vn 4853829

Figure 6.6 Frank Hurley. A canoe with its complement of warriors, Lake Murray. November 1922. nla.pic-vn 4853856

Figure 6.7 Frank Hurley. Vaieki, the coxswain in one of the giant fields of lotuses, Lake Murray. 24 November 1922. nla.pic-an23382099

Figure 6.8 Frank Hurley. The interior of the Great Dubu Daima of Urama. 6–9 January 1923. nla.pic-an23381999

7. The World War II and Middle East Diaries
(September 1940–October 1941)

Figure 7.1 Damien Parer. Imperial Airways Short C Class Flying Boat *Circe*, Lake Tiberias. 12 September 1940. AWM 003151/12

Figure 7.2 Frank Hurley. The Photographic Unit examines the wreck of an Italian plane near Bardia. 27 December 1940. AWM 005280

Figure 7.3 Frank Hurley. AIF in Italian medium tanks captured at Bardia. 23 January 1941. AWM 005042

Figure 7.4 Damien Parer. Frank Hurley and soundman Alan Anderson photographing the bombardment of Tobruk. 21 January 1941. AWM 005655

Figure 7.5 Frank Hurley. Men from D Company 2/13th Battalion at siege of Tobruk. 30 April 1941. AWM 007480

Figure 7.6 Frank Hurley. Men from C Company 2/13th Battalion on a daytime patrol, Tobruk. 30 April 1941. AWM 007481

Figure 7.7 Frank Hurley. The effect of a 1000 lb bomb on a small ship lying in Tobruk harbour. 5 September 1941. AWM 007579

4

Tour Diary – *In the Grip of the Polar Pack-Ice* (December 1919–January 1920)

3 December 1919

… The last night of the Sydney performance was given to a crammed house, Kings Cross, there being over 2200 filling seats, stairs, and standing. The story which all seem to say is unique and thrilling was received magnificently. It is some reward speaking to a couple of thousand upturned faces all eager, interested and intent. In these big theatres crammed with all classes, one does not hear a sound. All seem breathless. It is great. Tomorrow we begin the interstate tour. I take as assistant lecturer, Mazengarb and O'Shea, operator.

4 December 1919

… Left Sydney 3.30 a.m. by Brisbane Express. Tony and Matron O'Connor down to see me off. Our cases narrowly escaped catching the train owing to the faulty transport arrangements of Australasian Films. It was with some feelings of relief when we drew away from Sydney. The season has been an arduous one and not without some worry. It has, however, been a phenomenal success.

5 December 1919

Crossed into Queensland 9.15 a.m. Country drought stricken and in pitiable state… Arrived, Brisbane 6.40 and to Australian Hotel, a passable house with good table, small rooms and no pretty waitresses or maids. … Evening, the Union Theatre's publicity 'bug', Holt, carried me off to the *Mail* office where I had to give a column of my wretched experiences and adventures – which just now are becoming a bugbear. …

6 December 1919

Terry O'Shea and self make an early start at the Olympia, fixing up a buzzer control from the footlights to the box. The Olympia is a characteristic big barn, typical of West's theatres. It is only used for children's matinees on Saturday evenings and adults who can get in nowhere else on Saturday nights. It is a filthy, ill-kept, dirty and dusty house and the last place in the world to go in a decent suit of clothes. For talking in, a big drum would be better. One's words chase each other around the building and hurl themselves back at the speaker in a confused jargon. The heat! Thank heavens I am showing ice pictures, and even they thaw on the screen. The projector appointments are even below the standard of the rest of the house. The matinee filled the house with a prolific assemblage of children and second-rate adults. Whether they enjoyed the performance or not, I don't know. To me, it was an ordeal that had to be gone through as arranged in my contract. Whether it was their gladness at the sight of the relief ship which provoked such tremendous applause or the knowledge that it was the last slide, I am uncertain about. Anyhow, they applauded when the lights went up…

Contrary to what I anticipated, the evening performance was a great success. The house was packed from top to orchestra. The audience was one of the most appreciative to date and followed the story with keen interest and applause. My throat would not allow me indulging in elocutionary embellishments, as it was tired after the afternoon.

In these big barns one has almost to shout the whole time and pitch the voice high to overcome resonance. I am appreciative of my operator's efforts and the excellent results achieved with makeshift apparatus. The operating box made of galvanised iron and installed with two primeval machines, which had to be rewired and adjusted, got as hot as an oven. The slide lantern gave me qualms as the lens was held in by sticky tape and I had frequent apprehensions of it falling out. …

7 December 1919

Morning to Strand to fit up appointments for coming season. We found the scenery merchant hard at work converting the portico into an iceberg with the *Endurance* tossed up on the crest of a pressure ridge in her last throes. Over all waxes and wanes the aurora. I think the scenic artist must have had a very strong attack of hallucinations and drained 'many a draught'. His interpretation of an aurora is eloquent of the fiery squirms that haunt the brain of a delirium tremens. The entire arrangement is calculated to draw forth a one-shilling entrance from even the most reluctant. Afternoon to gardens with Mazengarb and O'Shea. The gardens are well cared for and tastefully arranged and the best has been made of the site. The band blared and blared. It reminded me of the gyppo band in the gardens at Cairo, each instrument vying with each other to make itself predominant. Neither execution nor melody. ... The outing gave us fresh air and interest studying the types of Brisbane beauty which so far I have not confirmed the existence of, and so to tea and to rest.

10 December 1919

Mazengarb delivered morning lecture and I gave afternoon matinee to a crowded house. The evening house was crammed to fullest capacity. The prices [at] one shilling dress circle and sixpence pit is absurd; quite readily double these charges could have been made. The evening recital was a great strain on my throat, but it held out manfully and I heaved a great sigh of relief when I came to the rescue. The house was greatly appreciative. The temperature was cruel and the perspiration oozed as though I had been in a Turkish bath. We are under a great debt to the manageress of our hotel – a Mrs Hunter – who always has a light snack and a big bumper of lemon squash ready on our return. This generous soul has lost both her sons at the front and her unselfish and motherly consideration has mitigated greatly the weariness of our tour. Queensland climate is frightfully enervating and one cannot help but 'go slow'. The Brisbanians are a weary-looking lot, minus dash and energy, and the women do not suffer from good looks to any noticeable extent.

11 December 1919

The great news that my friend Captain Ross Smith has reached Australia is the all-absorbing topic, far overclouding the coming elections on Saturday night. The flight was a glorious one. He left London on November 12th, just arriving in Australia in time to win the £10 000 prize. It is a fitting reward for his splendid services during the Palestine campaign. ...

13 December 1919

And so the season at Brisbane comes to an end with a record day and house. I addressed at the afternoon matinee and night. A more enthusiastic audience I could not have spoken to; during the afternoon they clapped and cheered wildly. The evening crowd was absolutely unresponsive until the end, when the applause was great! The picture season should have been extended at the very least another week. The advertising filled the houses the first days, but as time went on, those who saw the picture spread the news amongst their friends and so the advertising was unnecessary and the picture drew through sheer merit. ... [T]he audience were warriors to cram themselves into a theatre that was hot as an oven and badly ventilated. The picture story has stormed Brisbane and gripped the popular imagination. As usual, autographs are a curse of 'fame'...

15 December 1919

... We were up at five and ... took our departure. The day in the train was an ovenly ordeal. The sun blazed; and the drought-stricken country threw back the heat intensely. It was with much satisfaction that we crossed at Wallangarra into the home colony. A night in a prehistoric sleeper that jolted and jarred one's bones into disjointedness kept us awake.

16 December 1919

With daybreak, we observed a pleasant change in the country – the very antithesis of the burnt-up herbage of the north. Here were green trees and grasses, water and fat cattle – a parkland to a desert. Arrived Sydney noon and Tony waiting – home by car and to the two little nips, pictures of health and beautiful little angels. They have progressed well during the past fortnight and made great joy over the return of their dad. The garden grows well but there has been a plague of beetles that have done much harm to the roses. It is good to be home again, even though it be for moments.

17 December 1919

... Left home 9 p.m. to begin second stage of tour.

18 December 1919

A bad night spent in the train brought us to Cootamundra an hour overdue. Between Cootamundra and Junee, a steam pipe in one of the engines burst and held the train up for another one and a half hours. The passengers amused themselves inspecting the local country while awaiting the returns of our engine and an additional one from Cootamundra. The country is in fair condition owing to the recent rains. The wheat is being gathered in but the crop is small owing to the drought. We arrived at Wagga a couple hours late and visited the Strand Theatre, where the film is to be screened this evening. ...

Evening to Strand Theatre. The house packed and the audience one of greatest appreciation. It was a pleasure to recount to them. Here was the first really sensibly constructed theatre I have visited. The roof was so arranged in order that large windows might be opened and so effect sensible ventilation. Of course, there had to be the invariable yelping babe which disturbed the quiet and interest of the thousand. Why folks will bring infants in arms to such functions passes my comprehension altogether. This one and its mother were ordered to quit. ...

19 December 1919

And at the tiresome hour of five a.m., I turned wearily from my inviting couch to the long journey Adelaide-wards.

Once more aboard the train I found interest in the landscape of the Riverina... The crops have been fairly good, but in spite of recent rains, the country is miserably dry. Of course there had to be the inveterate hot axle so that our arrival in Melbourne was an hour overdue. ... An hour after arrival in Melbourne saw the party once more en route and off to Adelaide. The day and heat had subsided and the setting sun lit with a strong sidelight fields covered with ricks and sheaves. The hills were golden with ungathered grain and the evening mists were blurring the distant hills, making the landscape one of ineffable charm. Our quarters on the train were far ahead of our previous 'kennels' on the Queensland and New South Wales lines, so that I had a good night's rest.

20 December 1919

At daybreak we were climbing the Mount Lofty Ranges and nearing our journey's end. Arrived Adelaide 10.30 a.m., where I was surprised and gratified to see my dear old chum of the Mawson expedition Percy Correll awaiting. We jumped into his car and took up residence at the Gresham, an unpretentious hotel – comfortable and of good table. Before lunch, I visited the Olympia where we show on Monday. The usual great barn, typical of West's theatres, but kept clean and in order. The seating capacity is 2200 and should the weather be reasonable, there should not be the slightest trouble in filling it. Temperature today rose to 101° and was hot enough to drive all away from the swelter of a theatre. ...

21 December 1919

Morning to Botanical Gardens, which was much to my satisfaction and enjoyment. The gardens are exquisitely laid out and are splendidly cared for and, in my opinion, superior to Sydney; of course they lack the site, but this is made up for by the fine avenues and artificial ponds. ...

22 December 1919

Mazengarb's lecture this afternoon was a good rehearsal for this evening. The evening house was packed! The audience could not be better and I was in good voice. We have had trouble in securing suitable lenses. At present, the cinema picture is much larger than the slide projection, but I hope to correct this tomorrow. ...

23 December 1919

Spent morning in hunting up lenses. Visited Bonds and Kodak's where I had some trouble in getting away – for their tongues and questions were many and wearying. I eventually secured the lenses and found them to suit admirably. But the best laid schemes of enthusiasts gang off to die, and the new arrangement of optics nearly ended in the destruction of my slides. The picture, which is 30 feet wide, is projected 120 feet, necessitating 50 amperes of current. The heat cracked numerous cover glasses, but the careful O'Shea saved the slides. The audience was not worth the risk. They were the most apathetic and phlegmatic crowd I have ever spoken to. They were as cold as the frozen pictures I showed them. Why I don't know, because the temperature of the theatre was high enough, about 100 degrees. I would far rather have spoken to an empty house filled with logs of wood. ... The sociology of crowds gives one food for thought and I intend scientifically investigating the problem. This evening I repeated precisely the same words, projected the same pictures, was even more forceful in my rhetoric and yet last night the audience were on the crest of enthusiasm and tonight they fell into the trough of apathy. Under these conditions one becomes a pure automaton – a mere mechanical gramophone. It was with a sigh of relief that I fell into the lap of Morpheus and dreamt of new scenarios and squashy romantic films to suit this quixotic mob.

24 December 1919

A poor house, the mob preferring to flock the streets to visiting the theatres. ... I don't altogether blame them, for the weather has been sweltering. What to me is paradoxical is that heat produces a cold audience. And so this evening the house suffered from the heat and I got the shivers. It is about the most wretched occupation one can engage on, to speak to an unsympathetic mob about as emotional as a crowd of sea elephants. ... Adelaide for culture! I don't think.

27 December 1919

Our last night at West's, thanks be to heaven. ... One feels the impulse to be continually on the move. ... The house was packed early to full capacity and hundreds were turned away. Here, the authorities will not permit of the audience standing or sitting on the stairways, so one is entirely dependant on the seating accommodation. West's seats 2428 and every seat was taken. I found the audience splendid and could not have wished for better. ...

30 December 1919

The Pavilion depends on its rapid circulation for its turnover. The house is frequently filled as many as seven times per day and although the admission is but sixpence and threepence, the daily takings average about £300 per day throughout the year. ... The audience were all of the middle class and they seem to appreciate the hardships more than others. They are very demonstrative and although there were qualms about putting on a picture like ours at the Pav, which is to some extent educational, the success has been phenomenal and beyond any expectations.

31 December 1919

We ended our season here with enthusiastic and crammed houses – Webb, the manager, regrets we were not running another week. A hitch occurred in the projection this evening. The pictures were thrown upon the screen very poorly, the light fluctuating badly. This I attributed to my operator, who was the worse for the festive season, and I have threatened to send him back to Sydney, as I am unwilling to risk the reputation of the film, good faith with the people and my own reputation. ...

1 January 1920

By the 6.10 p.m. ... for Melbourne. ...

2 January 1920

We put up at Scotts in Melbourne, a place where one pays for toothpicks and 'swank'.

3 January 1920

The afternoon matinee was a huge success and the audience at the Majestic Theatre were more than splendid.

During the evening, I addressed to a house in which over 500 were turned away! Captain Davis of the *Aurora* and numerous other friends ... were amongst the crowd and I valued their criticism very greatly indeed. They announced the synchronised lecture to be the best thing they had listened to. The audience must have thought the same, for their applause was one continuous clamour. The best house I have so far spoken to. The theatre is the first with anything approaching good acoustics. ...

10 January 1920

Owing to the weekly change in programme at the Majestic, our season closes there. I suggested taking the Town Hall for the Saturday night. ... It was crowded! The seats were booked at three shillings and two shillings and the management [of] Union Theatres did remarkably well. The acoustic properties of the hall were wretched. It is a great echoing drum, but I quickly got into touch with the house and made every word understood clearly.

12 January 1920

From the aristocratic heights of the Town Hall, we have descended to the dungeon confines of the Britannia Theatre, a continuous house where we give four shows a day to a very mediocre crowd chiefly of servant girls, roughs and squawking kids. Outside, an organ drones away and a parasite sings. The sound filters into the hall and discords with the wails of half a dozen kids. One just goes ahead – like the *Endurance*, heeding nothing, grinding away at the icepack, [for] the audiences are just as cold and as capable of comprehension – until with a sigh of relief the end comes. One feels like the crowd; he could clap himself that it is over. Like begets like and the manager is a quality of 'stiff' and rough that looks more like a 'pub expeller'. Then on again in the evening. Bawling away to try and drown the cries of kids. Great heavens! It will be a relief when the season closes. ...

13–14 January 1920

Continued four sessions at Britannia, Mazengarb taking two and self two. The table from which one spouts is erected about 20 feet from the picture in a corner, and one feels more like an auctioneer babbling away than a 'dignified' orator! It is just a matter of grind away! grind away! until one finishes. ... [A] feature like this should not be run in a continuous show. The inflow – and occasional exit – of persons distracts the attention and spoils much of the effort. The manager, whom I originally took to be a 'Yankee stiff', is not such a bad fellow after all. He is none other than 'Diablo', the man who used to perform the 'loop the loop' stunt on the bicycle. ...

15 January 1920

... [B]y train to Geelong ... Thence to theatre, which I found to be quite a modern and splendid picture house, though of dubious acoustics. The evening house almost full and better than the house has had for a Thursday night since its opening. I found the audience rise to every applause and of great appreciation. They were a pleasure to talk to.

17 January 1920

Morning ... for a stroll around the docks, where several large sailing vessels are awaiting cargoes of grain for France. The lure of the sea came on me strongly as I trod the decks of these ocean greyhounds and I longed to be off with them. ... Shackleton's book is now out and has been well reviewed by the *Argus* (Melbourne). Return to Melbourne tomorrow by boat. Am much taken with Geelong. It is the centre of rich agricultural fruit and wheat growing and wool growing. What impressed me was the general air of prosperity and advancement.

18 January 1920

... An uninteresting voyage with a strong west wind following brought us into the Yarra, which quite lives up to the reputation of odour and desolation. Took up residence at Scotts.

19 January 1920

Morning occupied in arranging for a double show at the Royal, Richmond and the Palais de Danse, St Kilda. Mazengarb at former and self at latter.

The evening lecture was something to be endured and got through with as speedily as possible. The Palais de Danse is nothing so much as like a huge circular tank cut in halves and planted by the sea beach. The sides are open all around and canvas fragments try to keep out the weather. The seats have seen better days, but they still earn their money in spite of the decrepit appearance and old age.

The seating accommodation is about 4000! The biggest crowd I have hailed so far and the house was full. The proprietors are two Jews, judging by appearance and name, Phillips and Solomons. They are as dissimilar as it is possible to have Jews except in money affairs. Solomons looks like a sea elephant that has swallowed a barrel and is just about as apathetic. Phillips is a needle – a minnow. They are both repulsive. I envied the orchestra, for the noise they produced certainly filled the hall. They played from a gramophone-like recess in the side of the house about halfway up. I spoke also from this place and did my utmost to be heard by bellowing as loud as I could. Outside, the cable trams clanged and the hum of the cable filled the hall with a continuous din. With straining vocal cords, I pitched above this bass rumble; but there was another unexpected din caused by a scenic switchback railway in Luna Park just next door. These unrehearsed effects were farcical and disconcerting in the extreme.

Just as the *Endurance* was charging through the pack ice, the rumble of the approaching railway echoed through the theatre, and as the vessel came close and looked as though she was going to leap out of the picture, there was an ear-piercing chorus from the passengers in the train as it dived into one of the abysmal dips of the switchback. Every minute this recurred. When the dogs were killed, it synchronised remarkably. But it was mightily disconcerting and did not improve either my efforts or humour. I cursed the management and proprietors from the heads to the black cat which strangely always appears at these shows. ... I was glad when the show was over and I was back at Scotts.

'Adventure Films and the Psychology of the Audience' by Captain Frank Hurley

... The world's markets require so many millions of feet. America fills the spools, American machines unwind them; the shadows of America animate our screens whilst our Australian audiences gaze upon the shades of intangible idols entranced, enthralled and enraptured. ... What we want is more Empire, England and Australia on the screens and much of the sentiment that drifts American-wise might well be turned into national patriotism if it were compulsory to screen at least 50 per cent of British films during an entertainment.

Against the overwhelming captivation of the world's screens by American producers, there is only one class of production that forces a ready market: subjects that are entirely unique, sensational or adventurous. Judging by what we see, romance of the amorous kind rules America; it is astonishing that a nation which practically dominates the world's film output produces so little that is unique or of an adventurous nature. That there is an unsatiated craving for these productions is shown by the warm reception given to the travelogues of Burton Holmes and Martin Johnson. The Shackleton film, which was known in the States as *The Bottom of the World*, set American audiences agog. But to return to Australia – home audiences are the most critical and discriminating that I have ever spoken to. Characteristically Australian – they are candid – if they do not like your show, they tell you so and you play to vacancy. On the other hand, if you satisfy their wishes, there is no more appreciative nor desirable audience in the world. They are buoyant, eager, responsive, quick to appreciate wit and worth all the hardship and concentration entailed in producing an adventure film.

Of all my productions, the Shackleton pictures were the most successful, though *Pearls and Savages* is a hard rival. The former projected the shadows of a soul-stirring adventure, and two years of wild adventures and miraculous escapes flitted before the entranced audiences in an hour and a half! *Pearls and Savages* ... is the very antithesis of the Antarctic regions – the frigid desolation finds its contrast in gorgeous foliage and a dazzling ensemble of fantastic people. In my opinion, photographically it is superior to Shackleton and a better entertainment; still one's own opinions go for nought – the public are the judges and their judgement has been a generous acceptance of both. During the Shackleton season, I personally related the story to 200 000 people, my assistant lecturers spoke to a like number and the listed film entertained as many again. In motion picture theatres one meets every kind of audience and it has been a pleasant duty to study them. From the footlights, with two and a half thousand faces all turned up to you listening eagerly to every word, to feel that it lies within your power to carry them beyond the shackles of a city, to help them to forget the worries of trammelled civilisation and lead them along the magic carpet of romance to the godlike spaces of freedom, is a triumph and reward that any man might well venture his life a hundred times to accomplish.

The greatest tribute I have ever had paid, and the highest reward that any producer might desire, was tendered in Melbourne. The theatre was crowded and in the front sat two rows of returned soldiers. Their applause was of the heartiest and their unusual strained attitude at once attracted my attention. When the interval lights were flashed on, I more closely examined these appreciative listeners. A pang filled my heart – they were all blind. These men, heroes of an immortal past, bereft of life's greatest joy, found entertainment and solace listening to the adventures of a comrade. Needless to say, the only audience I knew [for] the rest of that entertainment sat in those two front seats.

On another occasion, the film was being screened in one of the poorer parts of Sydney and my managers had stage managed accordingly. I arrived on the scene ten minutes to zero hour. To my horror, there was a burly spruiker attired in apropos regalia blaring forth zoo-like on the portal, 'Ear yer are, com'n roll up and see the bloke as been ter ther South Pole'. Feeling less than the dust, I wished a zephyr could have blown me beneath the door chink, but they told me it was all in the show game and had to be gone through. It was, however, the last time I was deeply interested to see the audience and experiment on them. The crowd rolled up and overflowed the house – there was a riot to cram in. The women were carrying parcels and bags from market for the Sunday 'beano'.

A gazette opened the programme and the packets were untied and the shelling of the peas began. There was also a great crackling of peanuts. A football item met with disapproval and the screen was lustily pelted with peapods and peanuts. The audience was at least demonstrative! I wondered if they would pelt carrots or spuds at Shackleton. A chance joke about the football episode put me in touch at once with the crowd and as adventure followed adventure, the peas – both nuts and pods – were forgotten. The house grew silent and these people to whom life showed but the ragged and seamy side, who knew well the meaning of hardships and hunger, grew sympathetic and responsive. Their standard of education and culture was low, but a rough matrix encases hearts as fair as diamonds and these natures were as beautiful as the polished gems of cultured audiences. ...

5

The Torres Strait and Papua Expedition Diaries (December 1920–August 1921)

2 December 1920

I make this entry in my diary on the eve of setting out to the islands of Torres Strait and New Guinea. My primary purpose is to take cinematographic films and plates for a travelogue entertainment. ... I am cooperating with the Anglican mission who, in return for me taking a film illustrating their work in the region I propose visiting, will provide me with maintenance and transport facilities. The films will subsequently be lectured to by Lowell Thomas, I reserving the rights for Australasia. The Lowell Thomas rights will be subject to agreement previously made between us. ... So new adventure and faces lay ahead of me and I go out into the world knowing no one, into unknown places, yet filled with enthusiasm and feeling that success alone is with my own efforts.

3 December 1920

The *Taiynan* moved away from the wharf at 10.30 a.m. The wife and little ones and my old friends Allison and Lipman waving until we had passed beyond their vision, behind the wharves and warehouses. I then turned to the fo'c'sle head to watch the bows clearing away the free seas and to look out over the splendid harbour which nature has endowed our ugly city with. Calm sea and exquisite weather heralded our passage from the port into the open sea, and then northward in the eye of a light nor'easter for Newcastle. We arrived at the coal port at 4.30 p.m. ... I jumped ashore and visited a fine sailing vessel [the *Vimiera*] that lay just ahead. ... There is an atmosphere of perfect freedom, rest, romance and tradition about a sailing vessel that always excites in me a feeling of admiration and longing. The sailing ship holds a lure that is entirely lacking in steam, probably it may be because it is unmechanical; here man pits his own strength and skill directly against the elements. He is the master of his own craft and he maintains his mastery over storm and wave by his own will and strength of arm.

4 December 1920

... Whilst coaling operations were in progress, I had ample opportunity to study the activities of these lumpers. Scarcely have I been [so] disgusted with the habits and methods of any beings. The rampant Bolshevik trait was here more than apparent. Every movement and look bespoke more eloquent than words the iniquitous tendencies of this rabble. After loading a certain amount and while awaiting further truckloads, one arrogantly came forward and with threatening gestures and drunken articulations demanded 'whisky'. The insulting behaviour and arrogance of this object was but the reflection of the rest of the mob. Any effort to order or remove the spokesman of the gang from the passengers' deck would have resulted in the downing of tools and the calling of the ship 'black'. This wretched policy of intimidation is characteristic of the labour cause. God help the country from this control which at present dominates all progress and brings strife over the land. ...

5 December 1920

The *Taiynan* is 34 years of age! But she was built in the days when honest workmanship and quality were balanced with good shining gold. ... The attendants and seamen are Chinese. They are immeasurably superior to whites, being affable, diligent and ready to please. The table is excellent and the ship exemplary of cleanliness. ...

6 December 1920

One is appalled by the magnitude of our coastline and by the scant – almost destitute – traces of settlement. Overnight, we sailed along the margin of an unexplored country, so distant and far between are the evidences of man. ... Afternoon, I went over to the second class, where MacFarlane, one of the Australian Board of Mission's ministers, is travelling with his family. ... I ... will be travelling out to Darnley Island with him. We discussed the customs and habits of the natives... It appears to me that much valued information may be acquired during my tour of the island as well as many unique film subjects. ...

9 December 1920

... Townsville ... is built on an uninteresting flat, behind which a high granite ridge rises and culminates in the great boulder-shaped peak. The town has little charm about it, characteristic of most Australian towns, devoid of shade, surrounded by galvanised-iron shacks and materalising the unaesthetic temperament of the inhabitants. The people are an enervated lot ... and the women do not suffer much from comeliness. A relief to be back on ship...

13 December 1920

... Thursday Island at last. ... And so here the known trail ends. ... Steaming in from the straits, the first impression that courts the eye is of a large fleet of luggers riding at anchor. Drawing up and landing at the jetty, one cannot fail but notice the different and strange types amongst the little group gathered to welcome the ship. Long gaunt Australians, sun dried and tanned, shipping clerks clad in whites with dark felt hats, Aboriginals as dark as Nubians, Chinese, Japanese and half-breeds. The town is unimpressive, and in the glare of the tropic sun, objectionable. The town faces the beach and extends for some distance along an odoriferous waterfront. The main thoroughfare lies a street to the rear and some effort has been made to plant it with shade trees, which bear little evidence of thriving. A collection of galvanised-iron shanties, hideous and ugly, comprise the business and domestic edifices. The man who invented galvanised iron ought to be shot. Our outback towns and country homes are built exclusively of it. ... The poor unfortunates who dwell inside these galvanised monstrosities might as well seek comfort in an oven. A number of red poincianas in full bloom mingle with the bright tropical green colours, mitigating somewhat the ugliness of the rusty iron roofs. The populace are a heterogeneous collection from Malaya, China, Japan and natives from neighbouring islands. These intermarry and the offsprings are puzzles of racial complexity and mixture. The shops appear to be mostly controlled by Chinese and Japanese. There is a considerable white population, but these appear to be exclusively traders or lugger owners, the wants of the town being supplied by Asiatics. Thursday Island is a stain on the White Australia policy. ...

15 December 1920

The *Oituli* conveys our baggage and my equipment and is being sailed to Darnley by 'Wari', a seasoned old seaman, and a crew of four native boys. The *Herald*, belonging to Reverend John Doan, will convey Reverend MacFarlane, wife and three kids, Simpson [a government school teacher], self and crew [of] five native boys. ... The crew are all recruited from the Torres Strait Islands and are men of remarkably fine physique and I would back them against a white crew. Navigation in these waters is extremely intricate and precarious. Submerged reefs and coral shoals, rocks and islets are scattered over the sea in a maze. … We made good progress and had retired to 'shakedowns' in various corners and had scarcely fallen off to sleep when there was a crash. … [W]e had run on a reef. … Kedge anchors were run out, but all our hauling was without avail, and so all that could be done was to wait for the next high tide. …

16 December 1920

… As the tide continued to fall I rowed onto the reef and secured pictures of the mishap. Later, Doan came ashore and we waded over the half-submerged coral to a nearby sand spit. This was my first introduction to a coral reef, and I found it teeming with interest. … From the high sandbank, I had a remarkably fine view of the reef on which we had grounded. The sun was just resting behind a heavy bank of clouds, throwing beautiful reflections in the calm pools which extended for several miles around us. The ocean was littered with outcrops from the submerged reef and looked much like an ice-strewn sea. … The water was wonderfully clear and the seafloor was covered by a galaxy of every conceivable form and colour of live coral. It resembled a well-kept garden of shrubs ablaze with blossom. … Through this sublime expanse, fishes of fantastic form and unspeakable colour darted in shoals. There were shoals of electric blue, brilliant and dazzling – there were red fish and others striped with yellow and gold – colours so diverse and blended in such remarkable harmony and in such vast numbers that one felt entranced, [as if] gazing into the magic splendours of a wild morphic dream. …

At 4 p.m. we came in sight of Darnley Island and three hours later, began making the passage through the girdling reefs into land. … Mr and Mrs MacFarlane … under whose care these islands come, have been absent for nearly a year, and when the natives ashore heard of their arrival, there were wild demonstrations of evident delight from the shore. Embarking with them in the small dinghy, we were rowed into the shallows of the beach. All the amicable men and small boys swam and waded out to welcome the party shorewards. … The crowd caught hold of the boat and swam and hauled us along. Weird native cries and song greeted us, and on landing, the song changed to a missionary hymn, which sounded strangely incongruous coming from these people. … We formed part of a long procession, climbing up the hillside to the home of Mr MacFarlane. …

17 December 1920

… Darnley Island is about three miles long by a couple broad. Its inhabitants do not exceed more than 400. A well-made track skirts the western coast and links the villages. The coast is a series of spans of fine beaches flanked by a thicket of coconut palms and other tropical undergrowth. Behind, rising to a culmination of 600 feet, are rich-soiled grassy and undulating hills. The villages nestle in openings amidst the coconut palms and are constructed with grass rush roofs and plaited palm leaves. Bamboo split into strips form the floors which are elevated 2 feet from ground level. Climbing to the summit of the island, we had a glorious bird's eye panorama of the palm-fringed coast and out over the Torres Strait, streaked with green and blue tints marking the shallows and reefs. ...

19 December 1920

... This morning I went to the church and was astonished to observe the number of natives present. The missionaries have been established here fifty years and Christianity appears to have its sway. Perhaps there is a little too much of it. The hymns were sung with some accomplishment, but I was rather nonplussed when the scriptures were given in ordinary scriptural text, which is quite foreign to the native comprehension, and the sermon in pidgin English. I have not yet solved the problem as to whether the faith is embraced wholeheartedly, or whether it is simply a desire to please the whites. ... To me it looked more like a dogmatic teacher's holding forth to a class of naughty children. ...

22 December 1920

... [P]acked my outfit to accompany Messrs Handley and Clay on a beche-de-mer cruise. ... A beche-de-mer lugger is not a pleasure yacht, for on going aboard, I discovered only sufficient room in which to move about, the deck being hampered with three dinghies and the preserving gear, whilst down in the small cabin, bags of 'market fish' ... filled all available space except two narrow bunks, the size of coffins. Our crew was a volunteer one of eager islanders, all keen to be recorded on the movies... We headed a course ... out to what is known as the 'home' reef. ... The three dinghies were slid over the side, each being manned by a crew of three – one at the oars and two divers. Each diver is provided with a pair of watertight goggles... The rest of their attire may be nothing at all or just a loincloth. In the reef shallows, the boats separated so as to cover as large an area as possible. I accompanied two of the best men, and being armed with a viewing box, a light tight affair with a glass bottom, was able to observe the operations as well below water as above. ... 'Tom' puts on his water goggles ... and jumps overboard... The bottom is covered with a coral wilderness. ... Tom remains below water half a minute. I notice him snatch up a couple of cucumber-like objects and shoot up to the dinghy. A splash and up he bobs, his white teeth opening in a broad smile and a simultaneous gasp for breath. In each hand he holds up a fine sea slug or beche-de-mer. ...

Amidships, is secured a boiler with capacity about 100 gallons. A couple dozen buckets of seawater are boiling in the bottom and the beche-de-mer are thrown aboard and then dropped into the boiling water. One can observe them, through the sizzling broth, shrivel up like the deflation of a toy sausage balloon. An hour's cooking, during which time the odour of unsavoury soup reeks the atmosphere and the eyes have become much irritated through the damp wood fuel, 'the fish' are cooked. ... A boat remains out about a month, when she generally returns to Thursday Island to market the catch and refit. A few years ago, the finest fish which are generally found in deep water, sold for up to a maximum of £700 per ton. The same fish today fetch £300. ... The beche-de-mer finds a huge market in China where it is ... credited with the strange property of making old men feel young again. ...

24 December 1920

... A number of luggers have come in from the outlying islands to take part in the Christmas dances which form a feature of the year, and which are about the only original customs practised on the island. ... Infinite trouble is taken over the preparation and practising of the dances, each village competing in the dancing tournament.

26 December 1920

Up again at 5 a.m. to secure colour of the sunrise. The last week, on the average, I have had 4½ hours sleep daily and am beginning to feel the strain under these strenuous climatic conditions. Film development under these hot conditions requires special treatment. ... Frequently, the developer rises to 87 degrees. I find that the addition of 4 ounces formalin to 8 gallons solution assists the toughening during development. ... To develop six frames each of 65 feet takes three hours. ...

27 December 1920

... The Christmas dances were held tonight in the coconut grove just below the house. The site is ... a perfectly flat, elevated beach grown over with couch grass and facing the sea. Behind, there is a fine coconut grove – which takes the place of the greenroom. For the past fortnight there has been intense activity in the preparation of new dances, the making of toys and the composition of suitable songs as well as rehearsal. ... In the cool of the evening, a distant song through the grove and great excitement on the part of the gathered spectators announced the entry of the gladiators. Like a patrol, the song swelled until there came into view along the track, a body of handsomely decorated braves, their loins girt with 'lava-lavas' of coconut fibre, their legs camouflaged with raddle-like tartan, benecklaced and befeathered. They were indeed a grotesque assemblage; with much pomp they entered the square framed with a calicoed and motley gathering – kindled with enthusiasm and grunting approval. The orchestra seated in front each clapped in measure on bamboo rods – a weird overture chanted and the play began. ...

When dark came on, dry coconut leaves were banded together and ignited for torches. ... One dance – the flower dance – was extremely effective. A toy 4 feet 6 inches high had been made by each of the participators. A sliding bamboo ferrule opened and closed a hibiscus-shaped flower, the whole sliding into the ferrule when closed – and resembling a dance in which umbrellas were opened and shut. The flickering light from the torches, dancing queer shadows to the dancers, the breathless night and the moon rising down the grove behind all, is a picture that can only be felt by the seeing. The rhythmic clatter by the bamboo orchestra, the cadence of wild song rising at times to a female screech, the thump, thump, thump of stamping feet, the glinting torch fire on the sweating bodies, wild gestures and flashing eyes were all revivals of the primeval – before white men visited the island. ...

29 December 1920

... The morning we spent in loading up with provisions and equipment and shortly after noon, set sail for Murray Island 30 miles east of Darnley. In order to secure photographs, we visited Massacre Bay and Kemus Bay, the latter where Macfarlane, the first missionary, landed ... (in 1871) 50 years back. ...

30 December 1920

... We did the 30-mile run in about six hours and dropped anchor close inshore. The island, viewed from the sea, appears precipitous, rising in contour ... to about 700 feet. It is roughly 3 miles in length and populated with about 500 natives. ... 'The Black Brother Fraternity' conducted us to the church. Quite a splendid structure built of lime made by burning coral and roofed with galvanised iron. We then went up to the residence, a barn-like humpy built of the same materials, unfurnished but for a broken-down bed and a box table. ...

31 December 1920

Last night, terrific downpour driving me from place to place around the verandah, which was leaking badly. Storm cleared later in the morning, so MacFarlane and I ... climbed up to the summit... Looking down from this elevation, we had a splendid view of the interior and the coast. The island takes almost the form of an oval with two old volcanic cones at the wide end tapering down in altitude to the apex. Between the two ridges lies a rich belt of volcanic soil where the inhabitants have their gardens and coconut groves. Almost around the island a fine wide track has been made – a delightful walk through arching groves and trees with glimpses of sea and village. ... The people have few of their old original customs left...

1 January 1921

... The day was observed by dancing tournaments and the whole population congregated on the dancing ground with their baskets of food, infants and dogs. The dancing began with a humorous burlesque on the Thursday Island soldiery. Women and men armed with swords and knifes fashioned with skill from drifting cottonwood, went through military manoeuvres of their own conceiving. The while the orchestra beat time on drums and everyone joined in the singing. I must say the farce was well acted and staged. The women looked particularly amusing with tiny forage caps and multipatched uniforms. As soon as this turn was completed, a score of more gaily bedecked men, smeared with raddle and garnished with flowers, followed the exit of the previous actors, and so the 'grog' dance began. This comic opera was a burlesque, again on the Thursday Island community, depicting a drinking party toasting and regaling themselves. The hour ended in the dancers staggering drunkenly off the ground. ...

After the sun had set and the darkness gathered, the dancing assumed its full vigour. Lamps were kindled, and torches made of dry coconut leaf illuminated a weird and wild scene. No Drury Lane staging compared with this grand and imposing setting of nature. ...

2 January 1921

... The church just below the house where we dwell has been in full blast all day. I did not visit it, but the sounds of raucous discord with which the hymns were bellowed was at least an ear-splitting demonstration of wholehearted and throated fervour. The native mind is particularly receptive to the unknown and mysterious, and the superstition and awe of an omnipotent being appeals to them. Whether or no they embrace in full the beliefs and doctrines of Christianity I cannot discern, but usage relating to kinship and inheritance and other aspects of native social life appear to be little affected by contact with whites. Especially may the latter be observed during the dancing ceremonies, when a reminiscent expression comes over the faces of the old men and they live not in the present. The young men have the blood of their forefathers still hot in their veins, the wild look comes into their eyes, and their song and yells betoken the primitive man again.

5 January 1921

... I am indebted to Bauer, one of the councillors, and to Parsee, the mamoose, for their efforts in getting the people together and for their assistance in producing pictures. This afternoon, through their efforts, twenty-five dancers turned up and gave quite a splendid show. It is extremely kind of these people, for they spare no end of trouble in make-up without any remuneration.

MacFarlane left after lunch for Darnley. ... I am now the only white man on the island with 500 'native companions'. It is lonely enough – more lonely than if the place were deserted. ...

8 January 1921

... Punctually to date, the *Herald* arrived at noon and I cannot say I was sorry to see Doan and Simpson again. Hurrying down the hill, I got all my paraphernalia aboard and at 4 p.m. we sailed out to the home reef to examine the possibilities of securing pictures of the submarine growths. ...

12 January 1921

... In the *Herald* I am taking passage to Mabuiag – the home and centre of Mr Doan's activities.

17 January 1921

... Arrangements had been made the previous day for a dugong hunt, and so, with the best spearmen of the island, we made aboard the *Herald*... The fishing ground lay some 10 miles away... The lookout mounted at the masthead signed down 'a fish ahead' and we went in chase. Unfortunately, the light breeze sailed us so slowly that the fish disappeared before we could get up. There were no lack of dugong. Evidently they were feeding on the floating seagrass... The appearance of the mammal swimming resembles a sea elephant or Weddell seal...

I have not yet seen the actual capture, as our luck forsook us with the wind, and although several dugong were almost within striking distance, they sounded before the *Herald* reached them. The whole day I stood by the cinema waiting for the 'main chance' which did not come, though we intend a further hunt next week. The pursuit is filled with excitement and is reminiscent of the days when whaling was conducted from small whaleboats. ...

28 January 1921

... Great excitement was caused by the spearing of a turtle, which was brought ashore and cut out of the shell alive. In its dying throes, the fins and flippers were cut off and thrown into the boiling pot. Soon nothing remained of the turtle but the shell and the head still gasping. ... In ten minutes the turtle was deemed cooked; as a matter of fact, it was nearly raw. In another ten minutes it had all disappeared having been devoured by the cannibals! ...

30 January 1921

... I spent the day in writing up, for the *Sun*, the fourth article on Moa. The articles supplied to the present being Thursday Island, Darnley Island, and the two now going in with illustrations, Murray Island and Moa. ...

31 January 1921

... The spiritual welfare cry I consider is 'over-bellowed' and the natives require a good educational and industrial training to school them in their working of the islands. At present, the natives are a useless burden to the Commonwealth; instead, they should be adapted to some profitable purpose and exploited, with due fairness for the country's sake if not their own. An example should be taken by Java, where all are pressed into use to be of some value to mankind. The missionary business is very admirable in its way, but the beloved black brother policy is rather farcical and certainly is a deterrent to progression. ...

Climate forbids white man applying himself to manual efforts directly on the land in these fierce northern latitudes and the vast vacant places of Australia will remain destitute of population so long as the policy of white Australia is maintained. A few days away, we are faced with the teaming and overflowing millions of Asia. It is natural they must cast jealous eyes on our vacant tracts for their overflux of people, and the only way to ward them off is to populate the area ourselves by some of the Indian races who have served loyally in the times of the Empire's need. These people would become loyal citizens and a buffer betwixt the overwhelming north and the underpeopled south. The country's needs are too pressing for the process of white emigration, and even if the whole of the United Kingdom was tipped into Australia's undeveloped areas, there would still be room for more.

1 February 1921

... At night, gave an entertainment – 'The South Pole'. There was no doubting its popularity – being better attended than even the church. Experienced no small difficulty in making the immature intellects comprehend the meaning of the words 'ice' and 'cold', both being foreign and unknown quantities in these parts. ...

2 February 1921

... [S]ubjects photographic have been exhausted on this island (Mabuiag) and with Doan's continued sickness, transport to the other islands has been held up. As mine host is on the mend again, he has developed a great proclivity for making himself objectionable by an extreme peevishness, interpolating uncalled for interjections during conversation and a hypochondriacal attitude towards the household generally. ... Tomorrow we embark on board the *Herald* ... to Thursday Island. I will remain with the Luscombes at Moa – as 'a shuttlecock of the missionaries'.

15 February 1921

... I was astonished to observe, on our way to the anchorage, a great fleet of 100 luggers at anchor with the sails taken off as though they were all being laid up. It was a relief to put foot on the jetty and return to the 'world of beings', for one appreciates the change from the island loneliness, even though Thursday Island is an insignificant port. For 2½ months I have only seen half-a-dozen white men and even their company grows wearisome. ...

16 February 1921

... Business is practically at a standstill owing to the drop in inflated exchange. The markets where pearl shell, beche-de-mer and trochus were generally disposed of – China, Japan and USA – paid the local values for these commodities; with the evening up of the world's money markets, great falls have taken place in the money values of these specified countries, with the result that the producers are not reaping exchange advantages. The commodities have fallen nearly 50 per cent, rendering the working of the industry practically impossible...

18 February 1921

... Thursday Island at present appears at its best. The seasonal rains have covered the hills with verdant grasses and the trees are heavy with leaf. The streets which are not overburdened with traffic are strips of verdant green. The waterfront, however, is like a scrapheap; now that most of the fleet is at anchor, dinghies, luggers being careened for cleaning, copper and all the appurtenances and equipment of the vessels litter the piers or beach. Bedraggled natives add an air of general tatteredness and decay to the place, which sadly wants regalvanising or demolishing and rebuilding. Added to this the slump in trade, and the place appears unutterably forlorn. ...

19 February 1921

... At night, went to the movies, a pleasant entertainment, though the pictures had been worn threadbare and were of great age, many being of wartime and the first days of the armistice. These latter purporting to be of 'topical events'. All news up here, which gradually filters through, lays claim to similar antiquity.

   The local newspaper, wearing the dignified name of *The Torres Strait Pilot*, is a wretched rag, little larger than a single sheet of this book, printed on one side only, chiefly with 'ads' and at least one item of half a dozen lines of news! This latter brevity has been cribbed generally from any old newspaper! The price per copy is sixpence or one shilling per week!!!!

21 February 1921

Left Thursday Island for Moa Island at 2 p.m. ... On the morrow we head for Mabuiag and on Wednesday, for Saibai. I anticipate returning to Thursday Island by 5th March and will embark aboard the *Tamba* for New Guinea on 16th.

23 February 1921

... [T]he cabin of the *Herald* is more like a lavatory overrun with cockroaches, so in order to get fresh air, I laid me down on deck. Unfortunately, a rain squall came up, and getting wetted, thereby received a severe chill. At 2.30 a.m. we dropped anchor off Danan.

24 February 1921

Had excruciating headache and fever when I awoke, but this did not preclude me from going ashore and trying to photograph. Every step gave my head a painful jerk and my physical condition combined with miserable weather did not reap much in the way of results. ...

25 February 1921

... The anchor was heaved up at 10 a.m. and with a good wind, we made over for Saibai, which is only two miles distant. ... Two miles to the north stretches the coast of New Guinea, extremely flat and matted with mangroves. From the deck one can discern a small village and the fires. Saibai is the limit, however, of Queensland territorial waters and a landing may not be made upon the Papuan coast without first of all clearing the vessel at Daru or one of the government ports.

1 March 1921

... The *Herald* I am beginning to love with a deadly hate. She is a dirty, smelly, uncomfortable caboose overrun with cockroaches and I welcome the time when we arrive at Thursday Island, which terminates my voyagings in her. ...

5 March 1921

... Took up my residence at the Federal Hotel [Thursday Island] and received mail from home etc.

7 March 1921

... The *Tamba* does not leave for New Guinea until about 23rd, and how I am going to fill in my time in this damnable place is quite beyond me. Thursday Island is the tag end of the Commonwealth. There are indeed few people worth knowing and those have formed into cliques, and unless one's interest is pearling or trochus shell, you are quite unable to hold conversations. Of the outside world and its doings I am miserably blank. No news filters through and I haven't seen a newspaper for months.

14 March 1921

... The *Montoro* – a Burns and Philp vessel from Singapore – put in and I dispatched four cases of specimens and negatives – the records and collectings of my cruisings. ... I went aboard the vessel and envied every object aboard which will in eleven days time sail through Sydney Heads. ...

15 March 1921

... Spent the day with Mr Hocking at Wanetta, photographing scientific specimens of pearl shell etc. Hocking, who is one of the leading pearlers of Thursday Island, is a most charming gentleman and his freely given assistance is rendered without obligation. He is one of the extreme few who has studied the pearl-shell industry, its propagation and development, scientifically. In his home at Wanetta is a museum with pearl shell in all its stages, pearl shell from the entire world's fields and in fact everything from the first few weeks' growth to the mature shell manufactured into buttons. Altogether I took a couple dozen plates. I intend writing up the pearling industry thoroughly and am securing a large number of illustrations with that object in view. ... Tomorrow morning Hocking has promised to enact a 'stunt' depicting the collection of pearl shell...

16 March 1921

The day at Wanetta with Hocking on pearling, of which I took a large number of plates and cinema film. ... The film opened with the pearling lugger getting under way and sailing to the pearling ground. The Japanese diver (the entire crew are Japs) putting on his complete dress and going overboard. A bag of several hundred shells had previously been collected by Hocking's divers from their culture grounds at Goode Island, and so to save time, these were passed down to the diver and brought up with him. ...

26 March 1921

Punctually on the ring of four bells (10 a.m.), the *Tambar* swung out into the stream and the sea beginning to slip by, with the diminishing township of Thursday Island astern, kindled in me new hopes and anticipations. ... We carry about a dozen passengers, with perhaps two worth knowing amongst them. ...

The appointments of the *Tambar* have seen better days – especially the linen which is much discoloured. ... The food is passable and is prepared by a Papuan cook, the stewards being also Papuans. They are infinitely inferior in physique and general appearance to the burly fellows of Torres Strait, nor are they either as presentable in cleanliness. They display a wealth of hair like a black mop, and their arms and legs are decorated by small woven, band-armlets and 'leglets'. The skipper – Andersen – professes to be a Norwegian, though his accent is pronouncedly German; he is an uninspiring and weak individual...

27 March 1921

... Sunset, we came close inshore and dropped anchor off Daru. The shoreward prospect is uninviting, being absolutely flat and but a few feet above high tides. Mangrove trees fringe the inevitable mud foreshores; in the background, more mangroves and swamp, and mud and mangrove and mosquitoes for miles. A dozen or so luggers ride offshore, and in the centre, runs out a half-completed jetty. ... Then there is a beaten track to the half-dozen houses which nestle beneath the coconuts and crotons. An eagle-eyed and hatchet-faced official rowed aboard – a Mr Walker, the customs official, doctor, the landing officer and general nuisance of Daru. His appearance aboard was not greeted with a wild display of enthusiasm, being of such a pernickety nature and a charlatan for absurd details as to involve the ship's officers in a deal of unnecessary work and formality. We had nothing to declare, the ship being dry. I asked for permission to take my camera ashore, which naturally had to be scrutinised, and I was rather dubious as to whether I should not have to open the slides and pull the outfit to pieces to let him peer inside. Still, I don't wonder at anybody developing strange traits in such an isolated post as Daru. ...

28 March 1921

Anchored the night off Daru and owing to the stagnant heat, slept up on deck. The ship was visited by swarms of mosquitoes, which made sleep practically impossible. ... Daru is the first port of clearance for all small vessels or luggers coming from the west. We added another hundred passengers to our list – natives recruited from the vicinity of the Bamu River. These coolies are consigned to the mines at Bootless Inlet near Port Moresby. The recruiter is paid £6 for each boy signed on for 18 months and £8 for each signed for two years. These 'boys' take up the forepart of the *Tambar*. After all stores had been put ashore by means of a lighter, this crowd was brought aboard with their belongings – small bundles containing a sleeping mat and a little sago. Scarcely have I seen more destitution. The miserable wretches, clad in dirty singlets and a dirtier cloth wrapped about their loins, placed their meagre bundles on the hatch and huddled together like sheep. ... These Bamu natives are, on an average, 5 feet 7 inches. They are straight down from the shoulders, spindle-legged and devoid of muscular development. They manifest extreme primitiveness by their disregard for cleanliness, are infested with vermin and skin diseases. Laying on the iron deck like tired animals, they seem to care little for life or death. ...

30 March 1921

... We followed the coast, four miles from the beach, and gained a magnificent prospect of its coastal hills, jagged and hidden by low-lying clouds; behind the coastal chain in ascending terraces lay the great backbone chain of the Owen Stanley Range buried in the clouds. Through the slowly changing mists, their sky-reared summits occasionally peered. Just before forenoon, I had a fine glimpse of the summit of Mount Yule, 10 380 feet. This is the country of the Kuku-Kuku tribes, which are still in an extremely wild and cannibal state, a few miles behind the coast. It was with no small feelings of pleasure that Yule Island came into view... Rounding the 'home reef', we came to a beautiful anchorage... The headquarters of the Sacred Heart Mission Station is built on an eminence a few hundred yards from the beach, surrounded by fine coconut palms. In the background rises a small range of cupola-shaped hills, all of an exquisite green. To the right of the mission station extends a small beach, fringed with coconuts and terminating in a shapely bluff on which is built the government station. The mainland ranges rise up into the clouds to the north, and it is amongst these ranges that the mission actively operate.

Two boats came out from the shore; one, the government boat manned by native police attired in a loose navy-blue garment, and the mission boat rowed by nude natives. I was greatly attracted by the comely features of these boys, who are distinctly effeminate in their prettiness, wearing great mops of frizzy hair which is maintained in fine symmetrical trim, and also by their well-conditioned physique. ... On going ashore, we landed on a well-made stone jetty and I proceeded to climb the highest hill whilst the other passengers went up to the mission station. ... I was rewarded for my efforts by a charming prospect over the island and the splendid harbour which spread itself below like a placid basin surrounded by hills. I visited the mission station and was shown around by Father Van Goethen. I also met a Brother Alexis, whom I previously had acquaintance with on my way up to Java eight years previously.

The Sacred Heart station comprises some dozen well-built houses, wood- and iron-roofed, a church, convent, craftsmen's shops (a forge, carpenters, tinsmiths, etc.), school, laundry and living quarters. The priests are mostly French and Belgian, most wearing beards, and men of infinite kindness, of learning and I should say, peculiarly adapted for mission work. The sisters are sweet women and I should think that their very presence must alleviate the rigours and hardships of an ostracised life. Yet, these men are wed to the work; they are spoken of highly throughout Papua and by all with whom they have come in contact. I found the buildings far ahead of the Anglican mission of Torres Strait and the whole work is of a practical as well as spiritual nature. ... I dined with the priests, whom I discovered to be men of infinite charm and tender nature. I recounted to them my Shackleton experiences and spent altogether hours, which I shall always regard with honour. I left for the ship at 8 p.m. with an invitation to visit them at a future date and make an excursion into the mountains amongst their pioneers. If all the missions were of the calibre and practical ability of these men, I cannot but think that the Papuan and Papua would improve under their regime.

31 March 1921

... Port Moresby has grown since I was here eight years ago, though I scarcely think its expansion has been to its pictorial enhancement. Although I see it now in the best part of the year, it is a wretched place of galvanised roofed and walled dwellings perched anywhere on the hills, straggling and ugly. The wharf was packed with a great assemblage of coolies, though quite unpictorial and uninteresting, as most have lopped off their truly magnificent head mops and their garments are unclean. I climbed to the crest of Paga Hill just alongside the wharf and took a beautiful bird's-eye panorama of the town and the beautiful Ela Beach (bay) beyond. ... I am remaining aboard, as the transportation of my equipment and gear to a hotel would be a great inconvenience and would involve me in a great waste of time. I received two wires from Delhi from Lowell Thomas who is desirous of joining me here, though I am unanxious that he should come here at all.

1 April 1921

This morning I paid a visit to the Government Secretary, Mr Baldie, and the Acting Governor, Judge Herbert; both I found to be extremely delightful men, willing to assist and furnish with all official and private data concerning the Territory. The Administrator, Judge Murray, does not arrive from the south until tomorrow by the *Marsina*.

After arranging my official itinerary, walked round to the two native villages Hanuabada village and Elevala village – about two miles distant. These villages are of remarkable interest on account of their having been built out into the shallow water. Hanuabada village comprises over a hundred native huts built up on lanky piles. Communication is linked with Elevala by means of a narrow bridge-way, built about 15 feet above high tide; on either side of this narrow footway, plank tracks lead to the houses. The villages are laid out much as if on land, only the whole communication ways and houses are above the water. In front of each house is a platform-like verandah where the art of making pottery is carried on; behind this platform is a narrow sheltered verandah and then the house. The whole arrangement, with its waterways between the houses on which float many canoes, is intensely pictorial, though its fragility and ricketyness gave me qualms at every footstep. The water dwellers are of medium physique, the men about 5 feet 9 [inches] to 5 feet 10 [inches] in height and well proportioned. The women are much smaller, splendidly proportioned and many of infatuating beauty. Their rounded features and limbs compare with any of the types I have so far seen, and the great mop of frizzy hair, which is one of their characteristics, gives them great attractiveness. Many of the women are tattooed, which does not impair their looks, but gives to them a savage charm. The children are of wonderful prettiness. ...

2 April 1921

The *Tambar* left early for Bootless Inlet some 20 miles from Moresby to disembark our Bamu passengers which we have carried from Daru. ... Afternoon, went to Hanuabada village ... to secure pictures of types. The quaint houses raised on high piles above the water, the kaleidoscope of native life, the manufacture of pottery, the great canoes all combine to make a moving picture of Papuan life teeming with interest. The hideous skin disease sipuma is common in the village and one must thoroughly bath and disinfect oneself after having moved amongst the people and their houses. ...

4 April 1921

Visited the governor's secretary, Mr Baldie, and also Dr Strong, the chief medical superintendent, with whom I had an interesting discussion on the general health and anthropology of the territory. I am enlisting Strong's capable assistance in classifying native types etc. The *Marsina*'s mail contained a looked-for letter from home, and also one from Keith Smith telling me of their future plans for presenting the film lectures. Cabled Thomas not to come to Papua and also Kodak's for extra materials as there is a vast fund of work to do here. The *Tambar* completed loading the strangest collection of beasts and cargo I have ever seen massed in one heap. Horses, cows, goats, pigs, dogs, natives being quartered all together on the foredeck and a stranger collection of whites, planters, missionaries, pioneers, miners and sundries aft. ... Fortunately, the wind comes from aft and we miss the amalgamated stenches from the beasties forward. I have transferred from the fiery heat below to a deck cabin and more congenial solitude for writing my innumerable letters and articles. Scarcely a spare moment is left me. I am out to make a hit and win success and realise that I can only secure it by my own efforts. At 2 p.m. we drew out from the wharf... Heading east, we skirted close in coast and had a fine view of the lofty coastal ranges, and of the main Owen Stanley Range beyond, lost in the clouds. ...

5 April 1921

... By evening, we were off the Vilirupu River and as we have a few hundred weights of cargo and a cow to put ashore, the *Tambar* was headed inshore. Running a few hundred yards off a green bluff which we rounded, a glorious vista of a large lagoon opened up ahead of us. On our port bow, arranged on a green knoll with streets set out in draughtboard pattern, stood a large village. Whilst keenly interested in this unexpected sight, a number of canoes set off from the opposite bank, crammed with natives and garden produce and fruit. ... The bartering and bargaining lasted until it was too dark to discern if a fair exchange was being effected. In the background rose the Owen Stanley peaks with a mighty billow of clouds rolling over them. As the setting sun caught their crests, they glowed with a vivid salmon pink, again the calm waters of the Vilirupu River reflected the tint and the canoes floated upon waters of bewildering enchantment. The whole scene was of such extravagant splendour that one's mind seemed incapable of absorbing the scenic grandeur, the babel of voices and the sublimity of the skies. ...

6 April 1921

As I write, a parasitic gramophone is blaring away a jazz up on deck and is anything but congenial to writing. I went ashore whilst the *Tambar* was discharging cargo for upriver, being rowed by several filthy small boys in a filthier canoe. The village named Gabone is built on a hill slope overlooking the Marshall Lagoon. The river at this point widens out into an expansive lagoon some four miles in diameter. ... The canoe grounding on the beach, I hopped ashore with my reflex camera and made my way up the hill to the village. ... [T]he dwellers pass most of their daily life lousing and sleeping, for they are a dirty people, devoid of even the rudiments of cleanliness and while wandering amid their hovels, one needs must heed the footsteps, lest you trudge through faeces. The skin disease which makes them even more loathsome is quite common. A main thoroughfare passes along the crest of the ridge and the detached domiciles are built in rows on either side. From this main thoroughfare, passageways run at right angles, and more dwellings. Communication to the upper sleeping apartment is had by a small ladder which passes up through a trapdoor entrance.

The women are bedecked in small grass ramis quite insufficient to hide their ugliness and the men wear a piece of string tied to the top of the penis and drawn through the legs and fastened to a belt at the back. In their great mops of hair, which they frequently prick up with a small comb, a big rosette of feathers is worn. I was just in time to see the population moving out to their canoes to row away to the gardens, which are some distance up river – men, women and children, babes in arms, with skinny mongrels following in the wake. I took numerous studies of types, which were as endless as the trail of youngsters which crept in my wake. The launch returning from up river, the *Tambar* whistled, and I hurried back, for it would mean suicide to remain in such a filthy place. ...

10 April 1921

I am now seated in the bishop's study at Samarai. Having just gone through a great bundle of newspapers from the *Sun*, and have been delighted to find several of my articles contained therein, also to read news of the outer world for I have been isolated absolutely for the past four months. ... Nearing Samarai ... the coast becomes broken and the sea studded with numerous islets. Then one enters the glorious passage to Samarai, a small islet itself encircled by an archipelago of palm-covered islets. The glory of colour and clearness of water and purity of everything is like a peep in fairyland. A crowd had collected on the wharf and also a great collection of highly ornamented natives. ... The Reverend Benson bid me welcome... The *Whitkirk*, a large launch, has been placed at my disposal and for the next eight weeks I propose to occupy my time cruising the length of the northeast coast. I find the missionary people a charming people, who have seen enough of life to drop wowserism.

After afternoon tea, I took a stroll with the two reverend gentlemen, Messrs Hall and Thompson, around Samarai. I was bewildered by the exquisite beauty of the place. Samarai is a miniature Garden of Eden – it is my ideal of a tropical township. The glorious glades are avenued with the most gorgeous display of crotons conceivable. Walks are hedged with hibiscus of as numerous tints as the rose. A walk runs right around the island and it takes 20 minutes to encircle it. The labour is provided by prisoners from the penal gaol... Samarai is a gem set in a turquoise sea. It is as beautiful as Port Moresby is ugly. It is a glimpse of paradise and the grand culmination of my water journey from where I commence my expedition into the real New Guinea.

12 April 1921

The *Whitkirk* is owned by the Anglican mission and is used chiefly to convey personnel from and between their various missionary centres. ... A good passage favoured us across Milne Bay and by 6 a.m. we were off East Cape. ... At 2.30 p.m. we entered Goodenough Bay. ... A large crowd of natives had collected on the beach and Mr and Mrs Thompson, who went ashore first, came in for the ordeal of greetings and handshakings. ... From the beach to Dogura Mission Station is ¾ mile. ... The track up, owing to the heavy rains, was very mucky, but on reaching Dogura, I was pleased to find the place well laid out... I was duly introduced to the various identities, both native and missionary, and I hardly know which I prefer. Personally, I have little time for the latter. They seem to regard the native as a pet or prize puppy dog – 'Mark, do this' – 'Peter did this' – 'John is quite rude' and such inanities flood across the table and the talk reeks as much of native as the place does with their smell! The missionary is essential, or I should say, someone is essential to preserve the natives against ruthless whites. This could be as well done by the government as the missionary, an individual who makes a great pretence of action – leads an indolent life of uselessness – wears the skirts; and the women who are here don the trousers! ...

13 April 1921

Dogura ... is especially charming, being built on a plateau hill surrounded on three sides by the mountains and fronting Collingwood Bay on the fourth. ... From the guesthouse where I am writing, I look out over the coastal flat, covered with coconuts, scrub and isolated villages to Cape Frere. ...

Went down to the village Wedan, which lies just by the landing. The huts are mere grass hovels, built on the ground... The natives themselves are a miserable-looking crowd. The women have a strange custom of cutting their hair short when married, which does not improve their looks. I photographed a widow wearing a two-piece costume, grass skirt and grass cloak, which is the signification of mourning; also did much photographing amongst the people in the village.

Afternoon for promenade along coast and secured several fine glimpses. ... [A] long trail of small boys follow in the wake. They are not so forward as the children of Torres Strait, and as the mission school teaches them English, I can carry on a pidgin discourse with them. Further, they invariably carry my gear and are useful for foregrounds and figures. Everywhere I notice the natives willing to help cheerily. I don't know what could be done without them. Life here would be impossible without the natives to do our carrying, hard work and menial duties.

15 April 1921

At 11 a.m. the *Whitkirk* got under way from Dogura, bound for Ambasi, which we hope to reach on Monday. My companion is a young fellow named Homer, who knows more or less the coast... [R]unning in close to Cape Vogel ... we obtained a fine prospect across Ward Hunt Strait to the D'Entrecasteaux Islands. ...

17 April 1921

... [We] dropped anchor off the village of Emo in Dyke Ackland Bay. ... I was astounded by the strange assemblage that greeted us on arrival. What struck me at once was the strange makeup of the hair, which is of an extremely coarse variety like an astrakhan mat... The natives wear a great accumulation of ornaments made chiefly from shells, dogs' teeth and boars' tusks. The septum of the nose is pierced to receive bones, feathers and etceteras. The ears are similarly pierced and little bundles of shell ornaments distend the lobes into great loops. The filthy habit of chewing betel nut is indulged in to excess and the teeth are jet black. ... On going up to the mission house, which is built on a hill overlooking the village, Homer and I were welcomed by the Reverend F. Elder, a fine middle-aged fellow of powerful physique, though showing signs of weariness through the awful loneliness of his duty. ... Converts to Christianity are slow in this village. The natives' religion is animistic. They worship the spirit of the taro (which is a staple food), bats, crocodiles and a red flame tree. ...

In the evening, when the women bring in the root, the village drums and joins in chorus. These taro worshippers work themselves into a frenzy, drumming and twitching and apparently losing all control of their nerves and muscles. Finally, they roll on the ground in a paroxysm of writhing, yelling and crying and fall into fits. The display is so farcical and loathsome as to be amusing. However, this demonstrative worship, which is all ostentation, noise and display, has a powerful appeal to the primitive intellect, and Christianity asks them to give up this bombastic and sensual indulgence and in return, embrace a worship that is without display, is serenely peaceful and without show. ...

18 April 1921

Left the prettily situated little village of Emo with the solitary figure of Elder waving us goodbye and I doubt not, in his own mind, a speedy return. ... [I]n three hours, we reached Buna, where I landed and met the magistrate, Mr Wuth. ... He is arranging dances and subjects of native interest, which will greatly facilitate work on my return. It is a great help having the cooperation of the government, for the official just gave orders to his constabulary, which sent them to remote parts of the country to call the people into Buna to dance and perform for the cinema. This saves me the sweat and time of travelling to their remote villages in the hills – and even then, not being able to secure the same results. ...

I stayed as short a time as possible owing to the necessity of reaching the bad anchorage at Ambasi before dark. ... On going close inshore, the whaleboat came out to meet us, and aboard was a solitary white man, the Reverend Flint. It was a touching meeting in this wild spot that reminded me of our rescue when the whaleboat came ashore at Elephant Island. In these distant outposts, it is rare to see a white face, and I can well appreciate the gladsome expression in Flint's face when we shook hands and rescued him from the utter loneliness. Ashore, as usual, natives galore amassed to meet us. Dirtier perhaps than usual and evidently the more anxious to shake hands with a white intruder. Whoever introduced this strange custom of handshaking ought to have his head clamped in a milk-shaking machine and the machine set in violent motion for the rest of his life. Natives with skin disease – wizened dirty old creatures – bleary-eyed cannibals – tiny, nose-running infants, budding voluptuous virgins, all smelling like a hog's sty, came forward to grip my hand. ...

19 April 1921

... The day I spent in active photographic operations. ... An amusing event happened whilst I was photographing – an old warrior cannibal in war dress, carrying his shield and spear, befeathered and raddled and looking as fierce as a tiger, rushed out of one of the huts and bore down upon me and the camera. His savage mien and pointed quivering spear was so realistic that I think a weak-nerved snapshooter would have been put to flight. As I merely grinned and complimented the old warrior, I evidently went up in the public estimation. The old man – a thoroughbred old cannibal – was a born actor, and gave me a fine exhibition of war manoeuvres, combating an imaginary foe with terrifying grimaces and lunges. Had I been the unseen one, I admit I would have preferred a modern automatic to coming 'to spears' with this martial veteran. ...

20 April 1921

Five miles along the coast to the southeast flows the river Opi, 25 miles to the north, the Mambare and 20 miles south, the Kamusi. The mountains are about 20 miles inland and from the sea, a flat expanse of densely grown country extends to them. These rivers have cut their way through the most marvellous tangle of tropical vegetation I have ever seen. Palms of every description grow as prolifically as weeds. Tall cane grass grows in an impenetrable thicket, great trees tower here and there with festoons and tangles of parasitic growths, larger vines, staghorns, ferns, orchids and everything in the vegetable and insect world. The river Opi being nearest to hand, with Flint, Homer and a number of carriers, we made an early morning start, following a well-worn track. We passed through an old plantation where the Reverend King some years ago endeavoured to found an industrial mission plantation. ...

We chartered a native canoe for the day, paying two sticks of tobacco. ... With our vast quantity of material aboard ... the natives paddled us up the river. ... Frequently, we passed beneath great overhanging trees, and the pendant festoons of vines fell like a web around us. Trees along the banks were so thickly covered with convolvulus vine as to hide all their own growth – they merely became supporting trestles for bowers of matted vines. Some of the trees, when hidden by the vines, resembled castle ruins covered with ivy. There was one in particular which grew alongside the bank like a high keep, its fragmentary battlements formed by dead branches stood majestically reflected in the mirror-like waters. Then, through tunnels of the great sago palms with orchids and staghorns clinging to their trunks – all was just like a rich artificial hothouse with a river running through the centre.

A couple miles up, we landed at the Opi village. This is the most pictorial native village I have yet visited. What beautified it extremely was the great thicket of the elegant betel nut palms. These, rising to a height of 80 to 100 feet, swayed in the breeze, giving the whole atmosphere a feeling of enchantment. ... The natives themselves appeared a little cleaner, excepting one old woman that closely resembled a ghost at a little distance. She was smothered from head to foot with white mud. I learned that she was a widow and in mourning for the recent death of her husband. The hair had been clipped short and there she sat on the verandah of her small hut, the picture of abject misery, loneliness and hideousness. ... Purchasing a couple spears from the old men of the village; they brandished them at me and went through the whole imposing and terrifying manoeuvres of attack. ... They are just out of the cannibal stage and all the old fire is still there and only wants kindling into war flames. ...

21–22 April 1921

... Flint, Homer and self with an entourage of half a score carriers and a miscellany of cameras, moving-picture cameras, beds, stores and camping equipment left the Ambasi Mission Station for Koira village a couple miles up the Opi River, my intent being to secure films of the unusually beautiful tropical scenery. ... Our goods and passengers left very little freeboard to the canoe, on which we had to remain perfectly still to avoid overbalancing the outrigger and turning over. ... I mounted my cinema on a large box on the canoe platform, and as we rowed up river, I secured fine pictures whilst afloat. ... The native canoe is the gondola of New Guinea. To sit on the platform and glide downstream is surely the most pleasant transport in the world. Noiseless and motionless, drifting on the mirror bosom of the Opi through nature's own beautiful garden, far from all the cares of our alleged civilisation, is surely a glimpse into paradise. Why ever is it that these people sign on to enslave themselves under white man's yoke? ...

23 April 1921

After great packing activities, the mission boys carried our ton of miscellaneous camping and photographic equipment down to the landing and by lightering with the whaleboat, rowed it out to the *Whitkirk*, which came in early from Buna where she has been anchored for the past week. Flint and Homer are both coming on the tour of the mission stations and with the four boys they are bringing as carriers, I doubt not they will be of great assistance. ... I am sadly neglecting my articles to the *Sun*, not having had even a few moments relaxation to devote to them. Each day I average at least eighteen plates and a couple hundred feet of film. At every turn new pictures unfold themselves. The place is simply inexhaustible and I doubt not the eyes of the world will be opened by the extraordinary scenes and customs I am trying to depict. It seems incredible that within a few hundred miles of Australian shores, we dwell on the outskirts of the unknown. We are as ignorant of this enchanting and productive country as fools. ...

25 April 1921

... [W]e arrived at Buna at 9 a.m. Mr Wuth, the government resident magistrate ... has arranged all sorts of stunts for movies and has collected natives from far and wide for dances, fire-making, etc. ...

26 April 1921

... [I]t was 11.45 before the boom of the drums sounded up the coconut grove. In front of the government offices is a fine flat stretch of 'plucked' grass and thither the dancers, in colours as diverse as the sounds they made, gathered. Arrayed in war paint, bedecked with a burden of ornaments and crowned with a garnishing of feathers, my actors were indeed a brilliant and gaudy assemblage. The headdresses might grace the foremost beauty of the stage. Dazzling with plumage, one fell into admiration contemplating the accumulation of feathers, plucked from the most showy plumage, and amongst which the plumes of the birds of paradise outshone all. Some took up the form of a wide fan. Beaded in the front, then a fringe of small blue wing feathers, then a row of the black and red feathers from the black cockatoo's tail, then a cassowary backing, and behind all rose the glorious ethereal plumes from the bird of paradise. Others wore just a medley of the most gaudy feathers obtainable, arranged like the quills of a porcupine. Their faces were decorated with red and black raddle and through the armlets, croton leaves were threaded. Nothing could be more gaudy or riotous in colour than this wild kaleidoscope of savages. Each carried a drum and made a noise upon it. The accumulation of the noises was a bedlam which was only exceeded by the grotesque evolutions into which the dancers flung themselves. It was a wild, boisterous jazz. ... I took a large quantity of film and many plates of the headdresses. ...

28 April 1921

Packed up and aboard the *Whitkirk* and away by 11 a.m. Splendid calm weather and by 2 p.m., anchored in Oro Bay off the village of Beama. ... At the village ... we found a horde of gay-clad savages awaiting our arrival. ...

29 April 1921

... A deputation from the village of Eroro, a couple miles away, hurried our operations, as they came to tell us that all the surrounding villages had massed there to make a big dance for the movies. I rowed Flint and Homer in the dinghy, whilst our carriers walked around the beach. We discovered upon our arrival, that a couple hundred natives had assembled, all wearing their full dancing decorations. Our advent into the village was the signal for prolonged howls of 'Oroda!' (Welcome) and a thunder of drums. My actors were in merry mood, for dancing operations started before I could get my camera into position. I laid out a square with saplings to mark off the area in which they were to perform, but it was well nigh impossible to make them comprehend even with five interpreters and as many native police. It is impossible to stage manage a dance – 'It is not New Guinea fashion' to dance to order. ... A herd of wild animals would have been easier to control than this rabble. Five policemen were powerless to direct or influence it. ... There was a wealth of feathers and plumes amongst the dancers that would provoke the envy of the highest society. They are unpurchaseable from the natives, not only 'traditionally', but it is illegal to export or even have feathers of the bird of paradise in one's effects. ... At 3 p.m. the job was finished and with sighs of relief, once more aboard the *Whitkirk* and on the peaceful sea for Emo. ...

30 April 1921

Perfect weather is favouring my efforts and I am now completing the solid foundation work and concentrating more on specialised studies. Pictures present themselves at every turn. The Emo village, although quite small, has all the characteristic studies of native life and work going on. It is a village of activity. Clay pots are being made and baked, canoes are building, the tapa cloth makers are busy, canoes come and go laden with produce, and the cries of 'Oroda! Oroda! Oroda!' resound throughout the village as some new arrivals enter or [a] heavily freighted canoe comes downstream. The old women are busy on their low verandahs making nets or preparing meals. From within the dark interiors comes the boom boom of an occasional drum and a wild chant. Babes swing in the shade of the verandahs, slung in nets, and bright-eyed youngsters with mats of hair follow in my wake to watch the 'Dim-Dim' with his dim-dim – picture maker. ...

7 July 1921

This morning at 7 a.m. saw me embarking aboard the government whaleboat with 30 carriers, a native village corporal, a private native constable, together with a vast amount of equipment, cinema and camera gear. I carry sufficient food to last me at least fourteen days, sleeping gear and tent, developing gear and sufficient film for 2500 feet and 15 dozen half-plates, 200 pounds rice for the natives, shelter for them, cash £20 and 20 pounds trade tobacco. ... The carriers are of splendid physique, all big men wearing great fuzzy mops of hair and practically nude excepting for something less than bathing 'Vs'. ... Our journey to Ononge represents 250 miles (in and out). The road has been entirely constructed by the Sacred Heart Mission. ...

The coast from Daru to Samarai was taken up by the London Missionary Society, with the exception of the areas around Yule Island – Mekeo – on the mainland. The administration, observing trouble brewing for the future, passed an ordinance that the villages and districts held at that time by the rivals should be held exclusively by them. The Roman Catholics held but a small section which they had under control and the enterprising Bishop de Boismenu, looking around where he might extend his sphere of influence, ascertained from expeditions that there was a considerable population inhabiting the mountains directly in from his section. Thus, the road was started over 20 years ago ... the heart of an unknown country has been penetrated and the first steps to progress and development begun...

8 July 1921

I am now camped with Fathers Caudron and Bach in a small hut which stands in the middle of a large clearing hemmed in by dense New Guinea jungle. Outside, the carriers are seated around their campfires singing – contented after their evening meal. It is all unique and fascinating to me, reminiscent of early Canadian days with the redskins gathered around the pioneer's home. ... The temperature has fallen and it is decidedly chilly, but thoroughly exhilarating and pleasant after our long day's walk. The roadway throughout is well graded ... winding around the contours of ridges down to pleasant gullies, then gently ascending to razorback hills, all the while passing through a green tunnel of fine trees, ferns in endless variety, vines in a massed tangle, with the pleasant gurgling of mountain streams and sighing trees making music to one's ears. ... None of the labour was conscripted; the natives voluntarily offered their services and were paid for them. Occasionally, we had fine glimpses through the matted jungle of great ridges with small villages perched on their eminences and always of great trees burdened with vines. ...

9 July 1921

... The track much the same as yesterday, though growing much more hilly, for we are now in amongst the ranges. We met a small party of natives from Mafulu and they contrasted greatly with my Mekeo carriers, each of whom stands at least 5 feet 10 inches to 6 feet, the mountain men being short of stature, though extremely wiry. Whilst the muscles of my boys as well as their limbs are long and supple, adapted for long strides on the flats, the mountaineers are short and knotty and adapted to climbing. They wear extremely little clothing, men and women alike – one has almost to look for it. ... The mission station suddenly appeared on the crest of a high opposite hill – a mile as the crow flies, but before reaching it, we had to follow up to the head of a deep gorge, pursuing a track of great scenic charm, down to a mountain stream, the Takuluma, then to climb the rise again on the opposite side, when all of a sudden, as we topped the summit, the most wonderful panorama of mountain scenery burst upon us. On a cleared area stood the mission station, and over the lip of the clearing, falling to an abysmal gully, the prospect of a maze of noble peaks topped by scudding mists provided a prospect worthy of a world tour to witness. ...

10 July 1921

I am sitting on an old seat in a small clearing on the brink of a great gully that slopes down to a small mountain rivulet 1000 feet below. Up in the chapel behind me, the good Father Chabot is playing the organ and raising his voice in melody of praise. I am indeed near to heaven in more ways than one. ... Directly ahead on the far side of a green valley filled with lower peaks, rises Mount Davidson with heavy banks of silver-edged clouds drifting rapidly across, covering and unveiling its rugged summit. The winding course of the rivulet I can trace far away along the gorges and its song comes rising up to me from the depths. The abrupt bluffs that rise from the valley floor are covered with dense foliage of complex greens and browns. Right on their summits are tiny clearings and the small houses of mountain dwellers. In each of these villages, there is scarcely more than a score of small grass huts, looking like nests perched up on the crags. They were placed in these inaccessible positions to defend themselves the more readily from hostile attack ... In olden times, these tracks, which were the only means of access to the villages, were dug across, and a deep pit with spears pointing up was lightly covered over to make a trap. My vantage controls the whole sweep of the horizon from east to west and looks across a panorama of grand summits clad by nature in wealthy garb, green, brown and russet. This morning the valley was filled with glorious mists that fumed and boiled like a mighty hot lake. The mists rolled over the peaks like an angry surf throwing its spume in clouds to the heavens. ...

12 July 1921

... Daybreak, I was astir with my cameras, before the mists which still slept in the valley awakened to life. From the small mission, which is only visited at intervals, there is a magnificent prospect of great ranges on the far side of the valley, though not so extensive nor imposing as at Dilava. The roadway, after passing Deva Deva, takes a long dip down to the Kea River, a mountain torrent that gurgles over rocky banks, through forest glades of impenetrable luxuriance. The carriers enjoyed themselves plashing and bathing whilst I took cinema and nearly came to grief by falling off a slippery boulder, camera and all, into the waters. Fortunately, little damage was done, and beyond scaring my leg and damaging my tripod, little the worse. ...

13 July 1921

... It was my express intention to return home by the *Morinda* leaving Port Moresby on 1st August, but as I am now amidst scenes that are likely to present the highest success of my venture, and will later visit the people of Mekeo near the coast on my return, it would mean a hurried rush and purely superficial and extemporised results. Staying an extra three weeks will give the whole of my ten months work a grand finish and assure success. Furthermore, it will give me the opportunity of making a second show. So with the carriers I have sent letters home and made arrangements accordingly. Father Bach will accompany me forward and through the remainder of my trip, and this in itself will be a great help. ... Tomorrow morning we will push on towards our goal, Ononge, which is nearly three more days walk. ...

16 July 1921

At last we have arrived at Ononge ... 2000 feet below the Tafa Road which is 8000 feet above sea level. As one descends into the valley, the trees and foliage became much more luxuriant than that which grows on the bleak heights of the Tafa. The road, kept clear and free from all vegetation and overgrowth, is more like a road through a beautiful natural garden than a way into the heart of New Guinea. Sometimes, on the edge of a gorge, with the foliage 300 feet below, one can look across splendid vistas of alpine beauty to the most noble peaks of the Owen Stanley Range, to Mount Victoria's summit over 13 000 feet above sea level. ... Suddenly, the vegetation breaks clear and there is a distant glimpse of the mission station on a distant spur, standing in the midst of a vast gully. We have passed over the coastal range, which descends for several miles, without a rise, to the gorge of the Vanapa River, then rises again on the far side by a series of counter-ranges to the Owen Stanley Range beyond. ...

17 July 1921

... I went to the mass at 9 a.m. so as to see – I am afraid more than worship – the people massed together from villages within a radius of five hours. ... Father Dubuy held the mass and the opening prayers, sounded like a strange singsong chant, bass and euphonious. The voices massed together produced the strangest human tones I have ever heard. The congregation were just as bizarre. The Christians wear a lava-lava – just a cloth wrapped about their loins – whilst the other women and men wore something less than a fig leaf. Most of the men were bearded, short, sturdy, thick-set fellows, very robust and very dark. In face, many closely resembled our Australian Aboriginals. These people are the true aboriginals of Papua. The coastal people, excepting perhaps those of the Gulf of Papua and the far northeast coast are immigrants, believed to be from Melanesia. The densely packed assemblage in the small, confined church produced an atmosphere so reeking as to make one feel nauseated. The women with their babes, almost nude excepting the baptised Christians, who wore a loose-fitting overgarment (generally wide open at the back). The young girls with their hair decorated all over with small cowrie shells and the flat ground end of the *Conus millepunetatus* [sic], made an ensemble of the wildest Christians I have ever beheld. ...

20 July 1921

Up early and made phonograph horn from a couple kerosene tins, for I intend taking several records of the music of these mountain people this evening. Later, with Father Dubuy to the village of Evesi and took films and plates. The houses are small, pyramidal, wedge-shaped cots thatched with pandanus palm leaves and built 3 to 4 feet above the ground on piles. They are situated on the crest of knolls which rise from the innumerable low scarps which undulate down to the Vanapa River. The houses are small and built detached around the perimeter of a small cleared area. ... The old men were duly posed and photographed, together with their houses and whatever presented, though their arts and crafts are nil and they do little beyond making nets for catching wild pigs. ...

Afternoon, made preparations for taking a number of phonographic records of the local songs. This phonograph has travelled with me all around the coast from Daru to the Mambare, up the delta of the Papuan Gulf to Kikori, and now two carriers have brought it from the coast, 120 miles into the interior to Ononge. On opening the machine, it started without a hitch and the hermetically sealed tin of records was perfectly intact and without breakages. Father Dubuy entered into the work enthusiastically. ... The chorus of singers from the local villages stood around the horn in the kitchen. It took a great amount of patience and experimenting... The reproduction amazed the singers, but they soon got over their astonishment and regarded my machine as another of the white man's works – who can do everything and to whom nothing is impossible. The songs have a strange melody ... [and] the words are simple... Those I recorded were chiefly about the rivers, the birds, flowers and things with which they come daily in contact with.

21 July 1921

The day of departure has arrived. ... My leaving was shouted from ridge to ridge and as I passed along the road, the natives came out of the villages and hailed me farewell. ... I have grown to like these simple hill people; they are quite unspoiled by contact with civilisation and preserve yet all their original esteem for the white and will do almost anything for him. This, of course, is brought about by them only meeting the fathers, whose natures and ways the native only knows. No white man, except perhaps an annual visit from the magistrate, ever visits Ononge. ...

27 July 1921

... After breakfast, we move off for Dilava, I leading by half an hour on account of my crippled foot which has improved overnight. In the freshness of morning the forest is glorious; the sun streaks through the trees, spotting the track with sunbeams. The trees sparkle with dew and the spider webs spun overnight sparkle with dewdrops like diamond traceries. It is a pleasure to be by oneself and 'To mingle with the universe, and feel/What I can ne'er express, yet cannot all conceal'. ... After two hours, I meet a carrier bearing a little package of plates and mail. I sit down by the wayside and read of home and dear ones and of my new little daughter – born three weeks ago. It is good to hear all are well and I thank God. There is a letter telling me of Ross and Keith Smith and of their proposed voyage around the world. A letter from the *Sun* praising my articles and asking for one on the administration. A letter telling me of Shackleton's new expedition. Good news from Australasian Films telling me of the excellence of my cinema negative. All good news, and I go on my way rejoicing. ... I go on to Dilava... Later, there arrives Mr Baker, temporary patrol officer at Kairuku. ... We have much in common, for I previously met him at Buna and we crossed tracks, without meeting, during war service. In fact, I believe one of my pictures at Passchendaele actually includes him amongst the wounded! ...

28 July 1921

The prospect from Dilava Mission House is in my opinion the most imposing we have witnessed throughout the whole tour, not unlike the beautiful view from Echo Point, Katoomba, New South Wales looking across to Mount Solitary. But this New Guinea scene is far grander and more extensive, Mount Davidson standing by itself and presenting a titanic contour of 9000 feet altitude. Like the face of Mount Solitary, Mount Davidson presents sheer cliffs and is almost identical in outline. ...

3 August 1921

After breakfast, which is at 7 a.m., we went into the village to photograph, and there I met Camp, of the Sydney Zoological Gardens, just returned from his tour with a large collection of paradise and other birds for the zoo. He collected his specimens from near the foot of Mount Davidson and speaks of hardships and difficulties of portage and way. The large village of Inauaia has a population of some 350 extremely dirty people. ... In strict tribal law, the village huts are occupied by the women, children and the girls; the chief of the family takes up his residence with his sons in another hut behind that of the women. Bachelors and widowers dwell in a large house by themselves and do not take part in the civil life of the village. Married men may only pass down the main thoroughfare, the unmarried bachelors and widowers passing behind the houses of the village. The married men and their families thus enjoy the privacy of the area in front of their houses, their women not being susceptible to overtures from the young men, the bachelors or widowers who are suspected of ever being on the alert to steal the women away! Everything is done openly in village life – gossip attends to that – and one may see natives with various designs painted on their faces or wearing certain feathers in their hair advertising the fact that they are paying court or are up to something 'daring'. This painting of the face I once thought to be purely ornamentation, but it is one of the strange customs of acquainting others of secret intentions or doings.

6 August 1921

Packed up my equipment which lay at Aro Pokina from my mountain tour and left for Bioto where I arrived at noon. Found great difficulty in securing carriers, as all the people were gardening or hunting. After three hours ranting and waiting, I succeeded in getting a crew to man a canoe and I sent six others back to Aro Pokina to bring all my paraphernalia and carry it across the water by canoe to Yule Island. I had great difficulty in securing labour, but threatening the natives with gaol and a promise of reward if they carried, I eventually got a stir on. From Bioto, we paddled down the creek, a place of great beauty and wealthy foliage and eventually reached the Ethel River, a large tidal stream scattered with mudbanks and bars. After two hours rowing, we crossed the bar at the entrance, and passing between mudbanks ... on which many alligators were sleeping. ... As darkness fell, I reached Yule Island and forthwith took up my residence with the mission.

8 August 1921

The *Tambar* arrived just as I was exposing my last plate at 9 a.m. and hurriedly packing up, put my chattels aboard and bid farewell to my kind and hospitable friends. ...

9 August 1921

… [A]t 11 a.m., entered Port Moresby. The hills around the town are burnt so that there is scarce a blade of even dry grass and the place looks blasted and desolate. I secure several boys from the wharf and transport my belongings to the house of Mr Bertie, my kindly host when I visited this port some two months ago.

10 August 1921

Spent last night developing with results quite satisfactory and found that after two months, my plates have not deteriorated. The rest of the day I spent in arranging … matters prior to my departure for Sydney by the *Marsina*. I am gathering data for a résumé on the possibilities of development and problems of administration, which I will write up as time affords. I am looking forward to the time of leaving, for after ten months buffeting, I feel travel weary and am anxious to be reunited with my family.

15 August 1921

Left Bertie's house 10 a.m. and to wharf, where the governor's private launch awaited me. Government House lies at Konedobo, half an hour by water. His Excellency the Lieutenant Governor (JHP Murray) welcomed me to his home with that fine hospitality which I have experienced from the highest to lowliest in Papua. His Excellency is a tall, gaunt figure, bald on the pate and grey of hair. He is clean shaven but for a small moustache. Some 55 to 56 years of age. A man of great perception and keen intellect. Bodily, he is seasoned by arduous travel over his territory and is immune to most tropical ailments from which most suffer periodically. Simple in his ways, always with the bounden policy to protect the natives over which he administers, fearing no man and a Christian.

I like very much this man who has been vilified and traduced by the planters and traders for the greater part of his regime. His administration has been a path of thorns, for in his purpose to protect the native people, he has incurred the hatred and enmity of those traders whose object is pure exploitation. Government House stands on a high slope and looks out over the glorious blue of the port with coconuts bowed to the southeast trades in the foreground and a peep of the town to the south. In the west, the view looks down onto the native villages and to the distant reaches of the port beyond. Altogether a most delightful spot. Though lonely enough for [H]is Excellency, who is a widower, and dwells by himself with a few native attendants. …

17 August 1921

Spent most interesting social evening in discussion with His Excellency invited to dine with us. Much we talked of the Fly River and the early history of the colony, which I found to be deeply absorbing. I have now finished my filming of New Guinea and of my entire tour. I regard as most satisfactory the results I have obtained and achieved and can look forward to a really amazing entertainment. With the exception of a very few, I have met the highest to the lowest in the territory; I have met practically every missionary of the Sacred Heart, the Anglican and the London Missionary Society, most of the traders and planters and probably half at least of the entire population. ... I regard the country as one of the most productive I have visited in the world and the greatest of all tourist lands. Unfortunately, the tourist to Papua sees but Port Moresby and Papua and glimpses of the coast at a distance from the vessel's deck. He sees but a few of the natives of Hanuabada and goes away with an entirely false perspective of the territory. He sees nothing, [but] generally he goes back as an authority! The Papuan himself I like, having a decided preference for the aboriginal types of Mambare, the interior and the wild people of Urama – especially the latter. Altogether, my rambles through Torres Strait and Papua has been the most interesting, fascinating and productive of all my adventures.

19 August 1921

... [D]uring the afternoon I bid farewell to one of the best friends I have made in Papua, viz., His Excellency JHP Murray. My brief stay at Government House has been a pleasant climax to my voyagings and I go away feeling well disposed towards the administration. ... The *Marsina* left Port Moresby at 10 p.m., she having been delayed by a raid made by the customs officials to try and locate bird of paradise plumes which it is believed have been smuggled from Rabaul. ...

Arrived home 27th August and found all well after an absence since 2nd December 1920.

I consider my tour successful beyond expectations, having secured over 22 000 feet [of] films, all of which has turned out splendidly, and over 1200 still negatives.

6

The Papua Expedition Diary
(August 1922–January 1923)

The splendid success which attended the public presentation of the films, which I called *Pearls and Savages,* the picture records of my last expedition to Torres Strait … and Papua … has encouraged me to make another visit to this latter colony. My object primarily is to explore Western Papua – that unknown stretch lying west of the Kikori River to the Dutch boundary and extending from the coast to the old German boundary. … It is also my desire to further augment *Pearls and Savages* by eliminating scenic sections and replacing them with sensational and unique matter. My object in so doing being to exploit the films throughout the world and by thus doing, secure sufficient capital as will enable me to equip and set out on expeditions to various places without either government or private subsidy. This at once places my operations and movements beyond public criticism, and sets me entirely free to prosecute any programme I might feel inclined to embark upon. …

Owing to the impenetrable nature of jungles, swamps, mountains and rivers, the characteristic topography of Western Papua, I decided to undertake and carry out my work of survey chiefly from the air. … My opinion is that exploration of such a land can only be effectively and practically undertaken by aeroplane or seaplane. I placed my plans before Mr Lebbeus Hordern of Sydney and of whom I can only speak in eulogy. He at once decided to lend me a 'Seagull' – one of his Curtiss flying boats – for the undertaking; subsequently, he informed me that he considered the expedition would secure such valuable scientific data that he placed unreservedly at my disposal a 'Short' seaplane, known as the Fleetwings. The former is an American-constructed machine and the latter English. … In addition, I have the wholehearted backing of the press, which is in itself no small factor that can make or mar.

So that scientific research may be undertaken, I have engaged a small party of specialists, of whom Mr Allan McCulloch of the Australian Museum, Sydney, is in charge. I engaged as pilot for the seaplanes, Captain Andrew Lang, whom I consider to be the leading seaplane expert in Australia, and also his mechanic, AJ Hill, who also has had vast experience with these types of machines. So that lines of communication may be readily maintained, I approached Amalgamated Wireless, Sydney, for the loan of equipment, and the result has been that a complete transmitting and receiving set has been lent. The equipment is of a most complete nature and nothing has been spared to add to either our personal comfort or to invite success. ...

Owing to the bulk of the aeroplanes, it was found not possible to carry both at the same time on the one vessel. The Seagull therefore, went forward three weeks previously under Captains Lang and Hill. She was successfully landed at Port Moresby and is now undergoing assembly. The Fleetwings, under my charge, is at present on board the *Morinda*. ... I am indebted to Mr Styles of Burns Philp & Company for his deep interest and expert handling in shipping the machines. ...

29 August 1922

It is a deep relief to at last be aboard the *Morinda* and to embark upon the project [that] myself and companions have set our heart on. ... The equipment is all on board and the Fleetwings is lashed securely and snugly on the afterhold. ... She fits the space with barely inches to spare. All my intimate friends came down to join the wife and kiddies in saying goodbye. It was a cheery send-off – one that I will think of often during forthcoming adventures. ...

31 August 1922

At 10.30 a.m. we drew into the Brisbane River and moored up alongside that dismal river siding, Pinkenba. McCulloch and self went up to town and dined with Mr Longman, the director of the local museum. I then called on my old friends at the Strand Theatre and subsequently returned to the *Morinda*. ...

4 September 1922

... 9 a.m., arrived at Cairns. The town, built on an extensive flat at the base of a picturesque range of hills, is well laid out, and if only interest was taken in the planting of shade trees along the thoroughfares, would become undoubtedly the finest town in North Queensland. There is a magnificent fig in the main thoroughfare, with orchids blooming up in the branches and grown over with a wondrous garden of epiphytes and parasitic growths. It is to be deeply regretted that this tree is to be cut down because it threatens foundations with its roots! In such a climate one would have thought that every effort would be made to spare any tree giving shade. This is unfortunately the characteristic of many, in fact most, of our towns to destroy every tree in the vicinity, and erect as uncomfortable a galvanised shanty as possible to dwell in. ...

5 September 1922

... I received a wireless to stay with the lieutenant governor, which I gladly accepted. I also learnt by wireless that Lang had assembled the Seagull and had made a satisfactory trial flight. ...

6 September 1922

... At noon we entered the reefs that lie off the entrance to Port Moresby and after being passed by the doctor, drew up alongside the wharf. A large crowd of natives had collected to see the new machine being landed and a large number of canoes came out from Hanuabada village decorated with fringes of stranded palm leaves in honour of the event. The machine was swung outboard under the guidance of Captain Lang and mechanic Hill without sustaining damage and safely landed in water. As the machine tipped the water, the assembled natives gave throat to a prolonged war whoop and smote the canoe sides with their paddles, producing a deep-noted boom. As the machine was towed away from the *Morinda*, the natives circled around the Fleetwings, giving me the opportunity of securing some remarkably fine film. The amazing spectacle of the native canoes and man's supreme achievement – the aeroplane – moving off in procession across the bay, contrasting the most primitive and modern methods of progression, was indeed a unique and epoch-making event. ...

Lang made a trial flight with the Seagull yesterday and the event is today the discourse of the town amongst whites and natives alike. ... The roar of the engine called everyone out of doors; natives decamped from their work and rushed out in wild excitement to watch the Seagull racing across the water before taking off. They stood sceptically contemplating the machine, saying the white man was only making gammon and intimating that such a heavy mass of iron and wood could never rise into the air like a bird. Some of them had helped to lift the wings and hull and spoke to the others of the terrible weight. The trial was an object of ridicule. Lang having tested out the engine, decided to make a flight. Opening the throttle, the machine raced over the water gaining speed each moment; everyone looked on bewildered and spoke not, then as she began to lift and clear the water, the wildest enthusiasm prevailed. The natives yelled and cheered madly, which was taken up all over the town. The prisoners broke loose from the gaol. The court had to be forcefully adjourned, as the witnesses, police and prisoners rushed out to witness the sight. The greatest confusion prevailed, but everyone seemed glad.

There was no terror amongst the natives; they were glad and overjoyed. Lang is regarded as either a god or devil and the Seagull has become an object of awe and reverence. Work had to be postponed for the day, simply because the natives would not return but spent the remainder of their time discussing the undertaking and how it succeeded.

I noticed a certain amount of cold hospitality existing towards me amongst a certain class of town – the planters. This doubtless because of my attitude in the press towards them, I being a wholehearted supporter of the government and defending them against the accusations and slander of these exploiters. Of course, this matters not in the slightest to me, for I regard the majority as a narrow-minded, insignificant and unworthy clique. And as they can neither make nor mar my objectives, I simply ignore them. I am pleased to say that I have the wholehearted support of His Excellency, the Lieutenant Governor, (JHP Murray) and of the government officials. These are the only people that matter, and with them behind me, the undertaking rests upon our own shoulders. An unpleasant attitude of the commercialists – or rather exploitationists – was evinced during Lang's inquiries for a suitable cargo-carrying vessel. Prohibitive prices were asked up to as high as £300 per month for a small vessel! ... The impression that I am a millionaire to be fleeced is rather too amusing and I have already started the fleecing! ... I naturally must take advantage of the best offers and when I 'confidentially' put out that I was bringing a vessel from Thursday Island, the bottom suddenly fell out of boats. ... At the kind invitation of His Excellency, Lang, McCulloch and myself have all taken up our residence at Government House. ...

7 September 1922

... I chartered the *Kerema* for three months at £30 per month and also Bell, the engineer, for £30 per month. The vessel looks rather neglected, so I have spent £10 on painting her and small necessary repairs. The *Kerema* is fitted with a 25-horsepower engine and sails (threadbare). She has ample beam, light draught and is altogether a stoutly built and most suitable vessel. But she has been sadly neglected. We at once interviewed the wireless people and have made arrangements for installing the necessary apparatus. ... I expect, however, that it will be a fortnight before we will be ready to set out. Also interviewed various officials re maps and the securing of necessary permits to collect. ...

8 September 1922

... The *Kerema* has gone to a neighbouring island for careening... Port Moresby at present appears extremely barren and desolate. It is a homeless place and one feels sorry for those compelled to live here. The hills are burnt barren, it being now the height of the dry season, and the ceaseless winds which sweep over the place seem to fill one with depression. The wretched galvanised houses ... impress me as temporary dwellings that the occupants would be glad to leave at the first opportunity. The unusual dryness of the climate precludes much in the way of gardening, and home cannot exist without a garden. The only redeeming feature is the harbour itself, which expands from the town like a marvellous opal lake to the distant brown hills. ...

9 September 1922

I generally rise at 6 a.m., but breakfast is not until 8.45 a.m. after which we walk down to the boat pier and take the government launch into town two miles distant. Lang and Hill are busy on the Fleetwings whilst McCulloch and I have much other detail work to do. The Government Assistant Anthropologist, Mr Williams, has been added to the party by permission of His Excellency and the Government Anthropologist, Dr Strong. ... Red tape binds things here as strongly as in the Commonwealth, and were it not for numerous friends which I have in the administration, weeks would have been taken to secure permits etc., where it has been a matter of hours. ...

11 September 1922

The Seagull and Fleetwings were both towed across to the village and anchored in a small crescent-shaped harbourage formed by Elevala village and a small island. No better stage setting could I have desired than this remarkable site. The houses [are] built up from the shallows and erected on a forest of sticks with here and there, canoes moored. The machines were brought close under the houses whilst their occupants swarmed out onto the verandah stages to look on. On one of these stages I found a splendid site for photographing the subsequent manoeuvres. ... The wings of the Fleetwings were folded back and reopened, the natives lending their willing assistance and displaying greatest enthusiasm throughout. Lang tested out the engine and taxied the Fleetwings out of the village into the wind that was blowing. As he opened the throttle and the machine gained way, skimming the surface of the water preparatory to taking off, a large crowd collected on a neighbouring hill, wildly excited. As the Fleetwings rose from the water there was a wild display of emotion. ... Only the young infants which the women carried on their backs wore any semblance of self-control! The machine mounted high above the town of Port Moresby and after giving a display, landed at her moorings. Lang reported conditions aloft as being very boisterous and frequently, the machine rose and fell 400 feet. ...

12 September 1922

McCulloch and I spent the morning in the village, securing native types and pictures... There is much beauty in the village and my friend McCulloch appears very susceptible. I scarcely can blame him and were it not for the fact that I carry many charms with me, I doubtlessly would be similarly influenced. ... The popular village toy is now the aeroplane... These aeroplane toys made by young boys were remarkably neat and accurate to detail. The propellers were made by cleverly twisting a strand of palm leaf and in the wind, these rotated at a great speed. ...

13 September 1922

Passed through customs formalities, all expedition equipment and material being allowed in free. The *Kerema* has been hauled up on the government slip and is now being overhauled and the masts lengthened somewhat for wireless gear. Affairs for departure progress slowly, everyone and everything here keeping pace with the dullness and apathy of the place. ...

18 September 1922

The morning being reasonably fine and calm, we were up early and down to the Seagull. It has been my intention of making a test flight to Kapa Kapa to test out my apparatus and observe the stability of the machine. Lang took the Seagull off down breeze and then we climbed up to 1000 feet above the town. ... We headed east down coast to Kapa Kapa, securing a splendid view over the low coastal ranges to the main central mass of the Owen Stanley mountains. The mists still slumbered in the valleys and Mount Victoria stood out bold and clear in the early sunlight. ... I am delighted to find the Seagull remarkably steady and very suited for photography. ... On landing, I discovered myself to be quite deaf from the roar of the exhaust. Signed on Vaieki, the coxswain, and engaged two other lads for the *Kerema*. This will bring our complement up to McCulloch (naturalist); Lang and Hill, aeroplanes; self in command; Bell, engineer; and four natives. We expect to pick up Mr Williams, the Government Anthropologist, at Kikori. Williams has been loaned for the purpose of investigating the natives in the vicinity of Lake Murray.

19 September 1922

... Wrote article for *Sun*, 'The First Papuan Flight'.

20 September 1922

... McCulloch and I arranged to visit the main barrier reef off the entrance. At 9 a.m. a native canoe with a crew of six burly fellows waited for us at the government jetty, which is just below the house. My photographic gear and McCulloch's collecting gear was stowed aboard and we put to sea. ... The canoe is a hollow dugout, 30 to 40 feet long, to which is attached an outrigger by means of a number of spreader poles. The whole affair is securely lashed with vines and native rope. The sails now are chiefly made of canvas, which detracts much from their pictorial effect, but which adds greatly to their efficiency. ... This form of sailing is extremely exciting and is the chief sport of the whites, who hire the vessels on Saturday afternoons and hold regattas. ... I found McCulloch indispensable. There was scarcely a form of life that he did not recognise and know the life history of. This added increased interest to the material which I photographed and will make doubly valuable my future lectures. ...

30 September 1922

... Lang and Hill have been troublesome. They apparently find each other's company irksome. This I believe happened over some trivial affair in Sydney. Lang's disposition is a highly nervous one, a hypochondriacal nature that imagines himself as indispensable. ...

3 October 1922

I was up early after four hours sleep, and through the glasses I was pleased to see all hands working aboard the *Kerema*. At 5.30 the engines were started and without any ostentation the anchors were hauled up and she put out to sea. This is indeed a deep relief. The boat has been a severe handicap and time-waster so that I was glad to see the last of her round the point. She is in charge of capable hands and I have absolutely no fears for her safety. Her destination is Yule Island, where up to 100 cases of aviation spirit will be put on board. She will then proceed to Kaimare and await the Seagull. Lang and I expect to leave here early on Thursday. It is imperative to start out with the daylight, as when the sun gains altitude, the winds increase. The past week the winds have been very violent and quite unsuited to flying after 10 o'clock. Once the Seagull lands at Kaimare something will be accomplished, but one has to be careful of every move to avoid an accident that would ruin the entire plans. A single hard bump, a broken strut and a machine would be thrown out of action. Everything calls forth the greatest effort on the part of everybody and every step must be a winner. Spent the day in correspondence and finishing an article, 'My Coral Garden', for the *Sun*.

4 October 1922

At 8 a.m. I received a telephone message from the wireless station informing me that the *Kerema,* which I have re-called the *Eureka,* had arrived at Yule Island and ... will proceed to Kaimare during the afternoon. ...

5 October 1922

Up again at 5 a.m. and after a light breakfast, to the Seagull. I felt extremely tired and more fit to sleep for a month than go flying. A fairly stiff breeze was blowing, but ... we were determined to set out. The only gear which we carried was the photographic, and this weighs close on 100 pounds. ... The Seagull was towed down the harbour by the customs launch and started by the handle. She started remarkably easy, just a sharp down-pull and then off. Lang made a beautiful off-take, and then straight up over the town in the eye of the wind to gain height before turning in the direction for Yule Island. Just over Ela Beach, the sun burst through the clouds, throwing a silver ray across the sea, an omen which augers well. ... Passing over numerous villages built on piles along the foreshores or adjacent to beaches, where the natives assembled to look up in wonderment at us, we followed the coast to Redscar Head with the village of Mana Mana built around one shore known as Galley Reach. Not a single native was to be seen, they having all cleared out to the bush in terror. ... Nearing Yule Island, we ran into light rain and the visibility was remarkably bad. When just over Yule, the sun burst through the mist and I secured a few photographs. On the stone jetty, the fathers, brothers and a large number of natives collected and cheered us heartily as we landed. ...

6 October 1922

... In the air. ... Left anchorage 8.40, light northwest wind. Took mile run owing [to] dead weight and rarefied air. Wonderful view skirting close [to] shore [of] Yule Island at elevation of 100 feet. Thick verdured hills coming down to water's edge. Here and there native hut alongside miniature beach. Passed across to mainland. Visibility bad. Wonderful view over coastal hills of country behind, verdantly green. Later, coast fringed with coconuts, grey beaches and scattered villages ... where natives rushed out to look up at us. ... Heavy cumulus clouds and mist over land but clear seaward. ...

Crossing Orokolo Bay, dense mist and turbulent atmosphere. Prospect being obscured only 2 miles away. Nearing the five mouths of the Purari River, dense clouds encountered, shutting out prospect. Heavy rain fell as we progressed, pelting and cutting our faces like hail. The machine was tossed about wildly and added to the extreme gloom was the knowledge that we had to find a small village on an unknown river. Lang handled the machine with great skill, but I must confess at the low altitude of 1000 feet, I was much uneasy. Providentially, the following wind cleared the rain clouds and the visibility improved. The five great mouths of the Purari presented indeed a wild and grand spectacle. The seas were breaking on the various bars and great volumes of muddy water streamed out into the sea beyond eye reach. The foreshores were scattered with logs and timbers swept down by the river and stranded. In the background, the rivers could be traced winding amongst flat mangrove swamps and nipa palm until lost in the distant mist.

Whilst over the Baroi mouth, I noticed the top of a dubu through my 8x prism binoculars and so the machine was headed in that direction. Soon the familiar shape of the *Eureka* hove in sight and we had located the village. Passing low over a maze of winding waterways, Lang made a graceful sweep over Kaimare... The great ravis stood out boldly and as the tide was high and the mudflats covered, the village appeared as if it had been recently inundated by a flood. The structures seemed to rise out of the water, and the various 'suburbs', or isolated parts, were connected together by bridge-ways. A desolate, gloomy place – yet fascinating.

We swept lower and lower, receiving many bumps until we came over the fine waterway in front of the village. Lang made a beautiful landing right alongside the *Eureka*, frightening several canoe loads that paddled frantically out of the way. We touched water at 11 a.m., 2 [hours] 20 minutes from Yule Island, an average of 60 miles per hour. *The Eureka* had but arrived a few hours previously and the news of our coming had already been circulated through the village, so it was not astonishing that every man, woman and child came out to look on. ...

To me it has been a day of realisation. A scene that I had pictured twelve months ago. The wireless operating successfully. The reunion with the vessel and the great flight of the Seagull. It augers well after the wretched delay and worry at Port Moresby. ... After this somewhat lengthy entry, I turn in. The *Eureka* floats with her electric lights ablaze a few hundred yards away; McCulloch has just finished speaking via wireless to Thursday Island. The Seagull swings at her moorings nearby and around us rests the strangest of villages with its great dubus or ravis silhouetted against the moon. It is the realisation of a Jules Verne. The most ancient and modern resting by the shores of a time-old lake. White men and black men – the modern and the ancient strangely commingling. Truly, we seem to have entered another planet.

7 October 1922

The government rest house in which we are camped … is built up, like all the other native houses, on a great number of piles. The tides rise and fall beneath it so that at low tide the house stands above mud. … The way to the village is a pathway some 10 to 12 feet above the mud, made of mangrove uprights floored with mangrove saplings laid crosswise. A very rickety structure with the added disadvantage of flapping through into the mud if one breaks through or stands incautiously on one side and tips up the flooring. Furthermore, the sticks, being quite unsecured, have an unfortunate habit of rolling when one's weight is passing over them. These roadways of saplings and stakes pass throughout the village and similar roadways, though narrower, lead from the main thoroughfares to the individual huts. … In fact, Kaimare is a village of sticks, smells and slime. From the rest house the 'Styx' road leads over the mud, across a tidal creek and then between quaint native huts. … The huts resemble somewhat the forefoot of an alligator with the jaws open. The front is walled-in some distance back, thus forming a porch, where the family work goes on and the social life is conducted. …

Midway along the Styx road one observes the ravi, an immense structure that towers up to 65 feet from mud level to the entrance peak, and 500 feet in length. At the rear the ravi slopes down to some 12 feet high. … [T]he entrance is closed by a barrier of coconut leaves and the inmates are all busy making masks. These masks are beautifully manufactured, the detail being carried out with minute accuracy. The frame of the mask is made of cane lashed together with native string. Over the frame, which frequently measures up to 10 feet by 2 feet, the finely beaten-out bark of the wild mulberry (tapa cloth) is stretched and sewn on. … Great numbers of these masks are in course of being made and it is evident that shortly a great ceremony is about to take place. At the far end of the ravi was a partitioned-off section which none might enter. This was in charge of a very hideous old chief. He considered for some time the advisability of letting us pass this barrier, then apparently reluctantly, he bid us enter. In the darkness, we made out that the place was filled with strange masks. Something after the shape of a fish (known as chactodon). The masks were about 4 feet 6 inches long and 3 feet wide at widest part. … The entrance for the body is at the bottom end. The significance of these masks is quite unknown to me. … On emerging from this holy of holies, the old chief demanded kuku (tobacco). He informed our interpreter that unless a present was made to these spirits, we would most certainly become violently ill and would die!! Not being anxious just at present, we gave the old chief the tobacco as requested. Women on no account are allowed near the ravi …

8 October 1922

... McCulloch and I spent the day ashore in the village and in the ravi. I was particularly anxious to secure pictures of the forbidden holy of holies... I took with me my coxswain, Vaieki, to interpret. There were very few in the dubu so we walked to the far end... Whilst none were about, Vaieki showed his contempt for their beliefs by removing the barrier and screen so that 'the terrible spirits' stood revealed. There were eighteen strange effigies made of cane – evidently intended to resemble crocodiles. ... This section of the ravi was inexpressibly gloomy. The wind made a moaning sound through the leaf walls, whilst we disturbed hoards of bats, rats and lizards. I found it extremely difficult to photograph owing to the confined space. I exposed a plate by flashlight and we managed to re-erect the barrier without the inmates seeing us. ...

9 October 1922

Since landing it has been my desire to have a canoe regatta. Yesterday I called all the native village constables together and asked them to inform the people. As nothing happened, the coxswain, Vaieki, and myself went round the villages with the constables offering payment of kuku (tobacco) and threats of force from the government if the canoes did not come out at once. This latter had the desired effect and gradually the canoes began to row in. ... I made Vaieki admiral of the fleet, he being able to understand my talk and wishes and capable of seeing them carried out. Twenty-five canoes each with ten men comprised the fleet which was ample for my requirements. The Seagull was taxied to a distant point, and as she came up to the *Eureka*, the canoes followed in her wake, shouting and paddling wildly. It was a magnificent display, especially when the canoes formed up in line and made figure eights around the Seagull and the *Eureka*. ...

During the afternoon, McCulloch, Vaieki and myself visited another ravi which was lavishly decorated with 'Kaiva-Kuku' masks. I gave several sticks of tobacco to the old men on entering, which had a welcoming effect. There was a large number collected in the ravi, whom I included in the picture. I tried hard to arrange a dance, but ... anything which is not in keeping with the time-old traditions and customs would bring terrible consequences down upon those who participated in it. Happily, many of the young men have 'signed on' for various periods and many have returned from work with a broader knowledge. These manifested something of a contempt for the pseudo-beliefs of the elders and were for a dance, but the old men held out irresolutely. ...

It would appear that the old men strive to keep the younger men in constant dread of certain spirits which inhabit the crocodile effigies in the holy of holies... When a young man kills a pig in the hunt, he returns to the ravi and offers it to one of the spirits. The pig is then taken by the keepers of the spirits – the old men – and eaten by them! The hunter gets nothing! The religion and objective of the old men appears to be to terrorise the rest of the villagers. ... The old men are believed to be the chosen ones of the spirits and endowed with great powers of making puri-puri. The very mention of this word is sufficient to cause widespread consternation. I took several flashlights in the ravi, the exploding of the charge inducing the inmates to retreat very hurriedly. ...

10 October 1922

... [O]nce more I went the rounds of the village securing pictures of the intimate life. The people now are beginning to gain confidence in us... Lang, who has a false plate with two teeth attached, draws the plate back showing a vacant gap, then with a wave of the hand in front of his face, hey presto, and the teeth are back, always attracts an immense crowd who roll on the ground in convulsions of laughter. ... The women ... now show themselves, and today I was able to secure picture of one covered in mud. ... McCulloch collects all sorts of curios, which we buy at the price of one stick of tobacco, large or small. I always make a point of presenting half a stick when a picture has been taken, and it astounds me that the people pose without question or complaint or without even asking to see the result; in fact most do not even know what we are doing. ...

By lunchtime the weather had improved sufficiently ... to make a flight. The Seagull was made ready and my equipment was stored on board and the engine started up. Lang taxied the machine to the far end of 'the lake' so that he would have a clear mile in which to gain flying speed. A great crowd had collected to witness the event. As we swept along with increasing speed, a great cheer went up and there was wild excitement. The Seagull only gained flying speed when nearing the end of the course, but fortunately the river is some 400 to 500 yards wide and the machine took the bend beautifully and took off. Owing to the rarity of the air, it was a long time before any height could be gained; for several minutes we only cleared the mangrove tops... Flying down the course of the river was beautiful beyond words, but much of the aesthetic gave way before the turbulent atmosphere which tossed and bumped us violently. Frequently, we fell 50 to 60 feet and as we were only 200 feet up, the sensation was not a pleasant one. Lang made directly out to sea where the atmosphere was much more constant. The river mouth presented a particularly fine sight. Waves were curling over the bar and the shores were littered with stranded timbers and trees. Gaining height over the sea, I thought it advisable to land again as soon as possible, conditions being too hazardous and quite unsuited for photography. Turning back, we swept above the mangrove forests, threaded by a maze of tidal creeks and waterways, a scene that one might liken to a Martian landscape. ... The village appears from aloft to be afloat on the waters.

We landed safely, but the flight had a strange sequel. The natives, I subsequently learned, had invented a strange story which originated with the old wise men. The flying machine was going out to sea to bring back a big steamer filled with white men who were going to wipe out the village. The whole village was meditating clearing out to the bush, when Vaieki informed them that we had only gone flying to look at them from the air and to take photographs. This calmed them to some extent, but they thought it advisable to propitiate the spirit of the flying 'machine' by making a sacrifice of a pig to it. This ceremony is to take place tomorrow. I fancy this is the first time in the annals of aviation that an offering has been made to a flying machine. ...

11 October 1922

... During the afternoon, the ceremony of sacrificing a pig to the flying machine was performed. The pig was shot by the owner with bow and arrow in the side. The pig at once made off, pursued by a large crowd of hunters, all armed with bows and arrows. They chased 'Dennis' across mudflats, under houses and bridges and finally brought him to earth after firing many arrows. The pig was then carried triumphantly along the Styx road, much as a funeral procession, only the headmen taking part. Finally, the pig was taken aboard a canoe and rowed out to the machine. Lang and Hill were both aboard to receive the offering. A bag was placed on the bow and the pig laid thereon. The machine looked uncouth with this strange offering on the altar-like bow. The sacrifice was allowed to remain until dark when it was removed by us and presented to our native crew. This was the highest honour that could have been shown the Seagull. A pig is regarded as being more valuable than human life. The government has stopped the sacrifice of human life and the pig is now substituted. The natives fully believed the machine would devour the pig overnight, but if they could have seen the crew whacking into it, I doubt if we would have been so popular. We ourselves did not sample the offering owing to the filthy feeding of the Kaimare pigs. ...

15 October 1922

... I secured two canoes and lashed them side by side in order to prevent rolling whilst paddling, and went for a photographic excursion up a nearby creek. I secured several hundred feet of film showing the natives ahead of the camera, paddling the canoe up a narrow waterway with high walls of verdant mangroves on either side. The effect was indeed delightful, and this section should produce some of the finest film sections I have as yet taken. ...

16 October 1922

The *Eureka* towed the Seagull up river some 7 miles in order that I might secure pictures of the latter amid the beautiful river surroundings and also to make the pilot conversant with handling the machine on narrow waterways. The effect produced by the Seagull rounding the river bends in the wake of the *Eureka* was very beautiful. We filled tanks with water and returned to our old anchorage at Kaimare. I found a village constable awaiting me from Kikori with a note from Mr JE Williams, the government anthropologist. Intend flying to Kikori tomorrow, weather permitting, and dropping a letter on the government station in reply, asking Mr Williams to join us at Kaimare as soon as possible. ...

17 October 1922

... I spent the remainder of the day in photographing in the great ravi and secured many unique subjects hitherto and never likely again to be recorded. I managed to secure flashlights in the forbidden holy of holies ... in a strange and perhaps unfair manner. A person was dying in a nearby house and all the populace were either there venting their grief or else out at their gardens. Vaieki, the indispensable, and McCulloch accompanied me and finding the ravi empty, we at once moved to the holy of holies. The screen of coconut leaves we took down and re-erected some 20 feet behind us, so as to give me ample working space and to hide our movements... We discovered no less than seventeen huge masks made to represent alligators. These were all made of cane beautifully woven over a stout framework. They had four legs clawed at the bottom like a bird. An opening allowed a man to put his body through and so walk about with the mask covering him. Under each mask was a small packet carefully bound up in leaf. On opening, it was found to contain a number of pieces of thin wood ... which when whirled around the head make a roaring sound, the note according to the size of the 'bullroarer'. The sound produced is to represent the voices of the spirits of these mask effigies and terrifies the women and children. ... I am extremely fortunate in securing this picture, for in a few years all these things will have passed away.

No one appearing, we moved one of the great crocodile effigies out into a more open position so that a side view might be obtained. I secured a fine flashlight showing this individual mask and also the general arrangement of the masks in the holy of holies. The natives began to return just as we finished and came up to see what we were about. Accordingly, I handed

McCulloch a packet of tom-thumb crackers, which he ignited and rushed out amongst the 'intruders'. The crowd rushed helter-skelter in wild disorder pursued by McCulloch with the harmless crackers. The issue was a complete success for, by the time the natives had recovered, the barrier was back and the holy of holies restored. The natives took the affair as a huge joke and laughed heartily over the incident – so did we. ...

18 October 1922

Seagull was made ready for flying yesterday afternoon and at 8.19 this morning we took off for Kikori to drop a letter on the government station. Kikori is some 60 miles away and inland about 40 miles from the sea. The Seagull refused to take off downwind, so Lang headed back on our wake and we rose in the air after a half-mile run. The machine, however, failed to gain height rapidly so that he had to manoeuvre her, following the course of the river. This was extremely precarious as the river was narrow and windy and we were scarcely above the mangrove tops. I candidly admit I was mightily pleased to leave the Kaimare Creek and emerge onto the expansive waters of Port Romilly.

The landmark of Kikori Station, Aird Hill, stood out boldly, though 40 miles away... Heading then up the great Kikori River, we passed over vast stretches of nipa palm and mangrove, intersected with a myriad winding waterways... The country as far as eye reach is desolate swamp, covered with dense mangrove forests threaded by countless waterways. The whole aspect is what one might expect to see on the planet Mars. ... Amidst all this desolation of waters and swamps, I discerned the rooftops, minute in the distance, of Kikori government station. I had previously sealed up in a film tin a letter to Mr Williams and the Assistant Resident Magistrate, Woodward, asking that Williams should join the party at Kaimare as soon as possible. ... To the sealed tin I attached a lengthy streamer. As we drew near to Kikori, we noticed that numerous canoes had assembled in the riverway, crowded with natives to witness our arrival. As the machine passed over the station, I liberated the message, which was fluttering like a comet down to the station. Thus was the first Papuan aerial mail delivered. I had decided not to land at Kikori, but to return to Kaimare without hazarding a landing anywhere; consequently, we turned about and headed for Kaimare where we landed successful and without mishap after two hours flight. I was intensely relieved to be on board the *Eureka* again, for I like this country little for flying over. ...

19 October 1922

At noon Mr Williams arrived from Kikori. ... It is my intention of leaving for Daru Saturday morning in the Seagull, the *Eureka* following immediately afterwards. I expect the flight will take us three hours, the distance being 180 miles, and the *Eureka* to take two days. We will then proceed at once to Thursday Island and subsequently return to Daru. After this voyage, the machine and boat engines will be overhauled and we will then proceed on to Lake Murray. I expect to be back at Kaimare in six weeks time. The Seagull will then return to Port Moresby for shipment to Sydney and the *Eureka* will call in at various coastal villages collecting. ...

20 October 1922

... During the morning I went with Williams ... to inspect the ravi. Williams was desirous of securing certain information about a small bag which was placed at the bottom of several 'kwoi' plaques in one of the cubicles, or larava. The name of this bag in Kaimare is Amena Aku. Altogether it seemed quite a hopeless process of interpreting and questioning and cross-questioning. ... The people have a reticence to disclose their secrets, not [that] I believe that they are unwilling to do so, but the fear of evil falling upon them from the dread spirits which they have raised up and reared for themselves. ...

... McCulloch ... was also very anxious to secure a bundle [of bullroarers] for the museum collection. Numerous parlays failed to secure one of the bundles. The natives refused to sell or give, but it was suggested that one might disappear in the dark and a present left in its place. This was actually tried, but failed through other interested parties hearing of it. It transpires that each of the bullroarers belongs to a separate person so that no less than twenty persons were interested in each packet. This afternoon, all the old men were called together in the ravi to hold council. Some were for selling, others steadfastly refused. I explained through the interpreter that the things were wanted for record and museum purposes and to show white people how the Kaimarians lived. ... Eventually, McCulloch was allowed to open up each of the seventeen different packages and extract one bullroarer from each. The chief in charge of the holies refused to touch or assist. ... At last the selection was made, but it had to be wrapped up so that none might see. Bark was insufficient so McCulloch took off his singlet and wrapped up the parcel therein. Not a woman or child was allowed out of doors during his passage from the ravi to the *Eureka*. ... It is quite apparent that the whole affair was regarded ominously by the young people, a condition which the old men are very anxious to propagate. We are always careful of anything of an esoteric nature that we might collect, for the reason that if we made light of the beliefs, it would doubtless mean a fall in the prestige of these ancient swindlers and it would be the end of our collecting. ...

21 October 1922

Our operations at Kaimare are for the time ended. I have been going into plans for some time for the next stage of the journey to Daru, which I regard as one of the most dangerous stages of the expedition. ... In fact, it is rare, I am told, that an occasion presents itself when one might be confident of good weather the whole way. The coast from Daru to Kaimare is one extensive delta and in a distance of some 150 miles the great rivers, Purari, Kikori, Aird, Auro, Omati, Iurama, Bamu, Aramia and Fly have their outflow. The southeast trade winds meeting the moisture-laden atmosphere of the delta form low scud clouds and turbulent air conditions. Bad as these conditions are for flying, equally as bad are the waters for navigation. The vast amount of mud swept down by the rivers is responsible for the infinite number of low, flat, swamp islets and mudbanks which render this coast a positive nightmare. I intend to make the flight to Daru in one stage and for the boat to follow as near to our course as possible, so that in event of a forced landing, there will be a chance, minute though it might be, of being picked up.

Accordingly, our paraphernalia ashore was dismantled and stowed aboard the *Eureka*. The Seagull was made yesterday so that it was only necessary to place my cinema camera and aerial camera on board. ... We skimmed the surface at 45 miles per hour, then up to 50, but the machine would not come off. We made a hair-raising turn when we came to the end of the straight and then there was another half-mile clear run, but still the keel would not leave the river. ... It was a heartfelt relief to emerge from this jeopardy to the expansive waters of Port Romilly. ... We made directly across the waters from Kaimare Creek to Cape Blackwood, being most of the while 8 to 10 miles from the shore. ...

Our next objective was Bell Point at the mouth of the Turama River. Looking down onto the sea, I noticed everywhere the presence of shoals and mudbanks over which the seas were rolling, and I must admit I felt apprehensive in case our engine failed and also for the *Eureka* following behind us. We reached Bell Point at 10.30 [a.m.]. Heavy fractocumulus clouds over the land, a haze over the sea and visibility very bad. Our next course lay due south to the island of Umuda. Off the mouth of the great Bamu River, the visibility became exceedingly bad and we passed over banks of low scud cloud, which were only 500 feet above the sea. The flying now became very bumpy and disagreeable. The clear sky gave way to slaty grey and looked like rain ahead. The water hereabouts resembled liquid mud ... and mudbanks littered the sea in a maze.

We crossed over Umuda Island at 10.36; a swamp intersected with waterways covered by mangrove jungles, the same as the prospect further inshore. A place inexpressibly drear and dismal. We next headed across the north entrance to the Fly River, light rain being encountered, making for Sagoana, the southeastern extremity of Kiwai Island. Heavy rain was falling over the land and in patches over the sea. Lang manoeuvred the machine so as to evade large cloudbanks from which the rain was pouring. Great banks ahead, their crests crowned with silvery glory, almost barred our passage. They appeared to be driving in rapidly from the east. Could we pass through the narrow passage between these ominous storm clouds and the rain clouds over the land? If we failed, it meant that we must turn about and seek a landing. Providence rode with us and we just reached the passage and passed through this dread gap in the nick of time. As it was, we were violently tossed about by a squall just as we emerged, and looking down over the side, I noticed the waves swept white by a heavy gust. From now on, the skies were leaden and scattered rains fell over the land and sea.

We next made for the island of Parama, which we reached at 11.20. A severe easterly wind harassed us, causing the machine to rock alarmingly and taking all Lang's skill to keep her from turning over. Heavy rain compelled us to fly over the narrow passage between Parama and the mainland. We were halfway through when a violent atmospheric disturbance overtook us. The machine behaved like a small boat in a wild sea. We were pitched and thrown about and it seemed impossible to avoid disaster. For five minutes we lived through an age of great anxiety as the machine almost took charge and got beyond control. We fell from 1100 feet to 450 in half a mile and still we were going down rapidly when a great gust got beneath us, and as if by unseen hands, we were lifted again several hundred feet. Then, with a deep sigh of relief, we left the passage and were out over the sea on the last short flight to Daru. At 11.35 we came up with Daru and soon the small settlement lay below us. Lang made a wide sweep amongst the rain clouds and with great skill landed the machine under gusty and extremely bad conditions. There was a heavy swell rolling as we touched, but the Seagull behaved well under Lang's hand and soon we were taxiing up to the shelter behind the pier. … I write in great praise of Lang's pilotage. … Thus ended one of the most sensational flights I have made. The Seagull might be an admirable machine for most civilised latitudes, but her design is unsuited for the severe conditions one experiences here.

23 October 1922

Severe rains and wind through the night. The Seagull rode through safely and this morning looked comfortable in her bed of mud. I regret the machine is compelled to remain out in the open without shelter of any description. Since leaving the *Marsina* and her erection in Port Moresby, the Seagull has not once been under a roof. The rains and sunshine have played relentlessly on her fabric and I shall be mightily glad when she can be taken adrift and sent south again. The machine and the flying men have been a constant source of worry. ... Two more morose men I have not travelled with. Hill scarcely speaks to Lang and Lang to Hill. ... I have been scouting the horizon for a sign of the *Eureka*. ... [I]t is a worry, especially as the vessel has to navigate through such a wretched sea. ...

24 October 1922

I spent the morning writing articles for the *Sun*, in which I am sadly behind. I have decided to take the *Eureka* across to Thursday Island as soon as she puts in an appearance so that the wireless might be repaired. This will also afford me an opportunity of posting away my films. The Seagull will remain at Daru undergoing repairs and the rigging will be thoroughly overhauled. ... Lunched with Mr Riley at the mission house... A note was handed me after lunch with the good tidings that the *Eureka* had sailed into port and was safely anchored. ...

25 October 1922

I wrote last night till 12.30 a.m. and was up at 5.30 a.m. and went down to the *Eureka*. After putting a few stores ashore for Williams we heaved up anchor and put to sea at 6.45 a.m. ... It was a great relief to leave behind us the grey clouds of Western Papua and muddy waters for the clear seas and skies of Torres Strait. It was a deeper relief still to leave behind our two lugubrious pessimists, Hill and Lang, and to have only McCulloch and Bell, the engineer, aboard. For the first time since leaving Port Moresby I felt really happy. The *Eureka* made good speed and McCulloch recounted to me the doings on the boat from Kaimare to Daru. I further occupied myself writing my *Sun* articles, though I found it somewhat difficult to typewrite, as our vessel is a veritable tub in the least sea and throws one about harshly. ...

27 October 1922

... Torres Strait with its sunshine and blue waters, its sandy beaches and lovely little dream islets is a pleasant change from the mud and swamps, the leaden skies and dismal atmosphere of the delta. ... We arrived in Thursday Island at 1.30 p.m. with the customary yellow flag at our masthead. Soon, the doctor and customs officials came aboard and contrary to what I had heard in Daru, found them genial and not hidebound with officialism, like the Papuan officials. ... Thursday Island looks, perhaps, a little more threadbare, the roofs a little more rusty than when I was here 18 months ago. A large number of pearling luggers ride at anchor and the two ancient warships, *Phantome* and *Geranium*, engaged in charting Torres Strait, are also in port. ... We have decided to live aboard the *Eureka* whilst in port, as I am anxious not to waste time in social engagements.

28 October 1922

I forwarded films and mail today and also received several wireless communications from home and friends. ... Thursday Island, though a wretched place, is infinitely superior and ahead of Port Moresby. ... Farther, the distant view of Cape York always reminds one of home and this is part of Australia, the land we know and love. ...

31 October 1922

Our stay at Thursday Island would have been pleasant had it not been for the shabby garments in which we came clothed. ... I have been doing my best to evade my numerous friends, which have a habit of turning up at every corner and inviting me to dinner or other social function. ... We drew away from the wharf and dropped past the *Geranium*, with those onboard waving us off. I was muchly scared lest our engine might stop at any undignified moment and was mightily pleased when we drew well away from the ignominy of such a happening. ...

3–5 November 1922

Much has happened the past three days, so that I have made an unusual gap in my diary, through sheer want of time and worry. Both now have pleasantly arranged themselves and things which looked gloomy have irradiated. I enter my diary on Sunday afternoon, as the *Eureka* sits high and dry on a mudbank, where we have sailed her in order to scrape the bottom preparatory to ascending the Fly River. I will write the occurrences of the several days separately.

3 November 1922

At daylight on 3rd, the officious customs officer put off with a mighty sheaf of papers and we went through an absurd procedure of passing entries, bills of health and formality that was farcical in the extreme. It always seems to me that the smaller the place, the more trouble one is subjected to by officials, the narrower their intellects and outlook and the more mighty is the impression of themselves. ... Daru is a gloomy place made more inhospitable by the scowling officials. ...

On going ashore I met Lang and Hill who were awaiting our return. The former was wearing his usual dismal long face and Hill appeared little more cheerful. I called the two together and at once discussed the condition of the Seagull and of her ability to carry out further flights. ... [B]oth Lang and Hill have shown an absolute lack of initiative, and it is a mystery to me how they filled in their time doing nothing. Materials and unlimited labour were to be had for the asking, but neither of these two specialists made the slightest effort [to build] ... a shelter. Lang's unfortunate disposition and hypochondria have made him an impossible member. His utterances – when he makes any – are uncalled for and only to preserve harmony do we refrain from soundly tousling him. In my opinion, Lang's physical and mental constitution is unsound and I doubt if he could stand the strain of further operations in this region. All this I have given mature consideration to, and with the addition of treacherous flying conditions. I have decided to abandon further flying. I have therefore instructed Lang and Hill to get the Seagull ready to take off for Thursday Island at the first opportunity. ...

4 November 1922

... I have taken every possible precaution to ensure the safety of those on the machine and the safe transport of the latter. ... Had these two men pulled together more could have been done for aviation, but I sincerely feel that if the flying were to be proceeded further with, it would end in disaster and this would be extremely harmful to the cause we have set out to uplift and advance. Lang's health inclines me to the belief that he is in too nervous a state to be entrusted with a machine. ...

5 November 1922

At 6 a.m. McCulloch called up Thursday Island and the weather report was 'Fine – scarcely any wind'. Our local conditions were favourable and I decided the moment opportune to push off the Seagull. ... The entire population of Daru came down to see the start; the machine, after manoeuvring, took off. The effect was extremely beautiful, as a rainbow had formed and the machine passed through the arch. I took this as a good omen. A great relief came over me as I saw the machine grow to a speck and then disappear. Flying here has been one long hazard. The atmospheric conditions were quite unsuited to the Seagull and only a large machine, all metal and with sufficient horsepower to climb to an altitude above the mist and scud, is suitable for this country. Ten flights have been made and without accident of any description, which indeed is an achievement for pioneering in a tropical country where mists, rains and saturated atmospheres are the daily conditions. A considerable amount of observation and aerial photography has been done and the flying has been a success. ... We waited by the wireless equipment until the joyous reply was received that the machine had landed safely and crossed the straits. ... McCulloch, Bell and myself with five natives now comprise the party and the good spirits have revived within us. ...

6 November 1922

... Mr Riley (Reverend) of London Missionary Society, which has a post here, very kindly lent me a pilot. Malaki has an intimate knowledge of the passage as far as Mediri. The course is treacherous and shallow and as I have no desire to strand on a mudbank in the estuary of the Fly River, I thought it wise to carry a pilot whose local knowledge might save me weeks. We left Daru at 10.45 a.m. ... The mists which always hang like a screen betwixt Daru and the estuary of the Fly barred our way, but this time the screen which seems to hang like a mystic veil over this amazing river was less harsh than it appeared. A torrential downpour, and we were through into bright sunshine and calm.'... Once through Tauru passage, we turned north and entered the muddy waters of the Fly estuary ... [which] at the mouth is about 40 miles wide. ... Entering ... is like sailing on an inland sea. Fortune was kind throughout the day and she favoured us with splendid weather and a fair wind. At evening we dropped anchor off the little village of Daware. ...

7 November 1922

Anchor was heaved up and we got under way at 7.30 a.m. ... The riverbanks are still covered with jungles of mangrove with an occasional small village on whatever high bank offers. A remarkable feature about these so-called villages is the communal house. These strange structures are longhouses in which dwells the entire community. There are no detached houses whatsoever. So far I have not entered one of these abodes, but have only been able to observe them from the deck of the vessel. ... The people are rather diminutive in stature, with short curly hair, Semitic cast of features and black beady eyes. I don't altogether like their appearance, which impresses one as of great cunning. ...

At 1 p.m. we dropped anchor at plantation known as Mediri. This is the last habitat of white man on the river. The single figure of a white man looked inexpressibly lonely and outcast in this dreary place. We carried a small mail and half side of bacon for Beach, so McCulloch and I went ashore to meet and secure information from him about the river. The tide was rushing upriver rapidly, so that it took Dogai all he knew to make the bank. Beach greeted us warmly; we were the first white men he had seen for months. He is married to a native woman by whom he has one daughter, Frances, 10 years of age. The plantation impressed me as a failure. ... Beach has been at many things in his time: a recruiter, bird collector, prospector and other vocations which a ne'er-do-well might take up in these parts. He is, however, a strong and kindly character and he at once appealed to me. We dined at his bungalow, a fine large house made of native materials, which in these parts, is, to my mind, infinitely preferable to the usual galvanised-iron shacks. ...

8 November 1922

We waited for the tide until 9 a.m., when anchor was heaved up and we got under way. For economic reasons it is advisable to work the tides in the Fly as much as possible. ... [T]he engine gave more trouble today than usual. There was a continual spluttering and backfiring that was cruel to listen to. I remonstrated forcibly with Bell, the engineer, and told him that unless the engine could be made to work properly, I would abandon the project of going to Lake Murray (needless to say I had not the slightest intention of doing so). I therefore ordered anchor to be dropped and set him to work grinding the valves. One of the valves was in particularly bad condition and it took some hours to reseat it properly. All my work, thought and preparation has been seriously set back by this incapable impostor. Before leaving Port Moresby and later Thursday Island, I asked him numerous times what would be required for spares; but his lack of knowledge and lackadaisical manner procured the spares most unlikely to be required. I felt like shooting the man and pitching his carcass over the side for crocodile bait. ...

10 November 1922

... Of natives or villages we have seen nothing; nothing beyond point after point of the illimitable jungle. Always one wonders what lies beyond the distant point, and as we proceed and the prospect opens, another point lies beyond; nor is there hills, nor rise of any description, yet about it all there is an absorbing fascination and the knowledge that there is a goal of mystery and a planned objective that must be achieved. Every mile draws us towards this realisation and so we look forward. We dropped anchor in the starlit waters by the northern extremity of Alligator Island and began our first vigil on the Fly.

13 November 1922

... We entered the Strickland at 10.45 a.m. at what is known as Everill Junction. An unimpressive locality amongst low flat banks covered with reeds and stunted trees. The Strickland itself we found an immense river scarcely less wider than the Fly itself and the current swifter. The river is much more circuitous, especially near its unity with the Fly. Here we followed the course for four hours and at the end were only two miles north of the starting point, the river having described a complete horseshoe with the extremities drawn close together. ...

14 November 1922

I make this entry under very harassing conditions. The mosquitoes are hell and though I have wrapped several thicknesses of blanket around my legs and feet and donned a heavy, 'puncture-proof' Burberry waterproof, doused my hands and face with 'Buzz Off', it is all to no effect. We made the natives a mosquito-proof house from one of the tents. They, excepting Dogai, who keeps watch with me, are all inside, but the mosquitoes seem to be busy within, judging by the continual slapping and smacking. ... I, too, am terribly weary and tired, but a watch must be kept, as we are now close by the haunts of enemies, and a relax might enter in the whole destruction of the party. All day we have been forcing the passage of the Strickland... At 3 p.m. we entered the Herbert River, quite an unobtrusive stream which is the outlet to Lake Murray. ...

We are now anchored in the deep waters of the Herbert River and on the very threshold of Lake Murray. We all look excitedly forward to the meeting with strange people about which we have heard such distorted, fabulous rumours. ...

15 November 1922

We continued pursuing the course of the Herbert River, which the map shows to be merely a straight waterway draining Lake Murray, but which is in reality very serpentine. ... Naturally, the keenest expectation existed on board as to the nature of the lake and of its strange mysteries about which rumours are so prevalent. McCulloch and I kept a keen lookout from the mastheads, whilst Vaieki turned the wheel to our instructions and the crew kept the sounding lead busy the whole time. Then the trees along the banks dwindled away to reeds and then over the top of the swamps we observed the distant ramifying waters of this extraordinary inland sea. We noticed one canoe in the remote distance through the glasses – the first human life seen since leaving Mediri on the Fly estuary over 200 miles away!

My description of Lake Murray viewed from near its junction with the Herbert River is of a vast field of young wheat through which a flood has passed, leaving behind it immense pools. As we proceeded the waters expanded before us and swelled out into a vast sheet of water larger than Sydney Harbour! The distant shore could be observed in the misty distance and between it and our vessel a number of verdant islets beautified the scene. ... From the banks, large numbers of ibis, plover, terns, ducks and other birds arose as the exhaust of our engine awoke the solitude with its puffing. In the swamps in the immediate background and in fact all around, fields of beautiful lotus were in full bloom. ... What great work could have been accomplished if the Seagull had been here. ... The lake itself would have been a perfect landing ground, but alas! with the two men in charge – the thing was impossible. ... So on the very threshold of big success, the flying failed. Still, after all, it was not the all-important work, which is my photography and McCulloch's collecting and investigation. ...

I scouted every inch of the landscape for signs of a village and succeeded in locating a longhouse amidst a cluster of coconuts. ... The village resolved itself into one immensely long house on the only bit of dry land more than a few feet above the lake. It stood impressively on a hill some 20 feet high and looked quite hospitable with its small plantation and green reed surroundings. But not a soul was to be seen! The village looks too new to be deserted and I can only surmise that they have become scared and cleared out to what they consider safety. ...

16 November 1922

A truly remarkable and interesting day. The *Eureka* was headed in close inshore again and a party comprising self, McCulloch, Vaieki, Dogoda, Dogai and Jack all strongly armed with rifles and revolvers went ashore. The excitement was tense as we fully knew the people were watching us we knew not the moment a shower of arrows might come from the reeds or bamboo thickets which surround the dubu. We poked our way through the water grasses fringing the lake margin and came upon the usual track used by the villagers to reach the water. I led the party through the tall reeds, and finally we came to a more open space planted with coconuts and stood on the threshold of the village. I set the natives to guard strong points with their rifles cocked ready for attack whilst McCulloch and I foraged around and went inside. The general external appearance of the dubu ... bears a striking resemblance to the great houses of Kaimare, only the architecture and construction is wretchedly crude and inferior compared with them. The overhanging roof in the front resembles the conventional yawning crocodile design of the delta... I should have mentioned that before we reached the dubu, the track was 'closed' by a skull on a pole and arrows; these we removed and replaced with emblems of peace. ...

The entire population evidently dwells in this one great house which measured 223 feet long by 54 feet wide at the entrance and 25 feet high to the peak at the entrance – width at rear, 34 feet. ... We seem to be back in the remote Dark Ages amongst the prehistoric people dwelling on the shore of a primeval sea. ... We found numerous skulls and human bones, but the natives had evidently removed their treasured belongings during their flight. The whole abode resembled nothing so much as a very ramshackle shearing shed... The only sign of life that greeted us were the birds, which frequented the reeds in large numbers. ... The waters of the lake reach a temperature of 92° one foot below the surface and taken in the current. The day was sweltering hot and the temperature rose to 98° in shade with a humidity of 82 per cent. Numerous crocodiles idly swam about on the surface. ... As night drew on, we heaved up anchor and proceeded out into the centre of the lake again so as to avoid the attack – more of mosquitoes than the natives. ...

17 November 1922

... It has been a wonderful and profitable day. ... The presents which I left for the natives in the dubu in the hope that they might come and take them overnight and so make friends, were untouched, though there was evidence to show that the dubu had been visited during the night. We knew that we were being regarded from the distant thickets and not for a moment was guard relaxed. The unique opportunity to ransack the communal house and secure unusual specimens and photographs was too great to resist. So, setting the guard of my boys armed with rifles at strong points covering all approach, McCulloch and I made a detailed search in quest of ethnological specimens and to ascertain as much as we could of the native life and conditions. It is most probable that 'the treasures' such as skulls etc., were removed during their flight, but many things of greatest value to us were left behind and we secured a fairly representative collection. Everything of slightest value was ... suspended from the rafters or posts. The occupation of opening up these things was thoroughly unenviable. Everything was spun heavily with spider webs and covered with filth. We untied scores of these bags finding such things as grass ramis, stone axe heads, arrow points, yellow ochre, bits of wood – evidently the charms of puri-puri – mussel shells and sundry odds and ends of apparently no value whatsoever. ... We selected the choicest and took delivery thereof, substituting for the 'theft', axes, knives, tobacco, beads, red calico according to their value. ...

I secured a particularly fine specimen of a human head ... This gruesome object had the human skin stuffed and fancifully decorated. I am told these stuffed heads are greatly valued and are looked upon as the emblems of a warrior's power and wealth. The head and neck is severed from the body, so that the neck may be retained as long as possible. The skin is slit up the back and the fleshy parts extracted. I am uncertain as to whether the skull is utilised in the final stuffing, or whether clay is simply used as a cast over which the skin is strained. I am inclined to the former. The skull and skin is smoked for preservation and the hair is all removed. The shape is secured by stuffing with clay and grass and the skin is finally brought together at the back by lacing it together. The face is distorted ... being lengthened considerably. A large ball of clay is placed in the mouth, which is strained excessively open. The eye sockets are filled with clay and the external skin is decorated with red and yellow ochre. Surely, indeed, a gruesome trophy.

The bows were very interesting and formidable, being 7 feet in length and cut from the bamboo. The bow being formed by the straining back of the main member, the outer skin being on the inside ... and held in tension with a narrow strip of bamboo cane. The arrows are simply made from the reeds which grow in prolific abundance along the riverbanks. These are pointed with hardwood, or in the case of battle arrows, cassowary bone. These latter are also decorated along the shaft. One particularly murderous arrow was pointed with cassowary bone and barbed along its length for 15 inches with porcupine quills. Such a weapon would inevitably produce fatality if one happened to be hit with it. ... We successfully collected all the specimens aboard the *Eureka* and sailed out again into the centre of the lake...

18 November 1922

... The day we spent in endeavouring to locate passage through the lake, but so far have not succeeded. ... I intend carrying the soundings to the farther side of the lake tomorrow, which will definitely disclose if any deep water passage exists. I am convinced that a very considerable river must find its way into the lake, as there is a constant outflow and the evaporation over its vast area must be enormous. There is nothing I should like better than to discover this river. ... Looking through the glasses as we passed by the village disclosed that the natives have not yet returned home and I am chagrined as to how to get in touch with them. We have left ample presents and should they return at all whilst we are close at hand, I am sure they will be convinced that our intentions are friendly. I notice that as soon as we leave the anchorage that big fires are kindled at several remote points, which proves that we are under constant observation. ...

19 November 1922

... The lake proved to be of much larger dimensions than I had expected. Its extreme length must be at least 15 to 20 miles by 4 to 5 wide. The water is remarkably pure, and save for occasional clumps of lilies on the areas less than one fathom, it is all clear water. The banks for the most part are of long grass or reeds. The former grows out in the water and conveys the impression of a solid verdant bank; this deception readily becomes obvious when it is found that the grass is growing in at least one fathom and is deep swamp. It is extremely difficult to force a passage through this grass owing to the interlocking of the stems underwater, and once in, it is even more difficult to get out – owing naturally to the shape of the stern. For at least two hours we followed close along island banks, where we found the water deepest, it invariably shoaling towards the centre of the lake.

The course took us towards the western end of the lake amid scenery of indescribable beauty. We were now in waters hitherto untravelled by white man and every bend opened the portal to hopes and excitement. I was in great hopes that we might locate a fair-sized river, especially as the depth increased as the banks narrowed in. We were now amid scenes of sylvan enchantment. ... During the early night watch Vaieki reported having seen a firestick ashore; this was corroborated by two other natives, though they are great alarmists; anyhow, I was determined to take no chances and so fired three shots in different directions to scare them off. The phenomenal echo in the stillness of night produced an alarming and inspiring noise. ...

20 November 1922

... During the morning I had the crew build me a platform like a fighting top on the mainmast; this will be of great value in scouting, keeping watch and securing photos. ...

21 November 1922

... On the return from 'West Reach', I tried another arm that gave promise of a probable river entering its head. ... The reach frayed out into grassy swamps, so after securing a goodly collection of photographs and McCulloch of insects and butterflies, we turned back. We are now anchored in the centre of another extensive reach, but I am afraid that we will find no river, and that the lake is merely fed by the countless swamps and soakages around its shores. ...

22 November 1922

... We have met the people of the lake. For the past ten days we have literally been hunting the headhunters... When day broke this morning, we observed that we had been anchored all night close to a village which had been so perfectly camouflaged amongst the trees as to be unnoticeable, though I had scoured the place in the late evening with my glasses. Accordingly, an armed party rowed ashore in the dinghy and found on the shores footprints and fresh fish scales and every evidence of a recent occupation. Two canoes were also hidden in the grass and we felt that we were being observed. The rifles were loaded and we crept along in single file, wary of any pits or traps which might have been dug in the pathway. We found this village rather far away from the vessel and decided to visit it from another vantage which I deemed more secure. ... [W]ith a party of only another white man (McCulloch) and four very unreliable natives likely to decamp at the first signs of fight, every possible precaution must be taken. The rifle, when beyond arrow range, could hold off an army of headhunters, but ashore, with perhaps a hundred deadly bowmen to fight at close quarters, the contest would be against us. ...

Anchor was then heaved up and we proceeded up river. ... Scarcely had we gone more than 2 miles when I noticed through the glasses, two canoes. One was being rowed by eight men and the other appeared as if being towed. The *Eureka* began to rapidly gain and I noticed the two canoes begin to draw apart; one appeared to be abandoned, whilst the others rowed frantically for the riverbank so as to escape up one of the countless shallow reaches. As we drew close to the abandoned canoe, I observed it to be filled with bows and arrows and all the sundries which appertain to the Lake Murray village. The *Eureka* was drawn up alongside the prize and anchor cast. I remained on the platform frantically waving a piece of yellow fabric, that in 'Daru days' had served us for a quarantine flag, and calling out as loud as I could, the word 'Sambio! Sambio!!' This word we had ascertained previously to mean the equivalent to the word peace. It was the only word which we knew.

After much deliberation and hesitancy, one of the canoes began to slowly row towards us. The rowers and us hollering out to reassure one another 'Sambio! Sambio!' I admired the prowess of these few men immensely. They put down their bows and arrows and approached us – not knowing of their fate nor our intentions, but relying solely on the honour of that magic word 'Sambio!' Perhaps they were just as eager to ascertain what sort of creatures we were as we were to see them. ... The strange people, when they came alongside, fulfilled all the grotesque and fanciful ideas I had formed of them. Truly indeed they were prehistoric creatures, practically nude, covered with the hideous sipuma scaly skin and of the most amazing features. Their voices strange to say were pleasantly euphonious and comparable with the mountain folk of Mafulu, whom I consider the most musical of all Papuan tribes. The canoes impressed me greatly. They were shaped with a long 'clipper' taper, bow and stern, finely excavated and devoid of outrigger. One measured no less than 55 feet! The rowers stood erect and paddled their craft with very long paddles.

The cast of features of these people is remarkably Hebraic. In fact, were it not for their deep bronze, they might well pass for 'the lost tribe'. The hair is shorn off close in the front, but the back extends in a long luxuriance of pigtails, which are added to in length by plaiting them with fibre. This extraordinary hair decoration extends down to the rump where it terminates in teasled-out fibre. The penis was covered at the head with a small shell or hollowed-out seed secured by a string around the waist. Several men wore grass ramis, but they appeared more for effect than use.

We very speedily made friends with these people, or rather we appeared to, and began an active trading. I demonstrated the power of the rifle and its accuracy. At the report most jumped overboard in terror. ... Matches, the taste of sugar and salt alike astonished and pleased them, but what they clamoured for was the empty tins which we had saved for the purpose... These primitive folk are entirely destitute of utensils of any description beyond bamboo and a few water baskets made by folding the leaf sheath of the goru palm. For a few tins, we purchased a bundle of arrows, whilst the same currency bought paddles, stone clubs, etc. They were also very anxious to secure axes and knives, which we exchanged, securing great value for our tools.

After trading profitably to our advantage and their satisfaction, they directed us to their village with great zeal. I was muchly suspicious of this seemingly super-hospitable invitation, but my desire to see the people intimately lured me strongly. We accordingly sailed for the village, which we learned to be Dukoif and drew in close to the shore. The village ... comprised a large, flat, low-roofed house about 100 feet long and 35 feet wide. It appeared identical with that described on 16th November, excepting that the big house was open at each end and had no small entrances to the various cubicles from the outside. Our friends pressed us exceedingly to go ashore and I yielded to my inclinations and with four natives and McCulloch, we set out in the dinghy.

We found the foreshore heavily grown with waterweed, difficult to force the dinghy in and still more difficult to push it out should we be attacked. We also noticed that our friends appeared overexcited and showed themselves hysterically friendly. When a dozen willing hands went out to pull the dinghy up onto dry land, I waved them off, for I had premonition of danger. I motioned that I would bring the big boat in close, which pleased them greatly, and I think this strategy saved our party. We retreated carefully and slowly with those ashore calling 'Sambio' and we responded 'Sambio' – but their 'Sambio' sounded to my ear falsely strange. So we reached the *Eureka* safely and got on board, heaved up anchor and sailed out beyond arrowshot. ...

We noticed that neither women, children nor the aged were to be seen in the village and only the fighting men remained. Further, we noticed that bows and arrows were strewn about the ground, ready to be snatched up in a moment. At short range, the issue would have been our skulls adorning the dubu and our flesh a feast. Our escape was a narrow one and a lesson. I decided not to land, but to do my work from the vessel... So my hopes were realised. I had seen the people of the fabled lake for whom I had come nearly 2000 miles to see. The realisation was a supreme satisfaction and an accomplishment. This is the first time that white men have ever sailed these reaches, the first time white men have ever seen these people and the first time these people have ever seen white men. The manner in which they regarded us is as excusable as our curiosity towards them. They were much puzzled by our whiteness, the medium colour of our half-caste engine-room assistant and the dark bronze of the others, and the almost black of Ivoni from one of the Kaimare villages. ...

23 November 1922

Though we are now anchored at the entrance to the lake and far from the village of Dukoif, the cry 'Sambio! Sambio!' still rings in my ears. Almost before sunrise, a couple of canoes came down from the village and I noticed that those with whom we were especially friendly yesterday were in the lead. ... I lost no time in getting busy with my cameras and made the limit of my opportunities. We rigged up a blanket for a background and after great coaxing and persuasion, induced one to come aboard and 'pose'. I don't blame the poor chap appearing nervously brave and all the time wanting to peer round to see what was going on behind the blanket. I forgot in my desires, that this blanket would cause alarm. I can imagine our own feelings if a barrier were placed behind us in the village and we were coaxed to sit in front of it whilst suspicious characters with deadly weapons were moved about behind the screen. Then I found it well nigh impossible for him to keep still; he was unusually fidgety and not at all an easy subject.

Presently the sitter noticed his reflection in the lens; this again required many 'Sambios' and explanations to reassure him. Eventually, McCulloch brought out a few paper prints and I also let the native view his fellows through the reflex camera. This seemed to kindle an unimaginative intellect and as soon as what was wanted became clear, I secured an exposure. As there were many diverse types, I kept our decoy on board to reassure the others and then induce the various subjects one by one to come and 'sit'. But they were all very nervy and I had to make quick exposures. Most were of an Hebraic cast, whilst others resembled early Egyptians, but this impression was doubtless imparted by their strange hair. The chief was quite an aristocratic and kingly type, with his corona of bird of paradise plumes he would have passed for the reincarnation of

Solomon. Then there was Shylock typified, and judging by his voracious expression he would want even more than his pound of flesh. There were several very pleasant characters with whom we could have won a lasting and trusting friendship, but the shy and guarded nudges and expressions of several of the elders made me very wary and cautious. Even though these people had no weapons, they could easily have leapt aboard and overpowered us had we not been on the alert. Our strength lay in the range of our rifles and our capacity to keep the attackers beyond arrow range. I therefore instructed the crew to have their rifles loaded and in an unobtrusive position, ready for immediate use. Bell, from an elevated position, watched all movements intently. ...

After I had secured my types in the safety of midstream, I turned my attentions to the village, and so anchor was heaved up and we proceeded. I let the canoes have a good start so as to observe their movements. I noticed that they rowed in very close to the riverbank, and occasionally snatched bundles from the reeds; these I found were bundles of arrows which they had hidden. This was quite excusable, as obviously the depoting of arrows along the bank was intended as a precaution for defence. ... [T]he vessel was headed close in and allowed to drift past whilst I secured film. The men still remaining at the village, cried loudly 'Sambio! Sambio!' and the dogs set up a bloodcurdling yell that sounded like anything but welcome. Then we turned out into the stream beyond bowshot and anchored. ... They then began a fantastic dance and song to the accompaniment of a large drum and half-a-score benzine tins. Evidently they found these latter more suited for drums than for cooking utensils. The song was stirring and pleasant, and was the most like music that I have heard amongst the New Guinea people with the exception of (the mountain tribes) Mafulu and Ononge. McCulloch succeeded in recording the music and he ultimately secured the words, but what their import, we know not. ...

Our visitors displayed great curiosity in most things we did; my washing and lathering with soap produced no end of comment and evidently they thought that it was by this means I became and retained whiteness. ... [A]s I had now secured and hunted down and got in touch with these evasive people of the lake, once more we turned on our tracks, and in the fall of the evening made for the entrance again. ...

24 November 1922

... Early this morning, McCulloch succeeded, through sheer pertinacity and perseverance, in raising Thursday Island. ... It seems strange to be in contact with the exterior world, for here we are dwelling in far-off Dark Ages and seemingly on another planet. To receive news from our friends and to be able to transmit messages from the very threshold of a headhunter's village is truly uncanny and marvellous. McCulloch, self and several of the native crew spent the day ashore, or rather in the neighbouring swamp amongst the giant lotus lilies. ... Forcing a track through the shoulder-deep grasses, we came onto the field. We wandered beneath huge umbrella-like leaves and gigantic blooms in a floral wonderland. ... Many of the giant leaves grew 8 to 9 feet high, whilst the blooms were from 4 to 10 feet high. The flowers were in every stage from young buds to dry seeds. The blooms were nearly a foot across and of bewildering beauty. ... As we wandered in and out amongst the stems with the waving canopy of huge leaves above our heads, it reminded me of stories I had read – Stanley's [In] Darkest Africa...

25 November 1922

Evening is falling on the Herbert River as we turn down with the current to sail homeward. The low banks with occasional clumps of trees pass by in rapid silhouette against the setting sun. The still current runs like a river of fire, the clouds burn red and the day is done. We have left Lake Murray and are going home. A feeling of sadness came over me, for the mystery of this strange place holds me in its lure. ...

27 November 1922

We dropped downstream at daylight and again let out our anchor at the junction of the Fly and Strickland...

8 December 1922

At dawn the anchor was heaved up and we passed downriver to Mediri, where we arrived at 1 p.m. and were welcomed by Mr Beach. ...

9–14 December 1922

... On the upward trip, I have previously mentioned Mediri and the invitation extended to us by Mr Beach. We gladly availed ourselves of the latter for two reasons. Most important, my anxiety to dispatch and develop plates and forward films on to Sydney, the results of our voyagings up the Fly and our adventures on the lake. ... By good fortune, the *Aramia*, a 25-ton lugger, called at Mediri for a cargo of copra. I at once seized the opportunity to send all my films, as well as press negatives, articles and letters by her to Thursday Island. McCulloch likewise dispatched five cases to the Australian Museum. This is a great boon as the vessel leaves immediately and a minimum of time will be wasted in hastening my perishable records to Sydney. ... I was sorry to say goodbye to Beach, not only because he is a good fellow, but the sight of a lone figure waving from the coconuts, surrounded by the overwhelming loneliness of this remote place, seemed like forsaking an outcast being. We passed down the Fly, finding the low tide made the river treacherous with mudbanks, and dropped anchor with the darkness.

3 January 1923

... The dropping of the anchor off the village of Kerewa was the signal for numerous canoes to put off. The rowers were all in their dancing regalia and I seized the advantage to film them about the vessel. ... From the vessel an admirable view is presented of the great longhouse which extends along the riverbank for no less than 500 feet! This great structure ... is well and solidly constructed from lashed saplings and timbers thatched with the leaf of the sago palm. The edifice stands some 5 feet off the ground on quite a jungle of piles and is, excepting in height, the largest house that we have yet seen. The flat space between the house and the riverbank was abustle with the departing guests, whilst the river was animated with canoes returning to their villages. The hour was yet too early to use the cinema to advantage, but as soon as the opportunity presented itself, I went ashore.

The first objects that attracted our attention were small groups of skulls impaled on posts facing the river. These gruesome objects were tastefully decorated by a ruffle of palm leaves rolled into scrolls at the ends, which maintained a shivering movement in the breeze. ... The skulls were provided with very long noses, more like long beaks and the eye sockets were filled with clay and eyes made from small red seeds. The skulls were painted with raddle and were indeed grinning caricatures of death. We were extremely fortunate in observing this display, for such treasured belongings are hidden in the fastnesses of the long house and are only brought out on ceremonial occasions or to display to visitors the valour of the village. ...

The vastness of the hall causes one to loiter on the threshold in wonderment. Like a vast tunnel, the gloom extends to the far end where it is pierced by a star of light – the farther doorway diminutive by perspective. Extending down the entire length is a great promenade some 18 feet wide, which is kept clear of all impedimenta for the free passage of the inmates. On either side cubicles are arranged; mere areas bounded by uprights and cross-sticks without partition, as we understand the word; nor is there privacy from neighbours or passers excepting for the gloom which semi-obscures all things. Above each cubicle and extending the full length, is a narrow ceiling which serves for the stowage of goods and chattels. The tenants sleep on the floor, generally placing a palm-leaf sleeping mat beneath them for a mattress, and a log of wood for a pillow. Each cubicle has its small slab of mud for a fire and many contain small shrines on which clusters of skulls are placed. These shrines have a backboard carved with a crude human face and on a small shelf in front the skulls are arranged.

I expressed a great desire to purchase some of the skulls for the museum collection, and though I offered a pound a head, tobacco, rice, calico, etc., plus persuasions and threats, the owners were unwilling to part with them. They thus expressed themselves: 'The government now forbids us kill more victims and so we are deprived of the means of getting more and will not part from those which we have'. These, however, were only the old and ancient warriors; the young men, changed by contact with civilisation, would have sold the lot at a stick of tobacco a head. ...

4 January 1923

I had heard much about the immorality of Goaribari, but was scarcely prepared for so practical a manifestation as kept us from sleep the best part of the night. Scarcely had the moon risen before several canoes came alongside, rowed in some cases by a single man with a woman squatting therein, or by several men with quite a cargo of females. At first I merely imagined them to be casual callers as had frequented the vessel during the day, but when I observed the native crew in earnest barter and several women coming aboard, I took a tumble... It takes little to fire me in rage these days, having grown wily in native affairs, and the women hastily jumped over the side and the crew fled to its quarters below deck. But the canoes of solicitation continued calling, whilst I hurled them away with unseemly abuse... It was not until one o'clock that the canoes ceased their visitations, and it impresses me as a particularly degenerate race that purchases women for a few arm shells and trades them for a few sticks of tobacco.

When the light was good enough, we again went ashore and continued photography and collecting. I was gratified beyond words at our success in being able to purchase stone adzes from the natives. When they learned that we were willing to pay ten sticks of tobacco a blade, these souvenirs of their grandfathers came forth in great number, so that we made excellent choice of some magnificent specimens. These blades are shaped in perfect symmetry and are of highly polished basalt. The labour in a single blade must have taken months, yet steel supplanted it, and these worthless souvenirs of the young men will propitiate worthily the memory of their grandfathers in the museum showcase. Altogether we secured sixteen blades. One, a perfect gem, I would not exchange for a blade of gold. These young men have not improved with civilised contact, nor has peaceful government improved them. In place of stalwart warriors, deft in the use of the arrow and spear, whose life depended on their valour and strength of arms, the present-day youth signs on for 15 shillings a month and returns to his village, a loafer on the women, 'superior' in his dirty singlet, and cast-off apparel. ...

6 January 1923

At lunch, we eventually dropped anchor off the two villages Kinomere and Tovei. These two Urama villages are pictorially situated on the banks of a small tidal creek and present an enchanting picture. ... As usual, the running out of the anchor chain called out a fleet of canoes from the shore; most of these canoes were single-man craft, about 10 feet long and simply excavated trunks barely more than a foot wide. The hull was rounded, entirely without keel or outrigger, and the freeboard no more than 2 or 3 inches! The rower stood erect and used a single broad-bladed paddle to propel this extraordinary craft. The while, the paddle man maintained his balance instinctively, much as a bird on the wing. The canoe almost seemed to become part of the man, so deftly was it handled and balanced. I purchased the best of the single-man canoes about us for the museum, paying twenty-five sticks tobacco, one mirror, one rami and a string of beads. The owner took his craft ashore and re-raddled and decorated it. We then lifted it aboard – a single man lifting without effort – and placed the novel addition inside the large Aramia canoe which encumbers the vessel. ...

Urama is the name given to a group of villages in the vicinity of the people who were known on account of their warlike nature and the failure of the authorities to subdue them until recently; even now the villagers will have nought to do with traders or recruiters – which pleases me greatly. When it was explained that my object in visiting them was merely to study them, make pictures and purchase curios, we became very popular. ...

7 January 1923

Almost ere break of day the obedient spouses left the village in canoes and went 'bush'. The dance which the men were going to perform must not be seen by woman or child. ... As the men had the village entirely to themselves, I inquired if the Kaiva-Kuku masks might promenade for the benefit of the white people. The head of the dubu ... Gormier, discussed with the old men and finally, after much deliberation, they assented. This strange dance takes place but once every seven years. It has rarely been seen by whites and never photographed. Further the Kaiva-Kuku masks are not allowed to leave the dubu until after the dance, when they are all burnt. If any man should die during the interval between the dance ceremonies, his Kaiva-Kuku must be buried with him. So that it will be seen, the people granted me no small privilege in bringing forth these things which must never see the light of day until after the ceremony. Strange then, that the women might look upon the masks, but no woman might gaze upon them until the ceremony has bereft them of the insidious spirit.

The warriors arranged themselves in a circle and squatted down, chanting and drumming; the Kaiva-Kuku came from out the dubu and danced in short jumpy steps into the centre of the ring of swaying bodies and heads. Then began the same caperings, only turning round, facing one another, drawing close and then separating. Were it not for the extraordinary masks and their fantastic decoration, the whole ceremony would have been dull and uninteresting. The purport of the ceremony I know nothing of nor could I find out. ... These dances and the Kaiva-Kuku ceremony gives the culmination to my film. ... I gave the producer, Bormi, 200 sticks of tobacco to distribute amongst the people as a small present which they greatly appreciated. The day was well spent by the time I had finished and a blast from a conch shell informed the women that they might return. ... During the day, I exposed no less than thirty-six plates, 800 feet [of] cinema film – the most profitable day of the expedition.

8 January 1923

... It has been my ardent desire to secure a number of skulls, and re-establish them in the museum – an exact replica of the skull racks in the dubu. ... I made council in the remote end of the dubu and started preliminary negotiations for the purchase of a complete skull rack of twenty-four skulls, the gopi shields pending beneath it and the pig skulls which were arranged in a long row at the bottom. I must admit that this was an unprecedented overture to make, and was not surprised at the astonishment of the good Gormier. I opened the discussion by saying that we white men were travelling over the length and breadth of New Guinea, learning the customs and ways of its people, collecting their arts, crafts and all things appertaining to their life. That beyond New Guinea and the sunrise was a great world where the white people came from. I spoke of their great villages and of the enormous dubu made of stone that the great cities owned, wherein all things belonging to the native people all over the world were kept. That white people came day after day to look at these things and learn of other people. That all things were kept there for all time. That when Gormier died and his people died and new people came, the trophies which we would collect would live on and memories of them would never be forgotten. We had collected from everywhere and now we wanted the people of Urama to help us. The price I said they could fix themselves. I intimated that

I realised fully what these trophies meant to them. Each one was a record of a deed of valour, each gopi a tablet to a dead brother – each pig skull a treasured souvenir. If it was against the laws of the ravi, then I must go without, for I did not wish to impose nor digress from what might be their religion.

Gormier was obviously relieved by my last remark and ... asked questions about the museum and was satisfied that we were genuine. I said I should like to take the whole partition from the dubu – skull rack and all. I had photographed it and would erect it exactly as it stood in the great dubu of the white men. The old fellow left us and went down to talk with the other veterans who were seated smoking in the vestibule. A short while after he returned and said that the laws of the dubu did not allow of any part of its structure being removed. If the partition were cut out, a new dubu would have to be built. He had spoken with his brothers about the heads and other things and they all had agreed to do as he would do and desire. He could not give me his rack of twenty-four skulls. They were the inheritance of his children and must be passed on, but he would help me. The old man rose and took from the rack one of his best skulls, he pondered affectionately over the terrible object, then untied one of the gopi from its setting and selected one of the largest pig skulls; these he placed in a small pile and placed them beside me. Gormier then called the names of the warriors individually, they entered their small cubicles and did as he had desired.

It might seem strange that I felt rather sad about the whole affair; to secure a head from a headhunter might sound a permissible action to most people, but when it is understood that many of these skulls were relics passed down by ancestors – fine old warriors – heads won in fair combat by strength of arms and valour and objects of religious reverence, it is natural that many must have felt a deep pang when parting with them. One young man spent fully ten minutes allowing his eye to roam over the thirty-six skulls which his brave father had won. He must part from one of these heirlooms to the stranger; which one must it be? The expression was downcast and sad. What volumes of tragic story these racks could tell, what awful sights the eyeless things had seen. Awful to us who regard with horror the eating of human flesh, but infinitely worse are we who murder by the million. ...

The little bundles were all brought and laid down on the floor of Gormier's cubicle. On each I placed twenty-five sticks of tobacco, four bidi-bidi and one arm shell. I asked Gormier if the purchase money was satisfactory. He assented. Then the same question was asked of each; they all assented, and the transaction – surely one of the strangest trading incidents – was closed. Nor did the interest of the people wane here. They tore fibre from the dubu decorations and helped to pack the skulls and tied up the gopi. I expressed a wish to have a rack made exactly similar as to that of Gormier's. The old men went away and late in the evening the rack was brought out, complete in infinite detail even to the crude little decorations of queer figures and totemic symbols. This is the first occasion that I have experienced where such punctuality and contract-keeping has been adhered to by natives. The Urama people have topped the palm in my estimation and have my esteem and admiration. McCulloch is in his seventh heaven, for having secured such a prize has justified his accompanying me in the eyes of the museum trustees. I have added an improvise to my wishes concerning the exhibition of collections, and that is that the museum authorities will display the collection in the main hall and not bury it in the gloom of the cellar storeroom.

9 January 1923

... I paid another visit to the dubu during the afternoon and endeavoured to purchase two Kaiva-Kuku masks. Old Gormier informed me that this was contrary to the regulation of the dubu for the Kaiva-Kuku might not be disposed of until after the ceremonial dance. If a man died during the interval, the Kaiva-Kuku must be interred with him. The old chap intimated that there were several masks in the houses that had been used at the previous ceremony and that they would be repaired and repainted for me. This was accordingly done; and when evening fell the Kaiva-Kuku were brought out and paid for [with] twenty sticks each (tobacco). Our vessel is now becoming a floating museum and menagerie of native objects, cockroaches, rats and sundry vermin. ...

13 January 1923

... At 3 p.m. we entered Port Moresby and dropped anchor at the old moorings from which, four months previously, we had set out. ... We are living aboard our floating houseboat, which has become much of a home, and intend thus isolating ourselves from a place which I love little and [the] people less. Furthermore, we have much packing to do and desire not curiosity trespassing upon our secrets nor privacy. ...

14 January 1923

... Our decks have been encumbered all day with piles of cases and collections that lend the impression that we are embarking rather than disembarking. The governor being away in Sydney, his office is filled by the Hon. Staniforth Smith, a gentleman of jealous and obsequious disposition. During the afternoon the official launch came alongside, with only the launch boys aboard. They came to seek information concerning our past movements, which we garnished profusely. I suspect acting HE sent the lads across to ascertain the information. ...

15 January 1923

... McCulloch went up to make arrangements for the packing and official permission to take the collection out of the country and transmit same to Australian Museum. Mr Bell, in charge native affairs, later came alongside as the vessel was being brought into the wharf to discharge stores, and with McCulloch, informed me that the entire collections which we had made throughout the expedition were to be held up by the administration pending inquiries as to alleged irregularities concerning our gathering of same. I was not astounded by this information, having received a letter from the official secretary just previous to Bell's visit. Furthermore, we had received a wireless whilst in the vicinity of the delta, informing us that the cases which we desired the magistrate at Daru to forward to the museum via Thursday Island had been held up. ...

We are accused with practically being pirates, chasing and terrifying the people and robbing their villages! Such an absurd and fabulous rumour is a direct imputation against our honour and reputations. I am heartily wild and disgusted with the amazing excesses to which the administration indulges itself in red-taped officialism and its endeavour to harass all with whom it may have dealings. It is absurdly jealous of 'outsiders' trespassing on its sacred territory and prosecuting original work which the administration itself fails in doing. I have discussed the ignominious position in which McCulloch and myself have been placed with McCulloch, and we have decided to take up a dignified and hostile attitude to the imputations of which we are supremely innocent.

Mr Bell is, I feel, in nowise to blame, but I fancy that the ridiculous rumour originated with a missionary named Riley, of Daru, to whom I showed a number of negatives. These displayed my small party walking in the neighbourhood of a Lake Murray ravi with firearms. These latter were actually issued to us by the administration for defensive purposes, and further, we were instructed on no account to go ashore unarmed. Though several times in considerable peril, we happily made no use of the arms. Throughout, our venture was characterised by the friendly relations which we established with the natives everywhere and our freedom from trouble of any serious nature. So, soon as the stores were discharged, the *Eureka* was taken over to a small lee afforded by the village of Elevala. ...

16 January 1923

The ... letter I forwarded in reply to the chief secretary's, delivering it personally with McCulloch to the acting administrator with whom I further discussed the matter. I emphasised the point strongly that as all the crew were at present available as witnesses, an inquiry must be held without delay. As there is nothing to conceal, I have no fears whatsoever. My insistence elicited the reply from the administrator that I was not justified in demanding and insisting that a government should make inquiries. I therefore pointed out that the accusation was of so serious a nature that unless the administration at once complied with my wishes, I should at once wire to the Prime Minister and the affair would become a federal one. The administration then thought my idea quite an excellent one! That is, of an inquiry.

I informed him of the futility and absurdity of dispatching an officer to Lake Murray to inquire into our doings, firstly because he could not talk with the people – even though they might be found – no interpreters existing, and secondly, that as we had the exclusive charts of the unknown regions our sphere of operations would be quite impossible to find. I thus expressed myself; it would be far easier to burgle deeds from the safe deposit than gather information from Lake Murray. I also said that I could not leave the territory without exonerating my party from the imputations, and would not, under any consideration, agree to evidence being manufactured to suit the case by the magistrate of Daru, a man for whom I have the sincerest contempt, and who has shown himself ill-disposed towards our operations in his division. We put our case so strongly, that the administration, I feel sure, is much discomforted and ill at ease. Now that they discover I am not to be trifled with and have such influential backing south, I think the administration scents trouble and press ridicule.

The *Eureka* went alongside the wharf early this morning before the northwest wind arose and discharged the entire collection, which was carried by twenty prisoners up to the local muscum. We suspended packing and the entire mass of material, which we were preparing special crates and wrappings for, is now accumulated in a dump. What will finally come of it and how it is going to be packed and transported eventually, I don't know; however, time alone, I suppose, will solve the slow workings of this ludicrous and ignominious affair. The fact remains that goods which we have risked our lives to get and undergone severe hardship for – goods which have been bought and secured honourably – have been seized, and no means that I can exert publicly or otherwise will be spared to secure the goods and hold the administration up to ridicule. ...

18 January 1923

With McCulloch and our crew, I called on the Acting Magistrate, Mr McAlpine, and found him to be a man of insignificant looks and outlooks with an intellect in harmony. After I had recounted our doings for close on half an hour, this regrettable person asked if I wished to make a statement!! He said that he would be pleased to record it by the typewriter, an instrument in which he admitted his proficiency extended to picking out the letters from the maze of keys by a single poking. My time being of more value than being a partner in this recreation, I informed him so and went, parting with that I would send a personal report typed to save him the trouble!

McCulloch then gave his testimony, which absorbed the rest of the morning, whilst the native crew were not disposed of until next day. The recording of statements being eventually finished, the words and purport of the natives coincided exactly with the whites. The procedure did not take the form of an inquiry, but only a belated recording of statements. The acting administrator is a feeble weakling and impotent to take any decisive action. This, in fact, is characteristic of the officials, all of whom I am of opinion are infernally rotten actors! My statement ... places the facts in brevity and it can scarcely be said that I have hidden my attitudes to the superlatively ridiculous charges made against us.

19–25 January 1923

Little of incident has transpired during the week. Time has been all too brief, and the withholding of the collection has entailed us in much wasted time and irritation. In order to shelter from the northwest winds, we have been riding in the immediate shelter of Elevala village. McCulloch has had to walk two miles into town each morning to repack the collection and to tabulate them. I have not visited any of the government officials, preferring to allow an armistice in the feud until I can wage war through the press and theatre. The officials are cognisant of my intentions and have endeavoured to have the matter settled, hoping against hope to receive a wireless from the Lieutenant Governor, at present in Melbourne, to release the collection and save further trouble. This has not arrived, and I am now going to leave no stone unturned to harass the administration and exonerate all connected with the expedition from blame in any way.

7

The World War II
and Middle East Diaries
(September 1940–October 1941)

Arrival in the Middle East

10 September 1940

... [W]e reached the head of the Persian Gulf and came to the entrance of the Shat-el-Arab – the short broad river made by the conflux of the Tigris and Euphrates. The head of the gulf is an abysmal dreariness of mud – silt brought down by these great streams and deposited in the sea through the ages.

Abadan with its great oil refineries passed below and then Basra soon came into view; unfortunately, the air was heavy with dust whirled up from the desert by a 50 miles per hour headwind and visibility was restricted. The Shat-el-Arab at Basra is a magnificent stream at least half a mile wide, with docks and steamers and myriads of native craft gliding along with their huge white sails, like moths fluttering on a narrow mirror. The country for miles around is green with plantations of date palms, for it must be remembered that Iraq (old Mesopotamia) supplied the world with more than half its dates. ...

We practically stepped from the *Circe* onto the fine garden lawn before the Shat-el-Arab hotel in the late afternoon and escaped much of the blazing heat. After the usual customs formalities conducted in the inspection room of the hotel, we were into the lounge hall for afternoon tea. An Aladdin's palace in the wilderness! In this splendid hall the ultra modern contrasted queerly with the native attendants. One felt it only necessary to clap hands to see new wonders, and I did. My bedroom was worthy of a modern palace – cool air came from the air-conditioning cabinet, the furniture was of rich woods and chromium and the bathroom finer than I have seen in any of our city hotels. Then dinner at 8 p.m. on the lawn ringed round with coloured electric lamps and the Shat-el-Arab flowing just a few hundred yards away and the flying boat silhouetted against the moonlight path of ripples. ...

Basra was beginning to wake at 7 a.m. and the docks were stirring to life. White sails were gliding along the sunlit canals, which were as placid as quicksilver – colourful natives pause to watch us in wonderment disturb the calm with noise and speed. Then we climbed up above the date palms – the green sea of date palms – and headed north. ... [W]e came to the junction where the Shat-el-Arab splits into the two great streams, the Tigris and the Euphrates. The great streams separate to wind away amid the palm groves and brilliant green irrigation. A little above the junction is the town of Querna – a charming (from the air) village of mud-brick houses on the riverbank, reflected in the placid waters. Querna is the legendary site of the Garden of Eden. It is pretty enough for it. Here in an enclosure is the tree of knowledge. Then a little further along we come to enormous areas of green, grassy marshes with creeks and pools ad infinitum. This is the home of the Marsh Arabs; we passed above their homes flying low and picked out their homes – houses built of reeds, each family living on its tiny islet among the marshes. There was quite a big town, too, among the swamps – no doubt the capital of these isolated marsh dwellers. For perhaps a mile on either side of the Tigris, the land is irrigated – and maize and millet and berseme make a greenbelt through which the river flows.

Every mile of this ancient land has some fascination to the eye which is glorified tenfold by its ancient biblical and historical associations. ... It is pleasant to take breakfast in this comfortable plane, to eat peaches and cream and omelettes and to look down on this scene of ancient and modern history, but one's thoughts go out to the troops who fought in the blistering heat month after month with starvation around them, a cunning foe besieging and a relentless sun glaring with white-hot eye. ...

So the long flight draws to a close. ... We pass over the rugged wadi and ranges of Moab and look down onto the Promised Land with the Jordan winding away towards Jericho. It is a magnificent descent from the fiercely aggressive ranges down onto the blue waters of Galilee, surrounded by an imposing uplift of hills. Down we go, lower and lower, before the front of Tiberias city drowsing by the lake, and so we land on the waters of the miracle where the Master appeared to the fishermen, walking across the waters and where he quelled the storm. It is a kindly lake today – it reflects the hills.

Our pilot is taking us for a low tour over the waters – actually we are flying below sea level, for this lake is 203 feet below the Mediterranean. We touch – ruffle the calm waters – throw up an immense low wave and come to rest. So ends the flight from Rose Bay to the Sea of Galilee.

12 September 1940

I went ashore to the pretty little town of Tiberias and was met by Damien Parer and his driver – Parer has been carrying on the photographic work of the AIF over here for the past eight months. Passed through the customs without trouble and then with our paraphernalia aboard the car, set out for Jerusalem, a run of approximately 100 miles.

It is difficult for me here to set down my impressions as we hurried over the wonderful bitumen road through villages and garden-like countryside – everything has changed, the land of ruins has been rebuilt. Its wastelands have bloomed again. I don't know whether I like it better than the Palestine of the old time... Then at last we came to Jerusalem. It was dark when we arrived there; so far I have not seen the city but I recognised the way that led from Gaza to the Jaffa Gate of the Holy City. There have been unbelievable changes. We put up at the Fast Hotel – now the Soldiers Club run by the Comforts Fund. The old familiar hotel has been taken over. I stayed here during the last war – food was scarce then; the Turks in their retreat had ravaged the place for food and the people were in a state of famine. ...

13 September 1940

... Parer, myself and driver motored down to the headquarters. ... We remember Gaza as a place of shell-shattered ruins... Today it is humble but important, as the AIF Headquarters ... and this is where we put up in billets, these being two rooms in a rather fine villa which looks over the dirty old town. Spent the afternoon making contacts and getting the lay of the land. Met many of the HQ officers at mess during the evening – a fine crowd reminiscent of the old AIF.

14 September 1940

Again a crowded day, visiting at Gaza and making various arrangements. Met the GOC Sir Thomas Blamey, who is just as cheery and nimble in spite of his 56 years and considerable bulk. Sir Thomas is a fine leader and is universally liked. We talked over things generally and I was very pleased to find his attitude keen and helpful. I expect it will take at least a fortnight to complete the ground organisation and to make contacts and become familiar with the field generally. ...

The Assault on Tobruk

17 January 1941

Night at Capuzzo among the ruins. ... After a breakfast of Maconochie stew served on odd lids and the steel discs taken from the car wheels, we loaded up with our numberless cases of cameras and sound gear and set out for Bardia and Tobruk. The area betwixt Capuzzo and Bardia prior to the recent battle of Bardia was populated with infantry in dugouts and trenches and the roads were busy with transport. Today the dugouts are vacant and there is a great quiet – the war has moved ahead and the men and machines of war have moved up. This area is like the rest of the Libyan plateau we have seen, flat featureless and brown covered with low, parched shrubbery.

The main road to Tobruk passes by Bardia at a mile's distance. Along this vicinity is to be seen vast congregations of Italian transport. Large, powerful vehicles made by Lancia, Fiat and SPA. These trucks are considerably larger than those we use and are almost universally powered with diesel engines. I suppose the value of each in Australian currency would be from £1000 to £1200. Most have already been ransacked and looted and from many the wheels have been stolen. Looting is very rife and it appears difficult to check. It is not safe to leave one's car on the road without a guard, otherwise on return it will most likely have been stripped of everything movable, even the wheels.

After passing Bardia, the road has been badly knocked about by shellfire and wear for about 20 kilometres, then it becomes well surfaced and equal to our finest bituminised roads. One is amazed that such a fine road should be wasted in such a sterile wilderness. The distance between Tobruk and Bardia is approximately 116 kilometres and it may be traversed to within 24 kilometres of Tobruk. Beyond that point it is under shellfire and if one keeps going, you will soon be in Italian territory, or rather territory held by the besieged Italian army. Like Bardia, the Tobruk sector is completely hemmed round and only awaits similar tactics to those launched against Bardia to bring about capitulation. I duly arrived at Rear 6th Divisional HQ which is uncomfortably sheltered in sundry dugouts, tents, caves and underground cisterns. Camped the night in my truck, which appears as comfortable and safe as any other home one can find or build.

18 January 1941

Owing to our proximity to the Italian lines and aerodromes, I expected that we would be subject to night bombing – but since Bardia, the Italian air force has been almost absent from the skies. Recently, many have been destroyed in the air or on the ground and there is rumour of fuel shortage. Throughout the night, however, our bombers were active and also our artillery; generally this strategy is carried on for some days until the attack is launched. Today has been particularly vile, as it has been cold with a raging dust storm. This began early this morning and has been blowing almost uninterruptedly all day. The surface soil is very friable and the side roads have been pulverised into a brown flour-like powder through the passage of transport. In the high winds, these byways become rivers of dust which add ever-choking intensity to the ... trip. It is impossible to see more than a few yards ahead and there is the constant danger of head-on collision with some other vehicle moving along blindly like yourself. I am making this entry in the closed-in car on the plateau near headquarters. The storm has subsided a little, but the air is filled with murk so dense that even at midday it was semi-dark.

Within the confines of the very limited horizon, one gazes over a circular flat of light-brown rock earth, sparsely dotted with leafless shrubs not more than 12 inches in height. Through the pall of dust there are glimpses of scattered trucks and low stone breaks over which some covering has been stretched for small shelters. The dust-laden wind swirls and whistles, producing a picture dismal and bleak beyond imagining. I have seen nothing in the Australian desert quite so forlorn and cheerless as this Libyan prospect which has grown familiar to all of us.

I spent the morning with our mechanised cavalry who have recently become possessed of twelve Italian tanks. These are formidable weapons and mount a two-inch gun firing eighteen rounds per minute, and four Braeda quick-firing machine guns each capable of firing 1100 rounds per minute. Most of these tanks were captured at Nibeiwa during the Sidi Barrani campaign. Thitherto, the cavalry were equipped only with Bren-gun carriers; now they have become a formidable tank squadron and immeasurably improved their attacking power.

I did some filming, but the conditions were so unsuitable that after camera clogged and lenses clouded over with dust, I had to give up.

20 January 1941

Making contacts and ferreting out disposition of troops and endeavouring to secure information regarding attack on Tobruk, which is expected to take place in a few days. This is absurdly difficult in spite of the fact that I am the official photographer and expected to photograph and record all military happenings. My friend Major Hurley is very helpful in these matters, but like all others, he, too, indulges in the amusing procedure of looking wise to secretive, then peering all around to ascertain if the rocks and airs are listening, confides in sotto voce some information that I have already gleaned from drivers, cooks and batmen. Generally, however, by observing the movement of transport, artillery, tanks, etc., we are ahead to our conjectures and these are rarely short of the objective. During the morning, after several previous endeavours thwarted by dust and howling winds, I photographed and recorded an introductory speech to the Tobruk film by General Mackay, commander of the 6th Division which did such splendid work during the attack on Bardia.

The infantry were living in roughly scooped-out holes and slit trenches about 19 miles to the south of Tobruk. The plain hereabouts is very similar to Central Australia, being covered with a sparse shrub not unlike low clumpy saltbush. To the south, the escarpment, or the steeply rising hills that lift the coastal plain to the plateau, rolled away to the eastern and western horizon till lost in the ever-restless dust. A place of dismal loneliness inhabited by gazelles and Senussi, but now vanished into more remote wildernesses for fear of bombing and artillery thunder. I made arrangements to take my camera into battle with the first wave of infantry. This I hope will enable me to occupy an advanced position and have the cinema trained [and] ready for the tanks and the following lines of infantry which will continue the assault at dawn. Note: while I make this entry on the frightful rough Sallum–Sidi Barrani road near Buq-Buq, we are passing a long cavalcade of transports crammed with Italian prisoners taken at Tobruk. They are being conveyed to Sidi Barrani in Italian lorries, whence they will be shipped to Alexandria.

The area in which the British advances had imprisoned a garrison of 25 000 was protected by two formidable lines of defence – an outer perimeter of stone fortifications protected by mines, tank traps and entanglements and an inner chain of stone strongpoints linked with trenches. The enemy was cut off from escape to due west by strong British mechanised units, and the brunt of the assault was left to the Australians supported by the Royal Air Force, tanks and British batteries working in conjunction with our own artillery. The outer perimeter of the defence system approximates a curve of 35 miles, the maximum depth of 15 miles being due south of the town of Tobruk where the attack was launched at 5.30 a.m. on the morning of the 21st January after a fierce barrage sent down by the combined batteries.

Tobruk is ringed around with a scattered chain of defences, characteristic of all Italian military strongholds. These defences, known as Sanghers, are a combination of trench systems, and where the stony surface is too adamant for gouging, low walls of rock are built up in which are set embrasures for field … pieces, Braeda machine guns and for riflemen.

The … defences are deeply channelled with a broad trench about 8 feet deep and from 12 to 15 feet wide, which makes the passage of tanks impossible. Behind this perimeter gutter are barbed-wire entanglements generally protected with mines. These latter are interesting charges of high explosive contained in canisters about 30 inches long, 8 inches broad and 8 inches deep. There is an ingenious detonating device which is set off by the weight of a vehicle depressing the lid. This shears a thin wire which holds in tension the firing trigger. The mines are buried in the earth a few inches below the surface and form a complete cordon in front of the entanglements... However, it is not difficult to render them inoperative by removing a detonator cap. I had the good fortune to witness a car blown up by one of these mines and to miss going over a field through another's misfortune. I am pleased to say that the two occupants of the front car had a miraculous escape.

Then there are devilish devices known as booby traps. These are canisters about the size of a 2-pound jam tin charged with high explosive and bits of jagged steel. The firing arrangement is a trip plunger which extends a few inches from the top end. Lengths of string are attached to the trip trigger and these may be secured to any object likely to be lifted or souvenired. The traps may be set up also on the ground in any place to catch the foot of the unwary. I am strongly averse to the use of these latter devices and consider that they well justify reprisals. I have no illusions that the diggers will do this should any of their mates be killed in this way.

Collectively, I should say that the Tobruk defences are well planned and strategically sound. If manned by more courageous and determined troops, almost unassailable without superior numbers and equipment. The conformation of the land is such as to place the invader at a disadvantage, since he must advance over flats and skylines without cover against a well-protected foe who knows every wrinkle of the landscape.

21 January 1941

My intention is to advance into the assault on Tobruk with the first line of infantry – the 2nd/3rd Battalion[s] were frustrated by an unforseen incident. I arrived at the headquarters visited on the previous day as darkness fell, only to discover that the troops had moved on some 4000 yards to a more advanced position ready for the hop-off. In the darkness it was utterly impossible to proceed, as the country was gouged with trenches and very difficult to travel, even by daylight. As a matter of fact, this proved most fortuitous. Had I gone ahead as planned, the scope of operations would have been completely limited, whereas, as events transpired, the course taken at random enabled me to secure a record surpassing either that of Sidi Barrani [or] Bardia.

Disappointed as I was at the time, there was nothing to do but camp until daybreak. This I do by removing our paraphernalia from the truck and camping inside. 'Pambo' – Driver Morrison – boils up the billy on the Primus inside the truck, as one dare not expose light in this advanced position. ... One does not as a rule sleep soundly on the eve of a battle with the enemy a few miles away. There is always an apprehensive excitement to stimulate the mind and the constantly recurring question – I wonder how it will all go by this time tomorrow evening. One wonders, too, how one's own existence will fare in the entire scheme. The work of the official photographer is not devoid of risk. It is a vocation that constantly calls for a life stake and one must be prepared to play with chance, perhaps even more than in most branches of the service. One cannot crouch to shelter all the time. The infantryman and the gunner have at least the satisfaction of being able to shoot back, but we carry cameras to photograph them doing this, and unless one sets up where the barrage is sending up death shapes, then the camera misses the most spectacular symbols of war. It is through the lens that the world sees the contest, and so then it falls to one's duty to present as vivid and comprehensive a picture as possible. ...

It is a perfect starlit night and the close 'oomph' of occasional bombs echoes along the escarpment wadies and gullies like a thousand hand slaps. I am in grandstand position to observe all the amazing things going on along the Tobruk horizon. Occasionally, the dark north flickers brightly as bombs explode. Then you can count up to twenty before the deep 'oomph' of detonation begins drumming its echoes through the gullies. Those are our machines dropping bombs, the Blenheims that did such devastating bombing during the Bardia battle. Now and again they drop parachute flares – magnesium candles held up by parachutes – that drift slowly with the breeze and light the country for miles around. In retaliation, the garrison at Tobruk fire up 'ack-ack' shells in vain endeavour to bring down our birds and also the 'flaming onions'. These rise in high columns like roman candles shooting up strings of coloured stars... They compel pilots to fly high and upset bombing accuracy. It is a magnificent pyrotechnic display that appears to be more beautiful than effective.

And what of the Italian air force, this has not loomed in the skies for over a fortnight. Italian machines have been so conspicuously absent that we all wonder if there is some surprise catch behind it. True, the RAF has been destroying machines in the air and bombing them relentlessly on their dromes, but we have not so decimated the numbers the enemy are supposed to possess as to account for the complete absence. We can only wait and see if their pilots will again have the tenacity to face our fighter craft – somehow I think not; all indications imply that we have swept the Italian air force from the skies.

Repeating similar tactics to those at Bardia, the attack will be launched against the perimeter strongpoints south by west of Bardia, which is approximately 9 miles from the outer fronts. At 5.45 a.m. a lone star shell soared in vertical flight. The signal opened the barrage. The ridge ahead and to left and right blazed with fireball flashes that created a tumult of thunderings and reverberations that made our car quiver. We had a magnificent view of this grand preliminary that maintained a ceaseless coruscating flicker for 15 minutes, then the barrage was lifted and the gunners stoked up their hungry weapons as fast as breach could swing and lanyard fire the charge.

Then above this din of guns and shell whining, I heard the sound of approaching tanks like a metal surf ... on an iron coast. There is a rather terrifying sound in the approach of massed tanks that must strike fear and wavering in the soul of the enemy, had not rear gunners seen their armour-piercing shells ricochet without effect off the impenetrable steel of the 'I' Tanks and had not the quick-firing ... tank guns been as impotent as rifles. I watched the dark shapes of these monsters clank forward with exaltation. A little later the sun, as if wearing a red monocle, came peeping through the battle smoke and dust, turning our environment fiery warm and cheerful.

It was now light enough to get the cameras into the fun. My friend, Major Macarthur-Onslow, was in his chariot, a Bren-gun carrier leading his mechanical cavalry and a troop of Italian tanks with big white kangaroos painted on the gun turrets. I made some fine cine impressions of this formidable array silhouetted against the radiations of the upcoming sun. Then we hopped into the line with a tank ahead and a tank behind. It was noble stealthy going, but a little slow for us, so Pambo accelerated and we bumped along the trail taken by the infantry to 'I' tanks. The enemy was sending back an ineffective barrage and his shells were throwing up high shapes of yellow dust that hung like golden shadow ties in windless sky. Then the first batch of prisoners came trudging in ragged columns over the horizon and through the gap in the entanglements which our gallant 1st/2nd engineers blew up. There were several of our own dead near the gap, the victims of booby traps, and a number of wounded. Some distance ahead, there was a long stone-piled strongpoint bristling with cutaway machine guns – artillery pieces. At least one gunner had not thrown up his hands; he lay forward resting on the trunk of his gun... There was a tall observation post – a platform raised 30 feet on four poles – that commanded an extensive outlook. I climbed up to photograph – unseen until I reached the platform, the observer lay dead, still holding his field glasses.

There was nothing frightful in the grand battle panorama over which I looked. There was no obstructing tree nor feature to obscure and aid the attack or conceal the troops, and our troops were moving forward in a cheerful, resolute, optimistic way. There was no horror like we had in the last war – rather did this particular attack impress me as a spectacle made sublime by the great spirit of heroic men, many hailed me by name for the official photographer has become one of the most familiar figures with the men. ...

Today was cloudless and only a low haze of smoke hung around the horizons, those queer stemless shrub and tree-like shapes that shot up in brown eruptions where shells burst. I had my camera trained on a battery which the Italian gunners had accurately ranged. The shells were coming over in measured succession and you could estimate fairly accurately by their rocket SSSL sound where they would lob. I was trained on one of the guns, when suddenly the earth went up in a brown eruption around it. It seemed like a direct hit. Then, as the smoke cleared away, hands appeared and then broad grinning faces – no one was hit. It was one of those fine shots you catch in a lifetime. A nose cap landed with a metallic ring at my feet and bits of shell splinters fell among us, but strange as it may seem, the actual casualties from shellfire are comparatively small.

At lunchtime, we pulled up close to another battery, boiled the billy and divided up a big homemade cake for the gunners. They had temporarily ceased firing for lunch! It was our day and no one seemed to take the fact seriously that there were 25 000 Italian soldiers in the area. Towards evening, we reached the high cliffs that fall steeply down to Tobruk. Huge pillars of black smoke came curling up from below; the Italians had fixed the oil tanks and also a cruiser in the harbour.

The infantry, tired through their long march, came into range of the cine and I shot them as they went over the edge down the Tobruk slope. ... [A]s bullets came whizzing up from below, we crept back behind the shoulder of the ridge. Next morning, the tanks entered the town – Tobruk was now in our hands and we could move about the slopes with little likelihood of being sniped. While moving down a wadi with Pambo, about thirty Italians came forward with white flags and hands up. Evidently, they thought the cine a machine gun, so we shot them and directed them on their way. Everywhere, little groups were coming forward to give themselves up... We held up a column half a mile long, led by senior officers naval and military, to film it; there were no military guards in charge of these 2000 or more – one of the generals complained bitterly that cars had not been sent to carry them in – while most had batmen who carried their personal effects. Such extraordinary scenes suggest romanticism and had the entire grand picture been stage-managed for a film drama, I could not have been more satisfied. Everyone seemed so cheerful about it all; conquerors and vanquished bore no malice and I don't know how many times I heard our troops say 'I'm sorry for the poor blighters!' ...

There lay a pretty white town across the calm waters of a blue bay. A little distance east of the town, rolling columns of black smoke curled back from the oil tanks which were blazing magnificently. A cruiser nearby was adding black volumes to the smoky ceiling and in the foreground were two liners which had previously been gutted. I did all that lens and film could do with these scenes and then went down into the town.

Here indeed was a little dream city. I walked along the Piazza Benito Mussolini under gum trees with men from many of our outback country towns and found the comparison not in our favour. Everywhere, one saw exhibited a civic pride and charm of architecture that characterised an aesthetic people. From the sterile brown rocks and wastelands of Libya, these people had built a hometown of which I must say of a vanquished people, we admire them. The town has been considerably disfigured by bombings, but the damage can readily be repaired.

Menzies' Visit to the Middle East

26–31 January 1941

... I had hoped to spend a few leisure days after clearing up work before returning to the front, but it is not to be. Our Prime Minister, Mr Menzies, is visiting the mid-east on his way to England and it is very necessary that he should be assiduously photographed. Accordingly, I find myself setting out for more peaceful pastures, this time to Palestine as far as Lake Tiberias, which is near the Syrian border. Thus, I will have travelled from the northernmost limit of British territory to the most recently captured western area of Tobruk, points nearly 1000 miles apart. So, they say a change of scene is as good as a holiday, and that's just how I feel about it. The car has been completely overhauled – which it sadly needed – and with my cameras aboard, the scene shifts from military warfare to social hobnobbing with the Prime Minister and principals – with civic and military.

2 February 1941

Left Jerusalem for Tiberias at 7 a.m. ... The descent into the blue depth of Lake Tiberias or the Sea of Galilee is the most impressive climax of the tour. The lake is [686] feet below sea level and this morning was like a lovely blue mirror in a frame of green velvety hills. The town of Tiberias on the shores is arrogantly modern and is more like Manly or a similar popular watering place. Nevertheless, the lake does not lose any of its charm and the town is ... a delightful and peaceful spot. The lake is subject to violent winds, but today it was serene and unruffled. The airport, or rather 'seaport' for flying boats, is at the doorstep of the town; a rather fine café with a charming garden makes the landing very inviting. The flying boat carrying Mr Menzies, the Prime Minister, came up from the south and made a perfect landing, which the camera duly recorded. He was greeted by the High Commissioner of Palestine, Sir Harold McMichael, and the GOC Commanding AIF Middle East (General Sir Thomas Blamey). The PM and the GOC both looked fat and fit, the former more than worse for his long trip from Australia and the latter all the better for his sojourn at Gaza. ... Dined at the spectacularly and blatantly decorated King David Hotel...

3 February 1941

Kept closely occupied keeping ahead of the lengthy schedule drawn up for the Prime Minister. ... At 10 a.m., Mr Menzies visited the Australian Soldiers' Club, conducted by the Australian Comforts Fund. A large number of troops on leave made a splendid animated scene of the Fast 'Hotel' as they crammed balconies, the rooftops, and swarmed on the buses to give the Prime Minister a rousing welcome. I secured some fine film which should be a splendid propaganda item for the Comforts Fund, which this organisation really deserves. The party then moved off to the war graves cemetery. ... Mr Menzies placed a wreath on the memorial, after which I did much film work of himself and the GOC which should edit into an uplifting sequence. ...

4 February 1941

A very full day trying to keep ahead of the official schedule of the Prime Minister's tour. This is a very comprehensive one, each minute of the day being 'clocked' to pay a visit to some AIF unit. Even along the road while travelling from place to place, the PM inspects and handshakes. ... I did comprehensive filming and left for Egypt – the PM will be proceeding by plane tomorrow and it is essential to have the sound equipment on the drome before the plane lands. ...

6 February 1941

Left Cairo for Alexandria [at] 2.30. The Prime Minister is going to visit the fleet and I am anxious to have the gear set up aboard for his arrival. A vile journey from Cairo to Alexandria today, as a storm was blowing the sand in dense clouds across the desert. Visibility was very limited, especially when nearing Alexandria. Alexandria itself was under a brown pall from which buildings and traffic loomed as we proceeded. Alexandria, like Cairo, observes a blackout and this was further accentuated – if possible – by the obscuring conditions. Stayed at the Cecil Hotel, which is owned by 'Metzger', a family association with my wife's family which dates back to prewar days. ...

7 February 1941

We carried our paraphernalia down to 'quarantine steps', loaded it into a launch and made a wet passage over a joggly sea. The *Warspite* – the flagship. There seemed some uncertainty as to the programme and after meeting the captain of the fleet, we ferried back again to the *Perth*. Here we boarded an Australian ship and found the atmosphere less frigidly naval. I was greatly impressed by the officers and men, who formed up in lines on the afterdeck ready for inspection. Mr Menzies came onboard and ... looked over the vessel... We returned along the desert road to Cairo by car, preceding the official party, who travelled by plane, by nearly an hour.

16 February 1941

The Prime Minister, Mr Menzies, left Cairo on Friday and as this relieved me of further touring with him, I decided to return to Benghazi as soon as possible in case the troops might make a drive in the direction of Tripoli. ...

15 March 1941

My Eyemo camera arrived from Australia today and mightily glad I am to have it. This camera is light and quick to use. When I look back over the work I did with the heavy Debrie and tripod, I am amazed that we produced the results we did. To use this camera was a superhuman effort, but I believe we did a good job and produced some very fine historical material that will live.

The Defence of Tobruk

9 April 1941

... Vanquished Italy is being replaced by German forces and fighters so that it looks as if we will have to fight the battle of Libya all over again... All this war energy seems strangely at variance to the apparently peaceful face of Palestine. The cities of Arab and Jew bear little indication of war happenings a few hundred miles away. ... [T]here is little activity towards any major cooperative effort to assist Britain, upon whom the very fate of these people depend. There are thousands of young able-bodied Jews ... idling in the towns who might divert their efforts to raising a force for home defence... This trait has done much to turn AIF sentiment towards the Arabs. ...

12 April 1941

I had hopes of remaining in Jerusalem over the weekend to film some of the religious ceremonies, but owing to the invasion of Libya by German troops, I had to forgo this most interesting part of the year and hurry back to Cairo to go to western Egypt again. Having already followed the campaign from Sidi Barrani to Benghazi, I have little liking to go back to this dusty desert again. ... I had arranged with Major McGowan to stage a full dress parade for filming. We had over 1000 men, in column of line and in route, marching across the setting where Philistines waged ceaseless war with Israelites and whence the Light Horse drove the Turks northward. Just now, the prospect for the plains of these ancient battlefields is a glorious one. ...

13–19 April 1941

The week spent in Cairo at the rooms. Developed cinefilm taken during Palestine tour which turned out very successfully. ... This work completed, I decided to make a visit to Tobruk. ... The Tobruk forces are entirely isolated by land, but reinforcements, stores and ammunition are being supplied through the small port, ships running the gauntlet of air attack and mines. So the voyage is an even chance whether you reach there or get back. These bases must offer a dangerous obstacle in the German lines of communication, as there is every possibility of our forces ... cutting off the enemy forces between Tobruk and Sallum.

... Through the 'public relations' department I secured the usual movement orders that gave me authority to travel to Tobruk by the first boat. I decided to take Alan Anderson, the sound engineer, with me as assistant. So we left Cairo and duly reported to the movement control officer at Alexandria and after much parley and delay, found ourselves aboard the *Atid*. I have travelled aboard devious queer craft manned by queerer crews, but the *Atid* eclipsed most, and her crew the many. The *Atid* is a tiny vessel that looks like an attenuated barge with a short mast in front and a few deckhouses. She is very deeply laden with explosives and stores and has only a few feet freeboard. She is one of the few craft that floats the flag of Palestine, and her crew are all Jews! – Jews of diverse nationalities, but as I came to know them better, a most excellent lot, mostly refugees or immigrants from countries that have fallen under the ruthlessness of Hitlerism. ... Slept on deck aboard the *Atid* as she lay berthed alongside the docks at Alexandria.

20 April 1941

... The scene around us is of a harbour crammed with ships and of vessels alongside being discharged by hordes of native labour. A ship has just come in from Tobruk crammed with Italian and German prisoners. They are so filthy and dust-begrimed that it is not possible to distinguish one from the other. ...

21 April 1941

Several vessels came in from Greece this morning loaded with evacuees – almost entirely women and children. They appeared to be passengers of the well-to-do class who are making good their escape from Greece before things become 'too hot'. On one boat there was a fine luxury motorcar and on another a magnificent motorboat. Let us sincerely hope that this gallant little country which proved the

Italian battle thunder-wings to be so much squish-fizzling will, with our aid, hold back the ferocious and brutal invasion that threatens to overwhelm it. ...

The *Atid* heaved anchor at 5 p.m. and at 5.30 cleared the port... I spent most of the day making a newsreel item of the ship which struck me as being very unusual since the *Atid* is one of four comprising the entire Palestine mercantile marine. And her officers and crew gunman Jews, Polish Jews, Maltese, Free French, etc. The language spoken is German – the ship is German and the chief engineer was a submarine commander in the last war. ...

22 April 1941

... During the morning, we picked up the coast at a distance of 10 miles in the vicinity of Bardia. This is now in German occupation. One wishes the leisurely 7 miles per hour was 17 miles per hour as it is an 'unhealthy' distance between here and Tobruk and our slow speed makes us virtually a stationary target. All day we kept a constant watch on the sky and sea. ... We have two small boats which would preclude taking any equipment and as I have approx £1000 worth of my own gear aboard, I am anxious not to lose it. We sighted the headlands at 3 p.m. and then the buildings on the heights and familiar details of coast. ... By some real act of providence, we crept closer to port unmolested and eventually through the boom-protected entrance (which is a boom on line of mines held up by buoys) and tied up at No. 3 jetty. Tobruk harbour presented a very sad sight. It is a graveyard of ships sunk in all attitudes of dereliction, nose pointing sky up, masts only above the surface, others stranded and lying at abandoned angles. Altogether a pitiful sight, the result of magnetic and other mines dropped by planes and aerial bombings. ... The town has been severely wrecked since I was here some weeks ago and will soon be a heap of bricks and shattered concrete. I transferred my equipment from *Atid* to the dock store, as it seemed safer there, as the ships in harbour appeared to be the objective of raids. ...

23 April 1941

... At 5.30 a.m. air raid siren compelled all to hurriedly leave blankets and hasten off to the nearest air raid shelter. ... This shelter is a huge concrete-faced tunnel that bores into the rising slope on which the town stands. Some distance in, the tunnel swells into a large room which we are using as a hospital. Practically every bed was filled with wounded, practically all enemy. Poor wretched creatures, many just bundles of bandages from which peered tired heedless eyes. The sight was inexplicably cruel and horrible, but war hardens the finer susceptibilities, and most of those who crammed into this bed-crowded haven for refuge seemed quite oblivious to the bedridden and wounded around them. It was an evil-smelling atmosphere, noisy with coughing and yawns of tired men. We stayed in this place listening to the booming of anti-aircraft guns and bursting bombs for half an hour and then the air raid siren gave the all clear and we tarried not in the order of our going. I learned that Tobruk has experienced 166 air raids since 1st March ... an average of three per day throughout this period. ...

24 April 1941

... We had our first air raid shortly after noon, but not a great deal of damage was done. I took shelter in a small circular sandbag post occupied by three machine gunners. However, there was little to photograph; but an hour later there was a second warning and I took up the position again with the land cine. At the last moment, I was almost on the point of changing for another post up on a hill in front of Admiralty House. This time there were seventeen machines. We sighted them flying at about 18 000 feet, when in a direct steep line, they began to dive straight towards our pit. Everything in the neighbourhood began to open fire and the sky was peppered with bursting ack-ack shells; but still the dive-bombers came on. Above the noise of artillery fire and the rattling of machine guns came the ever-increasing screams of the dive-bombers as they cut through the air at over 350 miles per hour. I had the cine pointed at them and reeled in some film, but it was impossible to convey an adequate impression of the rather exciting experience. The bombers were not more than 500 feet up before they flattened out.

Every gun about was blazing away and the air was full of blazing tracer shells and bits of flying shrapnel. I dare not poke up above the bag for fear of collecting some of this stuff. ... The air was filled with bits of flying stone and masonry and much came down into our tiny shelter. One gave me a hard tap on the head and as I was not wearing a steel hat at the time, raised a pigeon-egg lump. Then the machines turned back and machine gunned all and sundry, but we escaped. It was quite a good experience while it lasted, but the kind to keep out of – if possible. ...

25 April 1941

... I was absolutely amazed at the quantity of the cargo which the *Atid* discharged onto the jetty. A large percentage appeared to be cases of beer... Only a percentage of 'beer' cargo ever reaches its destination. It is pillaged at every handling in an organised way and during the air raids on Tobruk, scores of cases disappear each time. In the cause of efficiency, it is nearly time 'the heads', whoever they may be, cut out this deplorable waste ballast from ships and troops alike.

... I have made my base at rear headquarters – known as 'Rear Cosy' – and here 'reside' a number of officers from area headquarters which functions at Tobruk. The office in Tobruk was hit by a bomb and the building mutilated. There were some extraordinary escapes and as Tobruk is the focal point of most raids, some of the staff decided to live away from the 'ruins'. Rear Cosy is about 2 miles from Tobruk in a small gully along the rocky foreshores. There are a few poor buildings with an air raid shelter burrowed into the hillside. ... The mess was in a burrow among rocks and reasonably bomb proof. The evening was very convivial, as all and sundry troops attached to HQ began to drop in until the burrow was packed. There was song and yarn telling and the usual popping of very many bottles.

26 April 1941

... I went up to the inner perimeter of the Tobruk defences to the 25-pounder batteries which did a fine job a few days ago by shooting up seven German tanks. Three of these were 22-ton tanks with formidable guns and heavily armoured. They are invulnerable – except to a lucky chance shot – to light anti-tank rifles and guns. These tanks made their way through the outer perimeter as the infantry was powerless to stop them. Then they came up against the 'crack' 25-pounders which effectually cracked most of them. The infantry dealt with the machine gunners which came in their wake and only a few tanks and enemy got back to their lines.

I then decided to visit the anti-aircraft 3.7 battery near the entrance to Tobruk harbour. This battery has been annoyingly accurate to enemy planes. As we passed through the ruined town, the air raid siren shrieked and we sped along at 60 miles per hour towards the battery. We timed our arrival exactly and hurriedly got the cine onto the stand just as the enemy planes put in an appearance in force. There were three flights of bombers escorted by fighters. At once, all the ack-ack guns opened fire and I was just about to 'shoot' up at the planes, when we noticed they began to dive from about 15 000 feet towards the battery. As we were in the open a cricket pitch from the guns, I took the cine from the stand and we made a dive for a slit trench nearby. We beat the dive-bombers to it as they zoomed down and dropped bombs all about our position. The ground shook with the concussion – and for five minutes, hell was let loose. Bombs, heavy ack-ack guns, machine guns and Bofors all made a fearful din and bits of rock, bomb splinters and shrapnel came tumbling down on our frail shelter. I expected the guns to be blown to hell, but the gunners bravely stuck to their posts and shot back. ...

We left the battery and motored round to the far side of the harbour to find a safer refuge from which to film bombing. We had only been there an hour or so when the air raid warning shrieked again. This time we were well away, but as there was too much dust in the air for our long-range lenses, we looked on from half a mile at the enemy planes diving onto the battery again and unloading their bombs. They were apparently 750-pound 'pills' and the whole area around was shattered with explosions from which big plumes of smoke and dust leapt skyward. I was fearful that the whole battery and my good friends there were wiped out. None of our planes went up to combat, for the reason that we have only one or two Hurricanes left here! The Germans have absolute supremacy in the air and we felt very bitter that this area has been left at the complete mercy of the Huns. ...

28 April 1941

... There was the wreck of a Junkers fighter, shot down by the ack-ack battery, which was so heavily engaged yesterday, and I decided to film it. We got some engine sump oil and lit a fire under it and redramatised the crash of a few days ago. While we were about this, another air raid warning made us hurry off to shelter. We dived for the nearest hole and found it to be a petrol dump, so we (Anderson and driver Dyer) laid down flat while bombs fell some distance away. There were only one or two machines, so this diversion was soon over. Then we went back to film the crashed machine again. I set up the camera and we were just about to light up, when the brutes came over again and this time we made a bolt for the seashore where there was good cover.

While watching three Messerschmitts coming up the coast in our direction, we noticed them suddenly dive onto a bomber. There was a flash and a huge cloud of black smoke and the bomber disappeared into the sea. At first we rejoiced, thinking the Messerschmitts were our own fighters which had shot down a bomber, but later we learned that it was one of our Blenheims, the mail plane which arrives each day. On board were several distinguished and important flying men who, I regret to write, disappeared into the sea with the bomber. The tragedy was too distant to photograph. A cloud of drifting black smoke hung over the calm peaceful sea where the Blenheim wreckage disappeared.

... It was no small relief to leave Tobruk ruins and the incessant bombing and return to 'Rear Cosy'... I am writing this entry sitting in a small cave that looks out across a small peaceful bay. The Mediterranean is making dashing and slapping and dashing noises in small limestone recesses and the sun is going dim over the peaceful sea. It all seems so utterly remote from war and yet, as I write, the rumble of guns comes from beyond the opposite ridge and air raid warnings compel men to retreat into holes like scared rats.

29 April 1941

Four air raids between 5.30 a.m. and 8 a.m. ... The position passes belief. We are using up ammunition at a great rate, dumps are being destroyed, transports shot up by machine-gun fire and we are not able to retaliate. There is but one Hurricane, which dare not take the air against so daring and overwhelming an enemy. It is a deplorable pity that we are not able to transport a gang of brass hats from headquarters in Cairo to this ceaselessly air-strafed hellhole and bring to the indifferent instincts the position which exists here. Even as I write, a plane now is brazenly skimming low along the waterfront on what seems like a pleasure-sniffing cruise. I have just retreated into my cavern like a periwinkle, lest stray machine-gun bullets come zipping by.

Today I was witness to another beastly sight that made me feel rebellious against the incapacity of headquarters to appreciate this deplorable situation. A fine ship sailed up the harbour and came to anchorage in the bay. I knew, as many others of us did, that this vessel would die among the others which have a grave in this impossible harbour. So, just after lunch, I motored to a hill overlooking the harbour and town with the ship in the middle distance. We built a small shelter of sandbags which were in the vicinity and roofed it over with baulks of timber. Scarcely had I set up the cine when the air raid sounded. Fifteen bombers soon came overhead and there was hell let loose as every gun opened fire at the hell-divers. ... I was watching everything through the rangefinder as the camera recorded this tragedy. Bomb after bomb fell alongside the vessel, her plates were smashed in and in no time she sank by the head. Fearful lest the boilers might burst, the crew jumped into the harbour and rescue ships went to them. Though my blood boiled at this sickening sight, the ship was a legitimate target and it demanded great pluck on the part of the Huns to dive through the terrific barrage. Those who send ships to this harbour should be tried for murder, for they are certainly sending men, vessels and cargo to their doom. ...

30 April 1941

Yesterday I made arrangements with Brigadier Murray of the 20th Brigade to visit his battalions in the front-line positions... This battalion was one which covered the retreat from the Benghazi debacle. They occupy the outer perimeter about 8 miles from Tobruk near the El Adem Road. I had filmed previously all round this barren, desolate desert area and it was strange to find the country on the Bardia side in enemy occupation.

The steel bars which fit into two massive concrete pillars bar the main road, which is mined. The barbed-wire entanglements stretch away to eye-reach across the rocky plain in either direction, and immediately in front of them there is a wide trench about 15 feet deep which prevents tanks from entering our side of the wire. Apparently, the enemy is some distance back from this line, as we climbed through an opening and wandered about unheeded far into no man's land. There were numerous derelict German tanks lying about, which indicate[s] that the last efforts the Germans made to break through did not go too well with them. ...

The front-line troops are ensconced in dugouts and strongpoints built of sandbags and trenches. They are also protected by the many deep concrete emplacements and underground tunnels built by the Italians as part of the outer defence system. ... Secured some fine film during the day and found the front-line positions comparatively free from aeroplane attack, owing to the dispersal of troops and the impossibility to inflict serious casualties. ...

1 May 1941

... Another small ship came into port today and she was tied up alongside a scuttled Italian, thus providing protection on one side at least. I watched the unloading and was amazed to observe that a considerable number of latrines was being unloaded, house and all complete. It struck me as being pathetically absurd to risk a ship and those aboard with such ridiculous cargo at this time. It suggests a complete lack of comprehension of those at headquarters. ... The offices are heavily overstaffed, overfed, over-entertained, over- officered and under-efficient, under-worked, and under-brilliant. ...

2 May 1941

... I visited the prisoners-of-war camp in Tobruk where there are a number of German prisoners taken during the battle of two days ago. They were in a grimy state, with faces encrusted with dust from which their eyes peered sullenly. ... I photographed them in 'propaganda' situations through the cage wire, being interrogated and so on. I was told that fifty-four or fifty-seven lorry loads more had been dispatched from the battlefront early in the morning, but they had never reached the internment cage – nobody asks any questions what has become of them. There is a preference here to bury dead Germans instead of taking prisoners.

5 May 1941

In the Tobruk area, we move along the roads thrillingly and apprehensively, for on overcast days you are ever expectant that a dive-bomber will swoop from the clouds and strafe the road with your speeding car as the bullseye. So we move about with one hanging on the footboard watching the sky while the driver accelerates as fast as turns will permit. I find that watching troops or figures on the landscape is the best indication. If they are running for cover, danger is above; if they are sitting about and indifferent, then all is safe. ... Everything is a target to destroy. Enemy planes bomb hospitals and hospital ships, recognising neither international law nor human creeds, and it is this ruthless attack which has developed in our troops a bitter hatred. We might, in our sorties against the blockading foe, take more prisoners, but one hears of a natural desire for reprisals and we wage war with a ferocity unknown against the Italians. ...

7 May 1941

... During the afternoon I visited the Australian field workshops situated near the base of a tall steel tower that looks down onto Tobruk. This tower is 200 feet high and from its summit there is a fine view over the desert to Tobruk. I was apprehensive about taking all the equipment up this open tower, as there was the possibility of being machine-gunned if the 'Jerries' put in an unexpected appearance. We hauled the gear up in stages and I eventually took the panoramas with one eye on the camera and the other squinting round the sky for planes. ...

8 May 1941

... This morning I finished practically all film I brought with me – 3000 feet – and called on the movement control officer for earliest possible passage back to Alexandria. Just when this is likely to be I don't know, but I am now on a two-hour notice to leave at any old moment. There are no ships in port at present. ...

10 May 1941

Waiting for ship to return me to Alexandria. ... Tobruk is the really bright spot in the news these days and as no other cine men are working on this front, the pictures we secure are in the nature of another world scoop. I have tried to convey a panoramic impression of life in the area during siege without resorting to the ugly side of destruction for dramatisation. 'Business as usual' is the tenor of the film and I think it should be very successful. The weather has not been the best for photography, as the air has been filled with light dust and mist producing a murky atmosphere that casts no shadow. In this land that lacks form and feature, these light conditions have made work more difficult. ...

I was not sorry to leave Rear Cosy, as the officers there, though decent enough fellows, were regrettably apathetic and through having nothing better to do, had resolved themselves into a drinking coterie of jittery nitwits. The camp commandant was a peculiarly arrogant egotist who had no great respect among his men and, though quite a good fellow at intervals, had got himself into a continual state of nerves and panic through liquor and indolence. The bang of a nearby gun or a hum that sounded like aircraft sent them scampering to the air raid shelter like rabbits to a burrow.

At 7 p.m. then, Dick Dyer, my driver, drove Anderson and I together with our paraphernalia down to the wharf to embark. There was an ominous stillness in ruined Tobruk as we made our last passage through it down to the waterfront, an evil place, as it was the focal point of bombings. ... [A]s the sun was setting through the desert dust and the full moon rising in the sea-haze, we slipped out of the harbour unseen. ...

Tel Aviv

1–7 August 1941

... I made the Ritz Hotel at Tel Aviv my convalescent home after three weeks sojourn in the 11th Scottish Hospital at Cairo where I dallied for three weeks through malaria. I chose the Ritz Hotel because of its pleasant proximity to the sea and the equable climate of Tel Aviv. ... The days passed pleasantly, with walks along the crowd-infested beach where one may find much entertainment in studying the strange things normal beings indulge in at the seaside. Perhaps most of these people are not quite normal as we Australians understand everyday circumstances of life. Many – most have immigrated – forcefully – from lands dominated by the ruthless decrees of Hitlerism. They are, of course, 99 per cent of Jewish blood and this seems to have 99 varieties in manifesting the divergent national strains and characteristics. Form varies from globular to spindly scarecrow and tints from creamy white to Nubian chocolate. A not unpleasant café au lait predominates as the Tel Avivians seem to spend the greater part of the sunny day in 75 per cent nudity, disporting along the sun-tanning strand.

They are a healthy population of sun worshippers who seem to exist in a state of perpetual holiday, walking about the busy streets – gazing at everything and nothing in particular, as if all their environment was a grand free show in which they themselves are unconsciously taking part. In moving with the crowd or sitting with the idlers in the café or lolling back in a deckchair along the beach as deeply absorbed as any in the pageant ... the impression one gains again and again is of a city of youth. The buildings all look fresh and young, the trees attaining adolescence; everything is in a condition of shaping, forming and maturing. The general effect is refreshing and startling – yet unsubstantial. It all looks as if the magic of Hollywood scene builders had conspired to raise from the sandhills a city of wonders and display. It would seem as if its architects had striven to break with the old-world ideas of architectural design and to evolve a distinctive design suited to the climate of their sunny new land of promise. ...

As far back as 1909, an institution of Jaffa Jews wished to establish a garden suburb suitable for European population. The Great War interrupted the project, which resumed activity round about 1921. Security under the British mandate and the Balfour Declaration kindled an enthusiasm in Jews of many lands and an intensive immigration quickened development which was further hastened by the ruthless Nazi exorcism of Jews in occupied countries. During this latter period, the influx was so excessive that houses could not be built fast enough. Thus, structures were raised that in the more sober discrimination of this great centre of 180 000 Jews of today would not be tolerated. In many of these outwardly modernistic family tenements, there are no bathrooms .... Still everyone seems happy; everyone here is free to enjoy the sunshine, to express his opinions without fear of brutish reprisals and free to work out his destiny. ...

I think the troops appreciate Tel Aviv because it is a European city where the people dress as Europeans, where most of the people speak English and where there is gaiety and entertainment. ... The city is wholesome and scrupulously clean and the inhabitants, though simply and inexpensively clad, irradiate a freshness that displays an innate pride in the individual, and this is reflected in the city in a grand scale. Though Jerusalem is Jewry's capital of the Promised Land, Tel Aviv is the chief commercial centre of the Land of Promise. It has countless small and considerable factories where most things displayed in the shops are made, and these range through foodstuffs, radios, wearing apparel and most things required in the home and everyday life. Here one will find men of culture and expert in all trades, for it must be remembered that in the Nazi exodus, men who were at the forefront of their professions and who ranked high in the competitive fields of Europe, have carried their artifice to this centre. You may find technicians and highly skilled experts – men at the zenith of their calling – working in a small, back-sunlit room, making their living, who would not return to the old regime. It speaks well for the administration and freedom of British control and one cannot help but admire and be sympathetic to the policy that gave these people a place to realise the long-cherished dream of their forefathers – to remake and reinhabit this ancient land which they have claimed as their birthright from earliest history. ...

5 October 1941

The Australians who have played so glorious a part in the defence of the Tobruk area for six months are being withdrawn... Our casualties have been heavy in Greece, Crete, Syria and Libya and it may perhaps be policy not to use the AIF as shock troops and so suffer further losses in Libya. The men of Tobruk have done a magnificent job and saved Egypt. Had they not held up the German mechanised advance, I think the enemy must have gone ahead to the canal. The Tobruk garrison was a ceaseless menace to severing enemy lines of communication and cutting him off from the main body to the east. The battalions, as they are withdrawn under cover of darkness, make the passage to Alexandria or Mersa Matruh by small destroyers. This is another epic feat carried out by the navy, as there is the ceaseless risk of bumping mines, encountering U-boats and bombing. ...

Index

253

Index